# Writing Irish History:
# The Four Masters and their World

Edel Bhreathnach
Bernadette Cunningham

EDITORS

**Word**well

Fig. 0.1.  Fresco of Florence Conry, from aula of St Isidore's, Rome (*above*).

Fig. 0.2.  FLK C 11. Foundation letter of St Anthony's College, Louvain (cat. no. 14) (*opposite*).

Ser.mo Señor fray florencio Conrrio Prouincial dela Prouincia de Ystanda
dela orden desanfrancisco meha Representado queporcausa dela persecucion delos
hereges ha venido engran diminucion esta orden enaquel Reyno pero q̃ nosobs.
tante esto y que han ydo derribando ydando algunos monasterios delos
que han quedado sehan buelto a Rehedificar yseconseruan quepuesto q̃
estar prohiuidos los estudios sehan acauado los Predicadores viejos q̃ auia
Supp.me que paraque q̃ detodo punto nose acauen y florezca enaquel Reyno
la Religion catholica ayudada depersonas doctas dela d̃a orden les haga
alguna limosna anual durante lapersecucion paraque enla Vniuersi
dad de Lobayna sepuedan sustentar yestudiar vn numero defrayles
moços de aquella nacion yporlas causas Referidas yotras Justas considera
ciones del seruicio de Dios les he hecho m.d ylimosna para el d̃o efec̃o
de M.l ducados encadavnaño todo el tiempo q̃ fuere mi voluntad
V.A ordenara que desde el dia dela fecha desta enadelante seacu
al retor opersona q̃ tuuiere acargo los d̃os Religiosos conlos d̃os
ducados alaño paraque q̃ puedan estudiar ysustentarse ysque se le
uen del dinero q̃se prouyere para elsustento del exercĩto q̃ por
tualidad que yo lotengo assi porbien sin embargo delas ordenes q̃
ay encontrario conlasquales dispenso para en quanto aesto quedando
ensu fuerza yvigor para enlo demas adelante N̄ro señor guar de aV.A
como desseo de S. L.or a XI de settĩe 1606

Buen Hermano de V.A

[signature]

[signature]

First published in 2007
Wordwell Ltd
Media House
South Dublin Business Park
Leopardstown
Dublin 18
Copyright © The authors

Published on the occasion of an exhibition in the Long Room, Trinity College
Dublin, autumn – winter 2007, on the theme of 'Writing Irish history: the
Four Masters and their world', featuring manuscripts and printed works from
the Franciscan Collection, located both in Dún Mhuire, Killiney, and in UCD
Archives, the Royal Irish Academy and Trinity College Dublin.

ISBN: 978-1-905569-12-0

Designed: Ger Garland
Copy-edited: Emer Condit
Printed: Graficas Castuera, Spain

Funding for this publication was provided by the Heritage Council.

Louvain 400 is part of the national celebration of **Shared Histories** organised
under the aegis of the Department of the Taoiseach and the Department of
Arts, Sports and Tourism.

# contents

It is a thing general and plain throughout the whole world, in every place where nobility or honour has prevailed in each successive period, that nothing is more glorious, more respectable or more honourable (for many reasons) than to bring to light the knowledge of the antiquity of ancient authors and a knowledge of the chieftains and nobles that existed in preceding times, in order that each successive generation might possess knowledge and information as to how their ancestors spent their time and life, how long they were successively in the lordship of their countries, in dignity or in honour, and what sort of death they met.

I, Michael O'Clerigh, a poor brother of the order of St Francis (after having been for ten years transcribing every old material which I found concerning the saints of Ireland, observing obedience to each provincial that was in Ireland successively), have come before you, O noble Farrell O'Gara. I have calculated on your honour that it seemed to you a cause of pity and regret, grief and sorrow (for the glory of God and the honour of Ireland), how much the race of Gaedhal the son of Niul have gone under a cloud and darkness without a knowledge of the death or obit of saint or virgin, archbishop, bishop, abbot, or other noble dignitary of the Church, of king or prince, lord or chieftain [and] of the synchronism or connexion of the one with the other. I explained to you that I thought I could get the assistance of the chroniclers for whom I had most esteem for writing a book of annals, in which the aforesaid matters might be put on record; and that should the writing of them be neglected at present they would not again be found to be put on record or commemorated to the end or termination of the world. There were collected by me all the best and most copious books of annals that I could find throughout all Ireland (though it was difficult for me to collect them to one place), to write this book in your name, and to your honour, for it was you that gave the reward of their labour to the chroniclers, by whom it was written; and it was the friars of the convent of Donegal that supplied them with food and attendance in like manner. For every good that will result from this book, in giving light to all in general, it is to you that thanks should be given.

As ní coitchend soilleir fon uile domhan in gach ionadh i mbí uaisle no onoir in gach aimsir da ttainicc riamh diaidh i ndiaidh nach ffuil ní as glórmaire, & is airmittnighe onoraighe (ar adhbharaibh iomdha) ina fios sendachta na senughdar, & eolas na naireach, & na nuasal ro bhádar ann isin aimsir rempo do thabhairt do chum solais ar dhaigh co mbeith aithentas, & eolas ag gach druing i ndeadhaidh aroile cionnas do chaithsiot a sinnsir a ré & a naimsir, & cia hairett ro battar i tticcernas a nduithce, i ndignit, no i nonoir diaidh i ndiaidh, & cred i an oidheadh fuairsiott.

Tanaccsa an brathair bocht durd S Fronseis Michel O Clericch (iar mbeith deich mbliadhna damh acc sccriobhadh gach sendachta da bfuaras ar naomhaibh na hEreann a maille le humhlacht gach Prouinsiail da raibhe in Erinn a ndiaidh a chele do bheith accam) da bhar lathairsi a uasail a Fherghail Uí Ghadhra. Do bhraithes ar bhar nonoir gur bhadbar truaighe, & nemhele, doghailsi, & dobhroin libh (do chum gloire Dé & onora na hEreann) a mhed do dheachattar sliocht Gaoidhil meic Niuil fo chiaigh & dorchadas, gan fios ecca na oidhedha Naoimh, na bannaoimhe, Airdepscoip, Epscoip, na abbadh, na uasal graidh ecclaisi oile, Righ, na Ruirigh, tighearna na toisicc, comhaimsir na coimhsinedh neich dibhsidhe fri aroile. Do fhoillsighesa daoibhsi gur bhó doigh lem go ffuighinn cuidiucchadh na ccroinicighe ar ar mó mo mhes do chum leabhair Annaladh do sccríobhadh i ccuirfidhe i ccuimhne na neithe semraite, & da leiccthi ar cáirde gan a sccriobhadh do lathair nad ffuighti iad doridhisi le a fforaithmet, & le a ccuimhniucchadh go crich, & go foircenn an betha. Do cruinniccheadh lem na leabhair Annáladh as ferr & as líonmhaire as mó do beidir lem dfághail i nÉirinn uile (biodh gur dhecair damh a ttecclamadh go haoin ionad) do chum an leabhairsi do sccriobhadh in bhar nainmsi, & in bhar nonóir óir as sibh tucc luach saothair do na croinicidhibh lás ar sccriobhadh é, & braithre chonuente Duin na nGall do chaith costas bídh, & friothailmhe riú mar an ccedna. Gath maith da ttiocfa don leabhor sin da thabhairt solaiss do chach i ccoittchinne as fribhsi as beirthe a bhuidhe.

Extract from Mícheál Ó Cléirigh's dedication of the 'Annals of the Kingdom of Ireland' to Fearghal Ó Gadhra, 10 August 1636, trans. John O'Donovan (37).

When the Irish Franciscans first began to think of how best to celebrate the fourth centenary of the founding of St Anthony's College, Louvain, we could not have anticipated the energy, enthusiasm, generosity and creativity that have met every invitation to help mark the occasion.

We should not have been surprised. After all, one of our own scholars, Fr Canice Mooney OFM, in 'The Golden Age of the Irish Franciscans', claims that the impact of the founding in 1607 of St Anthony's College, Louvain, on the development of the Irish Franciscans would be hard to exaggerate. He goes on:

> 'In fact, it can be fairly claimed that it was not without its effect on the general history of our country. It soon became an asylum of Irish learning, a rallying ground of Irish patriotism, a power-house of Counter-Reformation activities.'

Learning, patriotism and religion, all encapsulated in Br Mícheál Ó Cléirigh's memorable phrase: *do chum glóire Dé agus onóra na hÉireann.*

*Writing Irish history: the Four Masters and their world* is a key event in this year of celebrations and brings together manuscripts from the Franciscan Collection, located both in Dún Mhuire, Killiney, and in UCD Archives, and the Royal Irish Academy and Trinity College for the first time. Ní háibhéil ar bith a rá go gcuirfidh an taispeántas seo le glóir Dé agus onóir na hÉireann.

Caoimhín Ó Laoide OFM
*Minister Provincial*

10|11

The diversity of Ireland's past is recorded in thousands of manuscripts and books of Irish origin that have survived to the present day. The preservation of an important part of this legacy is solely attributable to the visionary thinking and extraordinary diligence of the Irish Franciscans in the seventeenth century.

During the sixteenth and early seventeenth centuries, a period of enormous upheaval in Ireland that included the Flight of the Earls in 1607, the Franciscans realised that if future generations were to understand Ireland's history, evidence of the past would first have to be rescued and preserved—using the best available intellects and the latest means possible. The task of the UCD Mícheál Ó Cléirigh Institute is to continue this great work and communicate it to new generations.

From their seat of learning at St Anthony's College in Louvain in the Spanish Netherlands—one of the most vibrant intellectual and technologically advanced regions in seventeenth-century Europe—the Irish Franciscans directed a mammoth project that involved the collection of medieval Irish manuscripts, the printing of books in Irish, the writing of Ireland's history, and the recording of saints' lives. The most famous work, the Annals of the Four Masters, a chronicle of Irish history from prehistory to AD 1616, was compiled by a team of scholars under the direction of Mícheál Ó Cléirigh, a Franciscan brother from Donegal.

As a modern, confident nation, we should celebrate our past and understand how past generations tackled the task of writing Irish history. This exhibition and catalogue, the fruit of a unique collaboration, offer the visitor a privileged insight into some of Ireland's most important and most influential works of historical thinking.

John McCafferty
*Director, UCD Mícheál Ó Cléirigh Institute*

Oíche fhliuch dhorcha i nDover Shasana. An scuaine don bhád farantóireachta go hOstend. Mé ag filleadh ar an mBeilg tar éis saoire na Nollag. Glaonn ball den lucht slándála i leataobh mé. Trioblóidí an Tuaiscirt faoi lánseol, fireannach singil. Caithfidh an póilín a dhualgas a chomhlíonadh. Tuigim dó siúd is nach dtaitníonn an cur chuige liom. Béasach borb. Cá bhfuil do thriall? Cad chuige? Oscail do mhála. Luíonn súile an phóilín ar an bportús sa mhála. Athraíonn a phort láithreach. Tuin an ómóis ar a ghuth. Would it be Louvain, sir? Mór idir sin agus a mhacasamhail breis agus trí chéad bliain roimhe sin agus é ag trácht ar na 'perfidious Machiavellian friars of Louvain'.

Mé fós i Lobháin in earrach na bliana 1977, leathchéad bliain go díreach ó d'fhill na Proinsiasaigh ar Choláiste San Antoine tar éis seilbh a chailliúint ar an áit breis agus céad bliain roimhe sin. Bheartaíomar gur chóir an deis a thapú chun an leathchéad a chomóradh. Chaith mé go leor ama sa Bibliothèque Royale sa Bhruiséal ag dul trí na lámhscríbhinní Gaeilge a bhain le Lobháin tráth. Bhí údaráis na leabharlainne an-tuisceanach ar fad agus cheadaigh siad dúinn dosaen lámhscríbhinn a thabhairt go dtí an Coláiste le haghaidh taispeántais. Gan de choinníoll acu ach go gcuirfí na seoda seo faoi árachas cuí i gcaitheamh an achair.

Is maith is cuimhin liom an drithlín uamhain a chuaigh tríom agus mé ag iompú leathanaigh Leabhar Inghine í Dhomhnaill. Díolaim filíochta a bailíodh do Nuala, deirfiúr Aodha Ruaidh, Rudhraighe agus Cathbhairr. Nuala a d'fhág Éire i dteannta na nIarlaí sa bhliain 1607, a bhí i láthair sa Róimh nuair a bhásaigh Cathbharr agus Rudhraighe agus a d'fhill ar Lobháin sa bhliain 1611 chun aire a thabhairt do Rudhraighe óg. Agus d'ainneoin cora crua na cinniúna níor chaill an deoraí croíbhriste seo an spéis san fhilíocht ba dhual dá haicme. Nó b'fhéidir gur mar fhál ar an uaigneas a d'fheidhmigh an fhilíocht di. Bhí an stair á gníomhú in athuair ós mo chomhair amach.

Maidin bhreá gréine bhí mé istigh sa Bibliothèque Royale. Bhí mé díreach tar éis litir a fháil ag deimhniú mo cheapacháin mar léachtóir sóisearach i Roinn na Nua-Gaeilge, Coláiste na hOllscoile, Gaillimh agus leag mé anuas ar an deasc í. Ansin chuir an leabharlannaí cúnta lámhscríbhinn le Mícheál Ó Cléirigh anuas taobh leis an litir. Bhuail splanc tuisceana ar an bpointe boise mé. Murach gaisce Mhichíl Uí Chléirigh breis agus trí chéad bliain roimhe sin, ní bheinnse mar Phroinsiasach ag saothrú i léann na Gaeilge. Lúb eile, dá leochailí féin é, i slabhra an dúchais.

Bhí na heachtraí sin folaithe sna póirsí is faide siar i gcúinní mo chuimhne, meirg agus deannach an díomhaointis orthu, nó gur iarr Bernadette Cunningham orm brollach a scríobh do *Writing Irish history: the Four Masters and their world*. Bhrúcht na cuimhní aníos ar an toirt agus thuig mé nach bhféadfainn diúltú di, arae tá scéal Lobháin fite fuaite le mo scéal féin ar bhonn pearsanta, ar bhonn Proinsiasach, ar bhonn scolártha.

Faoi lár na haoise seo caite bhí Mícheál Ó Cléirigh á mhórú mar eiseamláir Gaelachais agus slánaitheoir na saíochta dúchais. Léiríonn an leabhar seo cén chaoi ar tháinig ann don dearcadh sin, léargas is mó atá faoi chomaoin ag aeráid chultúrtha an stáit nua neamhspleách ná ag dianscagadh ar an stair. Ach má chuireann an saothar seo iachall orainn fáil réidh le híomhá rómánsúil an Chléirigh, is éachtach go deo an cúiteamh a bheidh againn dá bharr, gléthuiscint ar an teagmháil idir an seanchas dúchais agus cúinsí corracha na hEorpa sa chéad leath den seachtú haois déag. Ní fhéadfaí meabhair a bhaint as Éirinn anallód feasta gan ceann a thógáil de na coimhlintí reiligiúnda a bhí ag suaitheadh na Críostaíochta agus den bhéim ar na startha nua náisiúnta a bhí ag teacht chun cinn san Eoraip nua-aimseartha mhoch. Ní insint lom ar Éirinn anallód a bhí idir lámha ag Mícheál Ó Cléirigh ach athchóiriú ar scéal na hÉireann lena chur in oiriúint do choincheap náisiún Caitliceach na hÉireann, coincheap a bhí á ghaibhniú i Lobháin sa chéad leath den seachtú haois déag. Más údar díomá do léitheoir na leathanach seo an dírómánsú ar ról Uí Chléirigh, ní beag mar chúiteamh é cruinnléargas a fháil ar ról an bhráthar bhoicht i dtógáil an náisiúin.

Mícheál Ó Cléirigh's achievements, great as they were, would not have been possible but for the vision of his older confrère Flaithrí Ó Maoil Chonaire, *ollamh file*, adviser to Aodh Ruadh Ó Domhnaill, expert on Irish affairs at the Spanish royal court, provincial of the Irish Franciscans and archbishop of Tuam. Though described by Peter Lombard as more anxious to continue the war than the very officers themselves, Ó Maoil Chonaire's primary responsibility was the future of the Franciscan province of Ireland. With remarkable foresight, he successfully petitioned Philip III for permission to build a college in Louvain where young Irish friars could be professionally trained in the most up-to-date theology of Tridentine Catholicism. When the fledgling community took up residence in May 1607 there was no question of a publishing project. A number of happy coincidences facilitated a move in this direction, however. One was the reception of Giolla Brighde Ó hEoghasa as a novice into the community on 1 November 1607. A professional poet replete with an MA in theology from Douai, he was ideally placed to harness his literary and linguistic skills in the service of the Counter-Reformation. Just over three years later another significant event took place. When Fr Robert Chamberlain made his will prior to making his vows as a Franciscan, 7 February 1611, he left his pension from Philip III to the community:

> ... *re h-aghaidh an clodh Gaoidhilge agus neith do chur a ccló do rachas an onóir do Dhia, a cclú dár násion agus d'Ord San Froinsias.*

With Chamberlain's bequest phase one of the Louvain project was born, and Bonabhentura Ó hEoghasa (formerly Giolla Brighde) published his catechism in Antwerp the following summer, the first of a series of catechetical works. Phases two and three, the hagiographical and historical schemes—the subject of this volume—took another fifteen years to come on stream. This new development could not have occurred, however, but for the entry of professional Gaelic scholars such as Aodh Mac an Bhaird and Mícheál Ó Cléirigh into the Franciscans. The different phases were, nevertheless, very closely linked. Chamberlain's will is only the second known Gaelic text to contain the word *násion*. It is found for the first time in Tadhg Ó Cianáin's *Turas na nIarlaí as Érinn*, where it occurs eight times in all, once in conjunction with the word *Érinnach*. It is hardly coincidental in this regard that Flaithrí Ó Maoil Chonaire and Robert Chamberlain accompanied the earls on their journey to Rome in the spring of 1608 and that the latter entered the Franciscan order in Louvain on his return. There is little to choose between Chamberlain's words, for the honour of God and the fame of our nation, and Mícheál Ó Cléirigh's memorable phrase, *dochum glóire Dé agus onóra na hÉireann*. A worthy aim for a noble scheme. It is a tale worth telling.

Mícheál Mac Craith OFM
*Scoil na Gaeilge, Ollscoil na hÉireann, Gaillimh*

Where does history come from? Many of the fore-tales that tell of the circumstances leading up to what is probably Ireland's oldest and best-known historical narrative, the *Táin Bó Cuailnge*, begin with a question— a question to which the answer was 'It is soon told'. Throughout the Middle Ages the learned class in Ireland continued to tell stories, some true, some mythical, that recorded the experiences of people in the past. The decline of that learned class in the early modern period did not mean the death of *seanchas*, or history, but rather transformed it into something we can recognise as an ancestor of the modern discipline of history. Historians tend to build on the work of earlier generations of scholars, drawing inspiration from the enthusiasms and preoccupations of their forebears. In doing so they tell stories, and they still begin with questions. Their stories may not be as 'soon told' as those in the world of the *Táin* but they continue to be told. Telling ourselves stories about our past is part of the human condition, and the practice survives from generation to generation. This catalogue and exhibition are part of that process, presenting a story for our own time that explores how people in Ireland, from the seventeenth to the twentieth centuries, told stories about their pasts.

The 2007 exhibition on 'Writing Irish history: the Four Masters and their world' takes as its centrepiece the original autograph manuscripts of the Annals of the Four Masters written in the 1630s and looks at the sources and legacy of that version of the Irish past. The exhibition marks the quatercentenary of the founding of the Irish Franciscan College of St Anthony at Louvain, in Belgium, which was the intellectual centre of Irish-speaking scholars in mainland Europe in the early seventeenth century. Mícheál Ó Cléirigh, the principal historian involved in the preparation of the Annals, had joined the Franciscans at Louvain, and in 1626 he returned to Ireland to begin his work of scholarship. A prodigious scribe, his writings extend to thousands of pages of manuscript, now dispersed in various archives in Ireland and overseas. This exhibition draws together some of his manuscripts that have not been seen together for centuries. Not since the middle of the 1630s have the five manuscripts that comprise the two contemporary sets of the Annals of the Four Masters been assembled together in one place. The process of drawing manuscripts together is not just about the text of the Annals, however. When those manuscripts were written in a Franciscan friary in Donegal, the floor of the writing-room was covered with originals and copies of the source texts that the annalists used in their task. This exhibition includes some of those much older manuscripts also, and they too are brought together in one place for the first time since the Four Masters assembled them for their work the 1630s.

The process of reconstructing the world of the Annals of the Four Masters poses questions of context and linkages concerning the manuscripts that have been assembled here. While many scholars have explored and documented the histories of individual texts, the interrelationships among them and the circumstances within which they circulated in the past have rarely been explored. The medieval manuscripts in this exhibition include material from both secular and ecclesiastical contexts, manuscripts whose influence on the work of later scholars has been immense. The authority attaching to source compilations such as the Book of Leinster is daunting to contemplate, the high regard in which it was held in successive generations compounding its significance. The Franciscan texts that have survived from the medieval period are a reminder of the extraordinary longevity of the religious orders and their profound impact on the religious and cultural life of Ireland over many generations. By the seventeenth century, Irish historians of all Christian confessions were interested in the manuscript sources for early Irish history, not least because rival accounts of early Irish church history were in preparation. Historical chronicles and narratives were written from different confessional perspectives, and the interpretation of historical sources offered by Catholic and Protestant writers varied. Yet the essential concern to understand and preserve the authentic manuscript sources of the Irish past transcended religious divisions. Mícheál Ó Cléirigh and his associates were part of a seventeenth-century network of scholars interested in the manuscript sources for Irish history, an interest that persisted in later generations, though often in very different cultural contexts.

While so many of the manuscripts that once existed in medieval Ireland have been lost, the very fact of the survival of works such as the Annals of the Four Masters itself becomes a story worth remembering. These Annals have survived the ravages of time because of the value that later scholars attached to them as an authentic record of early Irish history. In addition to the endeavours of individual scholars, institutions such as Trinity College Dublin (established in 1592), the Royal Irish Academy (established in 1785) and of course the Franciscan order, which has had a presence in Ireland since the thirteenth century, have all contributed greatly to the survival of those manuscripts. It is fitting that these same institutions should collaborate in making possible this 2007 exhibition as part of the Louvain 400 commemorations coordinated by the UCD Mícheál Ó Cléirigh Institute for the Study of Irish History and Civilisation.

The final part of the exhibition examines how the seventeenth-century task of writing Irish history, especially the Annals of the Four Masters, was reshaped and recontextualised in the nineteenth and twentieth centuries. By the early nineteenth century works such as the Annals of the Four Masters had become the subject of intense antiquarian interest, as scholars were keen to make a more thorough study of early Irish history and to bring source texts in the Irish language into the public sphere once more. Through the publishing work of men such as George Petrie and John O'Donovan in mid-century, the Annals of the Four Masters took on the status of an iconic text for the emerging Irish nation. In a sense, this chronicle of Irish history can be said to have provided an important part of the inspiration for the late nineteenth-century 'Celtic Revival', and ultimately helped to shape the cultural climate from which the modern Irish state emerged.

History is a continuum, but it is also a chronicle of change. While the version of Irish history presented in the Annals of the Four Masters may have been constructed as an attempt to give weight to the idea of an Irish kingdom after 1603, by the twentieth century those same Annals were marshalled in support of a republic, a form of government for which the Four Masters would have had little sympathy. Each generation reinterprets the past in the light of present concerns, but the value of the manuscript materials that are the raw material of history remains undiminished.

Bernadette Cunningham
*Editor*

# Part 1. Essays

# Chapter 1

# The *seanchas*[1] tradition in late medieval Ireland

Edel Bhreathnach

The art of writing history was a long-established one in medieval Ireland, and the status of the historian in contemporary society was high. Mícheál Ó Cléirigh and his fellow scholars Fearfeasa Ó Maoil Chonaire, Cú Choigcríche Ó Cléirigh and Cú Choigcríche Ó Duibhgheannáin all belonged to families from the north and the west of Ireland who had practised the arts of history and poetry throughout the late medieval period. These families, and many others throughout Ireland, were members of the courts of the medieval Irish aristocracy. They sustained important schools of learning, were hereditary keepers of medieval churches, and possessed extensive lands and other wealth as a consequence of their profession and the nobility that accrued to it.[2] An essential element of the art of preserving and writing history in this world was an understanding of the concept of *seanchas*,[3] a word deriving from *sean* 'old, long-standing'.[4] The practitioner of *seanchas* was known as a *seanchaidh* 'a historian'. *Seanchas* consisted of the many traditions that related to the Irish as they were perceived in the medieval period—their origins and genealogies, their saints and their landscape. Briefly defined, *seanchas* was the memory and narrative of Irish history as preserved and written from the early medieval period to the writing of histories of Ireland in the seventeenth century.

In medieval Ireland, there were many terms associated with the practice and writing of history. Some were derived from Latin and from common forms of recording history, such as the compilation of annals or chronicles: these terms include *stair* (*historia*), *annál* (*annalis*) and *croinic* (*chronica*). Chronicles were compiled in Ireland from the sixth century AD. In the early medieval period they were preserved and updated in major monasteries such as Armagh, Clonmacnoise, Iona and Kildare. When the church was reformed in the twelfth century, the structure of learning was also reorganised. [Fig. 1.1] The task of compiling chronicles was continued by a learned class who had acquired knowledge of the art in the pre-twelfth-century Irish church but who practised in their own schools of learning and for secular patrons throughout the late medieval period. Although secular, these scholars were still closely associated with old churches, and some also with newly introduced orders such as the Franciscans. Hence, for example, the Annals of Ulster [Fig. 1.2] were compiled in the sixteenth century by Ruaidhrí Ó Casaide (d. 1541), archdeacon of Clogher and member of a family long associated with the island monastery of Devenish, Co. Fermanagh, and Ruaidhrí Ó Luinín (d. 1528), chief poet to the Maguires of Fermanagh. It was no accident that Mícheál Ó Cléirigh and his associates chose the chronicle as the form in which to present the history of Ireland since the beginning of the world in the Annals of the Four Masters (**18, 19, 20, 21, 22**). This was a well-trodden path and one that already had a given structure, although they added their own imprint and outlook to the medieval format.[5]

If a universal form of recording history provided the basis of the Annals of the Four Masters, a particularly Irish concept, that of *seanchas*, also informed the minds of the seventeenth-century historians. It could not have been otherwise, as their own training as historians was based on a detailed knowledge of *seanchas*. In its early medieval manifestation *seanchas* was linked to *scéal* 'tidings, narrative history' and to *reacht* 'law' and was subdivided into different branches, including *scéalsheanchas* 'the lore of stories', *laíodhsheanchas* 'the lore

Fig. 1.1. Book of Leinster. The *dinnsheanchas* of Tara. TCD 1339, p. 159 (cat. no.1) (*opposite*).

of poetry', *naomhsheanchas* 'the lore of saints' and *dinnsheanchas* 'the lore of places'. In practical terms, the memory of elders and historians concerning land-holdings, boundaries and legal disputes was essential in court proceedings: the *seanchaidhe* sat in the *taobhairecht* 'side court' 'because it is on the lore [*seanchas*] of the custodians of tradition and the clarification of the custodians of tradition that the court relies'.[6] In late medieval Ireland, despite the administration of the code of common law on behalf of the English crown and the use of formal legal documents such as charters and deeds, a parallel native legal system continued to be operated by the Irish aristocracy and to be fostered by legal families. The Annals of the Four Masters is replete with the obits of professors of native law (*féineachas*) and of lawyers and judges (*britheamhain* 'brehons') attached to the courts of Irish lords.

The right of a noble family to rule a particular kingdom or lordship was often supported by the *seanchaidh*'s recitation—and indeed on occasion creation—of an appropriate genealogy. According to the early Irish law-tract on the grades of poets, *Uraicecht na Ríar*, an *ollamh* or chief poet had to be competent in composing poems and in *féineachas*, and knowledgeable in *coimhghne*.[7] The term *coimhghne*, which can be translated as 'historical knowledge', pertained specifically to the memory and expertise in the construction of genealogies. A large corpus of the genealogies of Irish kings and saints survives in medieval manuscripts dating from the twelfth century, although the genealogies themselves can often date back as far as the sixth century. Many of the important manuscripts contain genealogical collections, including the twelfth-century Book of Leinster (**1**) and the late fourteenth/early fifteenth-century Book of Ballymote and Book of Lecan. The most extensive collection of genealogies was compiled by Dubhaltach Mac Fhirbhisigh (d. 1671), a contemporary of Mícheál Ó Cléirigh and a member of the great learned family of north Connacht, the Mic Fhirbhisigh. Ó Cléirigh, therefore, was following a long tradition of genealogical compilation when he produced his *Seanchas Ríogh Éreann 7 Genealuighi na Naomh nÉreannach* (Genealogies of the Kings and Saints of Ireland) (**23**) in 1630. In his own words, he had used the formula of the pedigree to present the sanctity and history of Ireland's many saints 'because it was impossible to trace the descent of the saints directly to their origins without first setting down the descent of the kings, for it is from these that the saints sprung'.[8] [Fig. 1.3]

*Seanchas* was not confined to practical uses such as legal disputes and proving the legitimate claim of kings and lords to their rights by reference to genealogies. It was a trigger for a society's memory of the past, best displayed in various genres of medieval Irish literature. The heroic deeds (*scéal agus seanchas*) of past heroes might be recited by a poet to inspire kings and armies to great deeds, as evident from the opening passage to the eighth-century tale *Cath Almhaine* 'The Battle of Almu'. On the eve of the battle, the poet Maigléne is brought before Feargal mac Maoile Dúin, king of the northern Uí Néill, who is about to face the Leinstermen in battle the following day. 'He related the battles and the contentions of Leth Cuinn and Leinster from the "Taking of Túaim Tenbad", namely Dind Ríg, in which Cobthach Cóel Breg was killed to the present. And they did not sleep much that night such was their fear of the Leinstermen.'[9]

This type of exhortation using the exploits of past heroes and their tales to instil bravery in contemporary heroes—a universal device not confined to Ireland or to any specific period—continued to inspire poets and to please patrons, as many bardic poems of the late medieval period demonstrate. The term *seanchas* frequently appears in their opening lines, thus presumably invoking memories of heroic ancestors and exploits in the patron and audience being addressed. An anonymous sixteenth-century bardic poem addressed to Mac Marcuis Mac Domhnaill opens with the line *Éist re seanchas Síol gColla* 'Listen to the *seanchas* of the descendant of Colla': by calling on Colla (the ancestor of the northern people known in the early medieval period as the Airgíalla) and his descendants the poet was immediately reminding the patron of his noble ancestry, of his family history and also of their enemies throughout the ages. Similarly Tuileagna Ó Maoil Chonaire, addressing Domhnall Mac Murchadha in 1603, opens with the somewhat provocative line *Cuiream suas seanchas Laighean* 'I present the *seanchas* of Leinster', thus again requiring the patron to face his province's and his family's history.[10]

Apart from noble patrons and heroes, landscape also evoked a society's memory. Places could be associated with many different tales and could be used to convey contemporary political messages. This branch of *seanchas*, known as *dinnsheanchas* 'the lore of place (*dinn*)', formed the basis for an extensive corpus of literature that in its ultimate form, as compiled in the eleventh and twelfth centuries, was known as *Dinnsheanchas Éireann*.[11] The corpus, written both in prose and in poetry, describes natural features (hills, rivers, lakes, woods, estuaries, bogs and plains) and also man-made features in the landscape (burial mounds, cairns, roads, forts, pillar stones). Typically a poem might begin with a verse such as in the case of one of the poems on the River Boyne:

> *A Mailshechlainn mic Domnaill*
>
> *do chlainn ingine Comgaill,*
>
> *adcós duit, a máil Mide,*
>
> *senchas Bóinde báin-gile.*

> O Máelshechlainn son of Domnall, of the race of the daughter of Comgall, I will relate to you, O hero of Mide, the *seanchas* of bright Bóann.[12]

By recounting the river's *seanchas*—including all its mythological associations with the goddess Bóann and the deities Daghda, Óenghus and Neachtan—the poet addresses Máel Sechlainn mac Domhnaill, king of the midlands and Brian Bóroimhe's great rival (d. 1022). While the composition of *dinnsheanchas* reached its height in the eleventh and twelfth centuries, it remained part of the canon of native learning into the late medieval period, as is apparent from the numerous fragments of these works preserved in manuscripts of that period.

The earliest entries recording the deaths of *seanchaidhe* (or *peritii*, the Latin word deemed equivalent by the medieval Irish) occur in the ninth century. Cú Roí son of Aldniadh of the church of Inishcleraun, Co. Longford, who died in 871, is described in the Annals of Ulster as *peritissimus historiarum Scotticarum* 'the most expert in the histories of the Irish'. Throughout the pre-twelfth-century period, notices of *seanchaidhe* increase, many of them poets or lawyers and most associated with churches. Increasingly they held the ecclesiastical title of *airchinneach* 'a hereditary keeper of a church and its estates', a title that continued to be held by many learned families in the late medieval period. The work of some *seanchaidhe* of the pre-Norman period has survived in sufficient quantity to gain a comprehensive insight into what they produced. For example, the work of Flann Mainistreach of Monasterboice—who died in 1056 and who is accorded the description *airdfher léiginn ocus suí senchusa Érenn* 'eminent man of learning and master of the *seanchas* of Ireland'—consists of poems listing the kings of various midland dynasties. They are formulaic, covering the length of each reign, the attributes and deeds of kings and in many instances how they met their deaths.[13] [Fig. 1.4]

Although carefully crafted to cover an extensive amount of material and written within a strict poetic metre, such poems were clearly devised as mnemonic aides to pupils learning the traditional lore of *seanchas*. Whereas scholars have argued for an independent oral tradition surviving in medieval Irish culture, this is highly unlikely: the survival of *seanchas* depended on a culture of writing and on memory as conveyed through a literate culture.

The late medieval entries in the annals, including those in the Annals of the Four Masters, consistently record the deaths of *seanchaidhe*, and especially of the prominent families involved in the practice of *seanchas*: the

Uí Dhuibhgheannáin, Mic Fhirbhisigh, Uí Chianáin, Uí hUidhrín, Uí Chléirigh, Uí Mhaoil Chonaire, Mic Cuirtín, Uí Chuirnín, Uí Luinín and many others. While often accorded the title of historian or chief historian to a particular family or in a particular medieval lordship, they are also given ecclesiastical titles and associated with other professions. The death is recorded in the Annals of the Four Masters under 1441 of Piaras Cam Ó Luinín, a learned historian and poet, and *aircheannach* (erenagh) of Ard and of the third part of Derryvullan, Co. Fermanagh. In 1373 Adam Ó Cianáin, an Augustinian canon and learned historian, who was chief scribe of the Ó Cianáin miscellany now NLI G 2–G 3, died at the priory of Lisgoole, Co. Fermanagh. Many were poets but others practised law and even medicine: the Four Masters record the death in 1478 of Tadhg Fionn Ó Luinín, a learned physician and historian. As members of the aristocracy, these historians were wealthy landowners in their own right, and it would seem that the highest praise accorded to them on their death was that their home was one of open hospitality: Dubhthach Ó Duibhgheannáin, who died in 1495, is praised as one of the richest learned men in Ireland in flocks and herds, who kept a house of general hospitality at his hereditary abode in Kilronan, Co. Roscommon. Being part of an aristocracy that was often at war meant, however, that an untimely death could occur, as happened in 1522 to Diarmaid son of Tadhg Cam Ó Cléirigh when caught up in the defence of the O'Donnell castle at Ballyshannon, Co. Donegal, against the O'Neills.

Mícheál Ó Cléirigh and his associates emerged from an education that was wholly dependent on *seanchas*, an encyclopaedic knowledge of the history of Ireland and its people that had been constructed during the medieval period. Their use of texts such as *Leabhar Gabhála Éireann*—the medieval narrative of the origins of the Irish and the chronology of their kings—and their identification of the primary sources necessary for their work demonstrate clearly that the bedrock of their scholarship belonged to this medieval form of historical writing. That this was the case is nowhere more obvious than in the controversy that arose when in the 1630s and 1640s his fellow Franciscan Tuileagna Ó Maoil Chonaire took issue with points of *seanchas* in Ó Cléirigh's work. The latter's colleague Fearfeasa Ó Maoil Chonaire, whose written defence survives, consistently refers to their adherence to the proper practice of *seanchas* throughout his argument and concludes with a valedictory description of himself as one by heredity not ignorant in the interpretation and setting down of the history of the Gaeil (*senchus na nGaoidheal*).[14] In reality, although historical texts were occasionally revived and renewed in Ireland into the nineteenth century, this controversy was one of the last episodes in which professional, noble *seanchaidhe* contended with one another in accordance with a long-standing medieval tradition.

1    Although many terms in this essay belong to the early Irish period, they are given Modern Irish spellings to conform with editorial conventions.

2    For a detailed account of the Mac Fhirbhisigh family and their medieval learned counterparts see Nollaig Ó Muraíle, *The celebrated antiquary Dubhaltach Mac Fhirbhisigh (c. 1600–71): his lineage, life and learning* (Maynooth, 1996).

3    For detailed discussions on the concept of *seanchas* see Francis John Byrne, '*Senchas*: the nature of Gaelic historical tradition', in J. G. Barry (ed.), *Historical Studies* 9 (Belfast, 1974), 137–59; Donnchadh Ó Corráin, 'Nationality and kingship in pre-Norman Ireland', in T. W. Moody (ed.), *Nationality and the pursuit of national independence: Historical Studies* 11 (Belfast, 1978), 1–35; Katharine Simms, 'Charles Lynegar, the Ó Luinín family and the study of *seanchas*', in T. Barnard, D. Ó Cróinín and K. Simms (eds), *A miracle of learning: studies in manuscripts and Irish learning. Essays in honour of William O'Sullivan* (Aldershot, 1998), 266–83.

4    Kim McCone, 'OIr. *senchae, senchaid* and preliminaries on agent noun formation in Celtic', *Ériu* 46 (1995), 1–10.

5    For accounts of the tradition of compiling annals in medieval Ireland see Kathleen Hughes, *Early Christian Ireland: introduction to the sources* (London and New York, 1972), 99–159; Gearóid Mac Niocaill, *The medieval Irish annals* (Dublin, 1975); Daniel P. McCarthy, 'The chronology of the Irish annals', *Proceedings of the Royal Irish Academy*

98C (1998), 203–55; Thomas Charles-Edwards, *The Chronicle of Ireland* (2 vols) (Liverpool, 2005).

6    Fergus Kelly, 'An Old-Irish text on court procedure', *Peritia* 5 (1986), 74–106.

7    Liam Breatnach (ed.), *Uraicecht na Riar. The poetic grades in early Irish law* (Dublin, 1987). For observations on the concept of *coimhghne* see Seán Mac Airt, '*Filidecht* and *coimgne*', *Ériu* 18 (1958), 139–52.

8    Paul Walsh (ed.), *Genealogiae regum et sanctorum Hiberniae by the Four Masters* (Dublin, 1918), 143–4.

9    Pádraig Ó Riain (ed.), *Cath Almaine*, Mediaeval and Modern Irish series 25 (Dublin, 1978).

10   RIA MS 23 G 8, pp 88–97.

11   E. J. Gwynn (ed.), *The metrical dindshenchas*, Todd Lecture Series (5 vols) (Dublin, 1903–35; repr. 1991).

12   *Ibid.*, vol. 3, 34–5.

13   W. M. Hennessy and B. MacCarthy (eds), *Annála Uladh: Annals of Ulster from the earliest times to the year 1541* (4 vols) (Dublin, 1887–1901), s.a. 1056; John [Eoin] Mac Neill, 'Poems by Flann Mainistrech on the dynasties of Ailech, Mide and Brega', *Archivium Hibernicum* 2 (1913), 37–99.

14   Walsh (ed.), *Genealogiae*, 147–53.

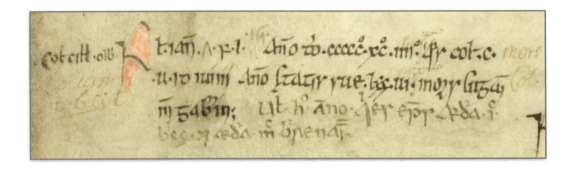

The *seanchas* tradition in late medieval Ireland

Fig. 1.2.   Annals of Ulster. Obit of Colum Cille, 597. TCD 1282, f. 21v (*above*).

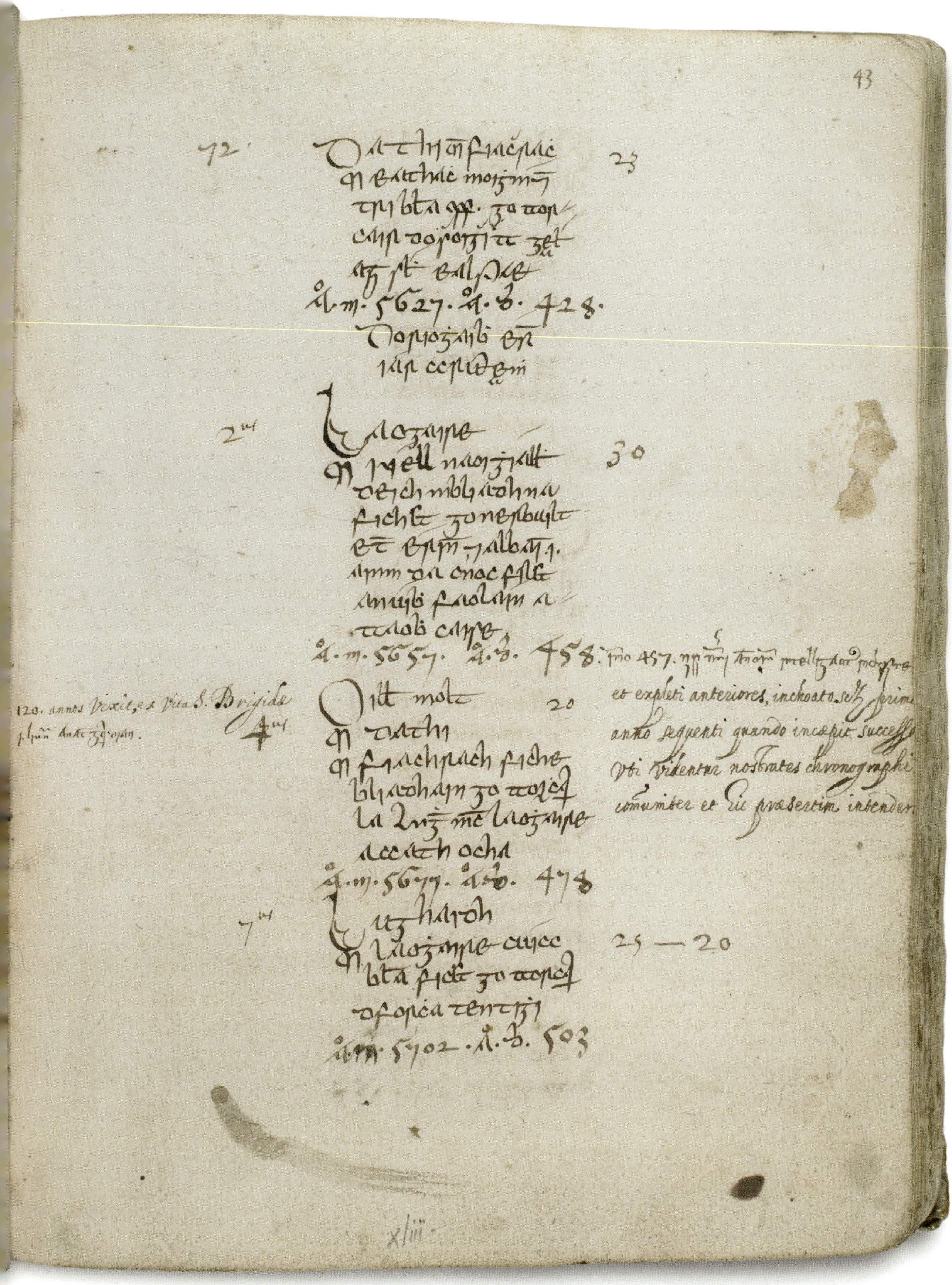

72              23

a.m. 5627. a.d. 428.

2ᵘˢ              30

a.m. 5657. a.d. 458.

120. annos vixit, es vita S. Brigida

4ᵘˢ            20

a.m. 5677. a.d. 478.

7ᵘˢ           25 — 20

a.m. 5702. a.d. 503

xliii

Fig. 1.3. Genealogies of the Saints and Kings. UCD-OFM A 16, f. xliii (*above*).
Fig. 1.4. Annals of Ulster. Obit of Flann Mainistreach, 1056. TCD 1282, f. 59v (*opposite*).

cua mc cte caimbelt comgb tod srais.

Cat ir piru alba paranu ropeo t mileo
dais alban ymib coly cristean. rropein in
pinciyn. loc ripoe oona irleib cuig toeliu
andso apice irsle miceal rorech irr gabail
ci ri auorail t abanciar;

Rian .i. p. lxxxra. Ano tb.m. lc.ii. Dom ruao
h. brias togb la. h. nisom. Aelmacrch maissin
com. comgaill. Coluis h. catail air riar ailegn
Oron h. meoais ain bza. gillapat ri oslais.
Fiac h. coren olc mono tbrisre. Mais riats
oelb h. mbrias pirich h. mbrias ropeo m.
c. ru coirruca olc. Cat marcrairi riaoib
oalesri com. palc. em lorris h. maelrect i com.
rines icot.c ou ropeo ili;

Rian .ii. p. lx. Ano tb.m. lc.ii. Caizac m zyn
zabai com. canris irarir. Clic cli cleinic
man sea. Leo h. roirchio qoc lerisri qo maca
i. bri. u. cearar rue ano inpace qe. gonzal ir
marcha inri ogcizrin plenr oiri inrlincerri
paurunt. Taro m melcirs h. scoba togb
urbmaie. Et m lobroa toir manie cirri
oroa oroar uit inrhirhinra m.2. Crle lam
all m maelrect roal naire cot xx.c rohuaib
it xx oiie robic. gillam a mocan irrame co
alea og morta 2. Flan mairrec qoc lerisri
rri rineza eri murca edna nerirrer. Tene rel
ci toizarri conogb cricorirunt cola im leis
in ocriuro iconobuir imile. Crle tocuaio
eoch h. rlaric qoce roolaie mon imais nira
cot.u.c bo uiii i. cohobrri muirri huaca racir
conuig

nabu irrobain riobaroe occ qxt oib incalena
morira;

Rian .iiii. p. lxxy. Ano tb.m. lc.uii. Fiall h. ere
nlean ri clic enoai air occiri qi. Durall h. tom
cha ri eocira cairi totiri lainch m mbriai cm
ulri. Pinore h. pinore riona man tociri la
maelrect h. mbrire. Cm qcac m enaia ain ouli
li clare tool oiaailri. Mais riarriaib h. riu
toaca oariaib rzillach cri h. rcel rrrbeach
h. aelruan h. roorral ri olrire eile totiri lainri
mbar. ciurriocac h. eyrie ri. h. mbqce m.2.
O nboalie h. cncroa ain conce riobqcac m prim.
com cot.c mono tbrirri. Dom h. riuic togb
laton m maelruan ri e manac.

Rian .u. p. l.ii. Ano tb.m. lc.uiii. Oirbleac ibri
roloircao colein ir oar hac icloicie. lulac m
zilla to oar qrrir alba togb lamael colri mon
cha icai. Mais rleibe ct riarriorac m mail
nambo prrnch m brriai roriec qb. h. hroai ain
irleca roam rirbqra m rcore ri ele rairir m.
zallbriac h. chbaril ririona rbirriac m.2. Colma h.
airlrriri com. tozaill. h. ct cua ain imleaca ibri
rrpace qea. ri beach m pirlaie qroq alb togb
lamaelrect m torcha icai:

Rian .ui. p. l.iii. Ano tb.m. lc.ix. Crle lam elrect
h. morabar rariraib com t.c.bo t paulo rri rro
rroqb zilla me m amilrriai me cte rrais. Aelrect
h. bric toriuch inuai lamaelrect h. rrelar. Leo
h. oiroar ri. h. noalzroa air occiri qi. Crle la

Roi expro. at deuchmarh lu do Airzzt. Loiser
Aile, seched, trijochatt, ase.

bn. michel oclerizh
Sinrus omcol conje
feaxfeasa omcol De
Creorzecche oclerr

conje oclerr

fr Bernardinus Terg
guardianus Dunglis

br. Nipyr ultach
bp Nipyr ultach

## Chapter 2
# Writing the Annals of the Four Masters

Bernadette Cunningham

In January 1632 four Irish historians came together in County Donegal to compile a new history of the kingdom of Ireland. The men involved were members of hereditary learned families within Gaelic society. The leader of the group was Mícheál Ó Cléirigh, a Franciscan who had spent time at the Irish College of St Anthony in Louvain in the 1620s.[1] He was assisted by three laymen, Cú Choigcríche Ó Cléirigh, Fearfeasa Ó Maoil Chonaire and Cú Choigcríche Ó Duibhgeannáin. They soon became known as the 'Four Masters'. All were trained historians from the north-west of Ireland, steeped in the heritage of *seanchas* that had been their families' profession for generations. They were experts in reading and interpreting Irish historical manuscripts, and they had assembled a significant collection of older manuscript sources that formed the basis of their work. They intended that their completed work would be published and become the first such compilation for Ireland to be made available in print. Circumstances prevented the work from being printed before the mid-nineteenth century, but the original manuscripts of the annals survived through the centuries as a testimony to the achievement of the Four Masters. [Fig. 2.1]

Though shaped by the tradition of their ancestors, the Four Masters were embarking on an innovative undertaking. The writing of the 'Annals of the Kingdom of Ireland' marked the coming together of the new European fashion of writing the history of nations with the older Gaelic *seanchas* tradition. The project, which was designed to ensure that the kingdom of Ireland would have a history such as other European nations had, was masterminded by the Irish Franciscans based at the College of St Anthony in Louvain in the Spanish Netherlands, but it was brought to fruition in Ireland where the necessary scholarly expertise and the source manuscripts were available.

It took the team of historians and scribes several years to complete their ambitious undertaking. The Annals of the Four Masters, at well over 400,000 words, were much longer than any of the older compilations from which they were partly derived. The approach of the Four Masters can be contrasted with that of Brian Mac Diarmada, who in the late sixteenth century had been responsible for compiling the Annals of Loch Cé. Like the work of the Four Masters, Mac Diarmada's annals were based on older annalistic sources of the Ó Duibhgeannáin and Ó Maoil Chonaire families. To these Mac Diarmada added sixteenth-century entries of his own, but in doing so his interest was primarily in his own lordship and his own family rather than in the history of Ireland as a whole. Mac Diarmada's annals commenced in AD 1014 and he displayed no interest in the theme of the ancient kingdom of Ireland that was central to the work of the Four Masters. Thus the annals planned by Mícheál Ó Cléirigh in the 1630s were much broader in concept and more ambitious in scale.

Work proceeded in stages over a period of four years. Much of what is known of the working method of the Four Masters is derived from the evidence of the autograph manuscripts themselves. The hands of various different scribes can be seen, including three of the four masters (the exception is Cú Choigcríche Ó Duibhgeannáin) and two scribal assistants, Muiris Ó Maoil Chonaire and Conaire Ó Cléirigh, who wrote substantial portions of the surviving manuscripts. There is plentiful evidence that the annals were carefully checked and revised, most

Fig. 2.1. Annals of the Four Masters. Signature page. UCD-OFM A 13, f. xxiv (*opposite*).

of the amendments being the work of Cú Choigcríche and Mícheál Ó Cléirigh. At least two sets of the annals were made, and when the manuscripts were completed in August 1636 those present signed their names to the finished work. Then Mícheál Ó Cléirigh obtained approbations from two other professional historians, Flann Mac Aodhagáin and Conchobhar Mac Bruaideadha, and four Irish bishops. [Fig. 2.2] These ancillary texts are quite innovative in an Irish manuscript context and provide a clear indication that the work was being prepared for publication. Once this ancillary material had been assembled, Ó Cléirigh took one set of autograph manuscripts (**20, 21, 22**) to Louvain,[2] while the other set (**18, 19**) was probably presented to the patron, Fearghal Ó Gadhra.[3] Later chapters will document the fate of the manuscripts since that time, as well as the story of their eventual publication.

The history written by the Four Masters contained entries arranged in chronological order by year, hence the name annals. They began with the aftermath of the biblical Flood and continued down to their own day, ending with the death of Hugh O'Neill, earl of Tyrone, in 1616. The annalists had calculated that the world was 2,242 years old in the year of the Flood, and hence their first entry was for *Anno Mundi* (year of the world) (AM) 2242. Under their scheme, based on the septuagint, the world was 5,200 years old at the birth of Christ. Thus the entry for the year AM 5199 was followed by an entry for *Anno Christi* (year of Christ) AD 1.

The earliest section of the Annals of the Four Masters is based on the origin-legend of the peoples of Ireland usually known as the Book of Invasions of Ireland (*Leabhar Gabhála Éireann*) [Fig. 2.3]. This early medieval text recorded a series of 'invasions' by Cessair, daughter or niece of Noah, the Parthalonians, the Nemedians, the Fir Bolg, the Tuatha Dé Danann and finally the Clann Mhíleadh. Versions of this origin-legend were recorded in a range of medieval manuscripts that were available to the Four Masters, and that text was fundamental to their understanding of the ancient Irish past. The annalists prepared their own new recension of the *Leabhar Gabhála* and used this as the basis of their annals, assigning each 'invasion' a precise *Anno Mundi* date.[4] Thus the arrival of Parthalon was dated to AM 2520, that of Nemed to AM 2850, the Fir Bolg to AM 3266, the Tuatha Dé Danann to AM 3303, and finally the arrival of the sons of Míl was dated to AM 3500.

The year of the world 3500 was taken to mark the beginning of the reigns of Irish kings and thus was of special significance to the annalists. They drew attention to it by writing the date in extra-large letters in their manuscripts. They noted a similar watershed over 2,700 years later, when they recorded the reign of the last Irish king without opposition under the year AD 1022. After that, they recorded 'kings with opposition' down to the coming of the Normans. Thereafter it was Norman/English rather than Gaelic kings that were noted by the annalists, beginning with King Henry II and continuing in a systematic way down to the accession of King James I in 1603.

The pre-Christian entries are generally very short, often recording nothing more than the regnal year—the name of the king and the number of years for which he had reigned. Where additional information was available it was included, as the following typical examples illustrate.

AM 4175

The year of the world four thousand one hundred and seventy-five. The sixth year of Roitheachtaigh.

AM 4176

The year of the world four thousand one hundred and seventy-six. After Roitheachtaigh had been seven years in the sovereignty of Ireland, lightning burned him at Dunseverick. It was by this Roitheachtaigh that chariots of four horses were first used in Ireland.[5] [Fig. 2.4]

These entries about successive kings of Ireland were derived from older king-lists available in manuscript sources. The Four Masters prepared a new version of the *Réim Ríoghraidhe* (Reigns of Kings) (**23**) and this was then used along with the *Leabhar Gabhála* as the basis of the chronological framework of the annals.

The coming of Christianity to Ireland was an important event for the annalists, because theirs was a history of the kingdom of Ireland written from a Christian perspective. They paid particular attention to the coming of St Patrick, which they recorded under AD 432. It is interesting that in the Louvain manuscript of the annals (**20**) the folio containing entries for the years AD 431 and 432 was cut out and replaced by a revised text. The revised text contained information derived from the published work of a Continental historian, Cardinal Caesar Baronius, and clarified that Pope Celestine had sent Palladius to Ireland in AD 431, while Pope Sixtus had sent Patrick to Ireland in AD 432.

Records of the lives and achievements of famous men—and some women—form the core of the late medieval annals. There were two main kinds of entries: narratives of battles and other military exploits, and obituaries recording the deaths of significant individuals. Reflecting the nature of society in Gaelic lordships, men dominate these accounts. Nonetheless, almost one in ten of the obituaries relate to women, mostly the wives or daughters of prominent men. Recording the careers and deaths of prominent men was an important function of the annals. These included lawyers, historians and churchmen as well as the secular political leaders of Gaelic society. Some of the more elaborate obituaries include an account of the territories under the control of a lord at the time of his death, as well as naming the chosen successor as head of the lordship.

The annals were not conceived of as propaganda. Rather, the text was crafted so as to be a formal, matter-of-fact account of historical truth. In spite of this, a certain political bias can be detected in the work of the Four Masters. Special prominence is given to narratives of the military exploits of the O'Donnells, lords of Tír Conaill, now County Donegal. Sometimes, stories of particular battles that were told from an O'Neill perspective in older annals such as the Annals of Ulster were retold from an O'Donnell perspective by the Four Masters. The explanation for such a bias is easily discerned. Within the Gaelic lordship structure, the Ó Cléirigh family of Tír Conaill had traditionally been employed as historians to the O'Donnells. Thus Mícheál and Cú Choigcríche Ó Cléirigh were merely following a time-honoured tradition within their family by eulogising the achievements of the leaders of the O'Donnells.

The final section of the Annals of the Four Masters is largely based on the Life of Red Hugh O'Donnell (**24**) written in the early seventeenth century by Lughaidh Ó Cléirigh. This contemporary section is more political than earlier parts of the annals. It reflects the real concerns of the annalists and their contemporaries amidst the social and political upheaval that accompanied the decline of traditional Gaelic society. But while the annalists lamented the deaths in exile of two Ulster leaders, Red Hugh O'Donnell in 1602 and Hugh O'Neill in 1616, the overall theme of the annals was a positive one about the antiquity and longevity of the kingdom of Ireland rather than despair at recent losses.

While adhering to a very conventional form, authenticated by tradition, the annalists succeeded in offering a new, accessible and comprehensive account of Irish history set within a context that had special relevance for seventeenth-century readers. Its grand scale, its rootedness in authentic sources and its particular emphasis on Irish kingship were its most appealing characteristics. It was taken for granted that the history should consist of the doings of kings and nobles, saints and ecclesiastics. The common people had no place in the record of all that was honourable in the Irish past. That accorded with the European norm, and was part of a belief that the purpose of history was to enhance the honour of the nation. A key objective of the annalists was to ensure that the kingdom of Ireland would have a history that would bear comparison with similar histories of other countries that were then in circulation in print. That objective had been clearly expressed by another Irish Franciscan, Patrick Fleming, in a letter to Hugh Ward at Louvain in August 1624: 'What more remains, other than to make a history of the kings of Ireland with their reigns such as other nations have'.[6] Indeed, the desire to show that the kingdom of Ireland was of equal status with other nations was at the core of the entire research project embarked on by the Louvain Franciscans into the lives of Irish saints as well as the secular history of Ireland.

The annalistic form chosen by the Four Masters was the simplest form of historical writing, one that had a time-honoured pedigree. While their work may appear more old-fashioned than that of some of their contemporaries, such as Geoffrey Keating (**25**), who opted for a discursive prose narrative, the format allowed the story of the past to be presented in a comfortingly familiar framework, and readily evoked a sense of continuity from ancient times. By dealing with the recent past within the grand sweep of history from the creation of the world, the upheaval and change documented in the late sixteenth- and early seventeenth-century entries were set within the context of an Irish kingdom of great antiquity. The objective of the annalists was to offer a comprehensive record of the origins and history of the contemporary kingdom of Ireland, and in that they certainly succeeded.

After the annals were completed, the chief compiler, Mícheál Ó Cléirigh, left Ireland for the last time, returning to the College of St Anthony at Louvain, where he lived for a few years until his death in 1643. He took with him the text of the completed annals, as well as other manuscripts relating to the secular and ecclesiastical history of Ireland. The fruits of his labours were used by John Colgan in his work on the saints of Ireland (**28**). When Colgan published the first volume of his Lives of Irish saints in 1645 he made special mention of the work of Mícheál Ó Cléirigh. Indeed, it was Colgan who first called the four annalists the 'Four Masters'.[7] His words of praise were endorsed by later scholars, and the history of Ireland produced by the Four Masters continued to be held in high esteem. In later generations, the Annals of the Four Masters were perceived as having captured the essence of Gaelic lordship society, recording in minute detail the personalities that had come to prominence in politics or learning or the church, and placing them within the framework of a kingdom of Ireland whose noble origins were as old as recorded time.

1    Brendan Jennings, *Michael Ó Cléirigh, chief of the Four Masters, and his associates* (Dublin and Cork, 1936).

2    UCD-OFM MS A 13 and RIA MS 23 P 6–23 P 7.

3    RIA MS C iii 3 and TCD MS 1301.

4    See the fragmentary copy, now RIA MS 23 M 70, in the hand of Mícheál Ó Cléirigh, and an extended version transcribed by Cú Choigcríche Ó Cléirigh (RIA MS 23 K 32). The latter formed the basis of a partial edition by R. A. S. Macalister and J. Mac Neill (eds), *Leabhar Gabhála: the Book of Conquests of Ireland: the recension of Mícheál Ó Cléirigh, part 1* (Dublin, [1916]). Ó Cléirigh's dedication to Brian Ruadh Mág Uidhir, together with the address to the reader, survive in TCD MS 1286, and were published, with translation, in Eugene O'Curry, *Lectures on the manuscript materials of ancient Irish history* (Dublin, 1861), 169–73, 552–7.

5    UCD-OFM MS A 13, f. 90r. The scribes sometimes tired of the repetitive annual entries on the reigns of kings, and in the example given here the scribe of C iii 3 abbreviated the king's name to his initial 'R' only (RIA MS C iii 3, f. 78r).

6    Translated from Latin in Pádraig A. Breatnach, 'An Irish Bollandus: Fr Hugh Ward and the Louvain hagiographical enterprise', *Éigse* 31 (1999), 11.

7    The term 'Four Masters' had already been in use in an earlier Franciscan context. The *Expositio Quattuor Magistrorum*, or Exposition of the Four Masters, was the name given to a medieval commentary on the Rule of St Francis.

Fig. 2.2.  Approbation from Bishop Roch MacGeoghegan for the 'Annals of the Kingdom of Ireland'. UCD-OFM A 13, f. xxxii (*opposite*).

De hoc opere (quod intitulatur Annales regni Hyberniae, in duas
partes diviso, quarum prima continet à Diluvio ad annum
christi millesimum ducentessimum vigessimum septimum:
Secunda vero continet ad millessimum Sexcentessimum
octavum) quem fr. Michael O'Clerij ordinis S. Francisci,
ad coëm patriae utilitatem collegit; no aliter cense-
mus, quam Censores ab eo ad pium Proum eiusdem fratris,
Scilicet d. Florentius Kegan, et d. Cornelius Brudyn pro
eodem opere inspiciendo, examinando, et approbando,
vel reprobando asignati indicaverunt, et decreverunt.
Nos en eosdem tanquam peritissimos Linguae Hybernicae,
ac in oibus historijs, ac patria chronologijs versatissi-
mos existimamus. Quapropter, illorum Censurae et
iudicio de ipsato opere fris Michaelis O'Clerij in omnibus conformamur. In quorum fidem his manu propria Subscripsimus. Date in loco nrae mansionis
die 8o Jan. ano dni 1637.

                                     fr. Rochus Kik

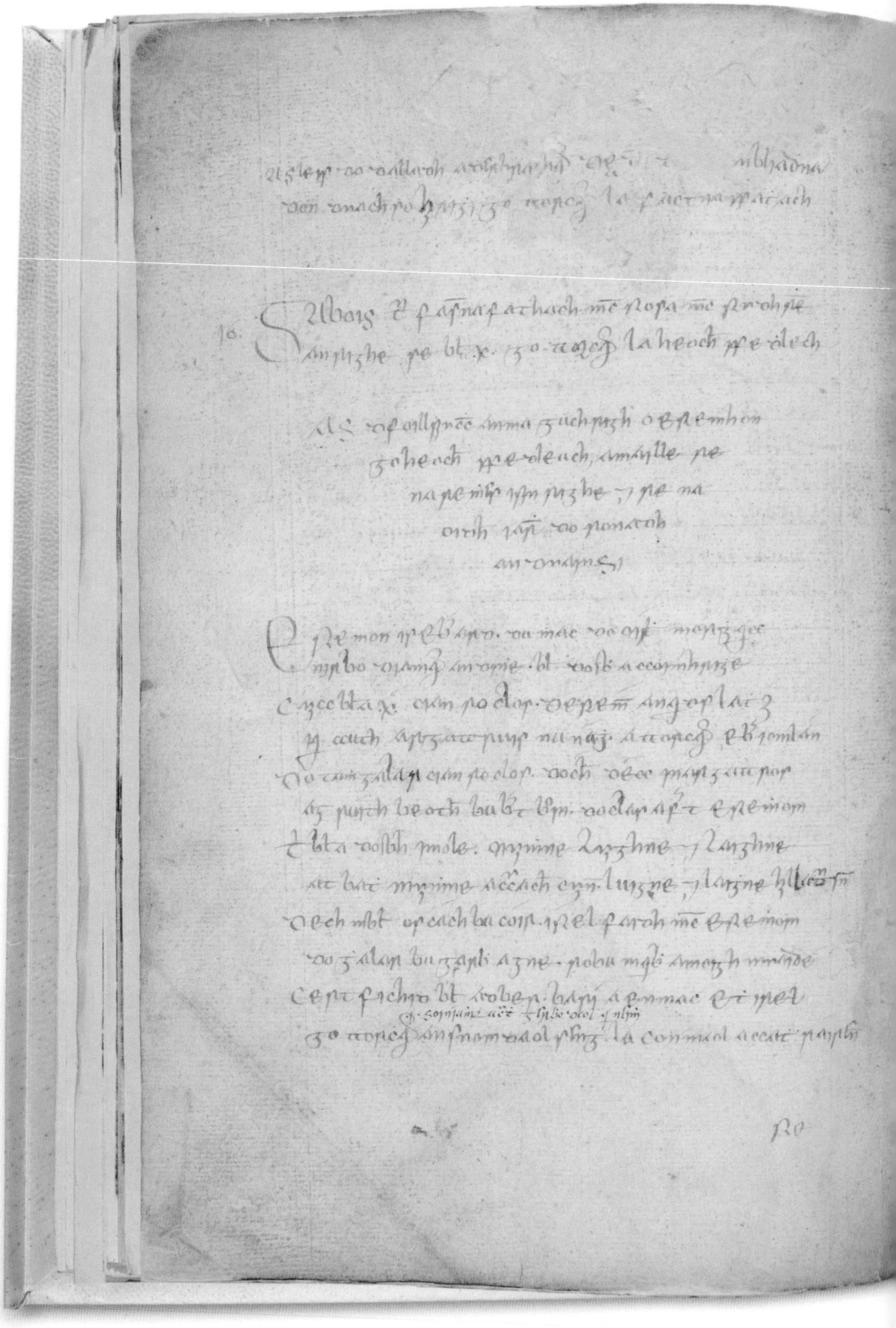

Fig. 2.3. Mícheál Ó Cléirigh, *Leabhar Gabhála Éireann*. RIA 23 M 70, f. 83v (*above*).

Fig. 2.4. Annals of the Four Masters, entries for AM4175–9. RIA C iii 3, f. 78r (*opposite*).

Aois dom. 4175.

Aoir dom. cicpe mile, ceo, seachemo аспи. an pеrp blioo R.

Aoir dom. 4176.

Aoir dom, cicpe mile, ceo seachemo аспе. RꞂꞂ mbec pеаp mbliccona hi pipe nеꞂ oo poceachc Ro loipec cem zealum e hi nom robanpce. As lapen Roceuchc po anpiche cаꞂp cеcꞂpe nbch ꞂꞂ cz pеꞂ

Aois dom. 4177.

Aoir dom. cecc milu, ceo, seuchemoꞂ apeachc. Enbliuo oelpи aill f paꞂ paeachca mc poceucc hi pizhe neꞂ, zo coꞂchuap Ꞃp opicho nu bliconu hippи la zꞂallch mc oiltu olchꞂоꞂ. Ro peap piꞂeuchca moꞂ zo mbluꞂ f Ꞃonu Ꞃsи mbliꞂoꞂ, As ane oo zapch aill f paꞂ peuchcu oepꞂ

Aoir dom. 4178.

Aoir dom. ceicpe milh, ceo, seuchemoꞂ иhochc. An ceo bliuo oo zꞂallch mc oiꞂolla olchꞂоꞂ mc siоꞂи Ꞃpizhe neꞂ

Aoir dom. 4179.

Aoir dom. cicpe milh, ceo, seuchemoꞂ an coi. an oꞂ blioo zꞂallch

S. COLVMBA

# Chapter 3
# Saints' Lives

Pádraig Ó Riain

Few early seventeenth-century Irish scholars were made the subject of casual, almost conversational comment, but in a letter sent in February 1629 to Hugh Ward, Malachy O Queely, vicar-apostolic of the diocese of Killaloe, had this to say of the 'poor friar' Mícheál Ó Cléirigh:

> As I was teaching at Cassell uppon your patron his festivall daie [feast of St Francis, i.e. 4 October], there
> I met your brother Clery who made a collection of more than three or foure hundreth Lives [of saints].
> I gave him some Lives I collected, and sent him to Ormond parte of my diecese to write there for a
> time, from whence he promised to com to Thowmond, wheare I undertook to get many things for him
> … soone I do expect his comminge who shall be wellcom truely to me.[1]

Since the extant Lives of saints in Ó Cléirigh's hand run to about 50, the number cited by O Queely appears to be greatly exaggerated. His comments, however, capture a fleeting image of a friar who, between about 1626 and 1637, travelled the length and breadth of Ireland in search of manuscripts. His search was no random one; he was acting on the instructions of his clerical superiors, whose main concern was the advancement of the so-called Louvain scheme for the preservation and publication of Ireland's early literary monuments, both civil and religious.

The scheme was launched in Paris in 1623, at a meeting attended by one secular priest, Thomas Messingham, rector of the Irish College in Paris, and three Franciscans, Aodh Mac Aingil (**40**), on his way to Rome, Patrick Fleming, who was accompanying Mac Aingil, and Hugh Ward (Aodh Mac an Bhaird) of the Irish College in Louvain. Moreover, the first publication to follow the launch of the scheme, a florilegium of Lives of saints (**26**), was also published in Paris in 1624 by Thomas Messingham (**26**). [Fig. 3.1] Dissension with regard to the destination of transcripts of relevant materials soon led to the virtual exclusion of the Paris College from the scheme and the assumption by the Louvain Franciscans of full responsibility for it. Accordingly, with the approval and, where possible, the financial assistance of the Irish Franciscan province, all necessary steps were taken under the direction of Hugh Ward for the collection of manuscript and printed sources on which the success of the scheme ultimately depended.

The plan was roughly the same as that published by Heribert Rosweyde in *Fasti sanctorum quorum vitae in Belgicis bibliothecis manuscriptae*, which went on to inspire the great Bollandist enterprise for the publication of the *Acta Sanctorum*. Coincidentally, Rosweyde's booklet was published in 1607, the same year that saw the foundation of the Irish College in Louvain. Almost immediately after the meeting in Paris, transcription began of hagiographical materials relating to Ireland in the principal libraries of Italy, France, Belgium and Germany, and among those most active in this work were the Franciscan Patrick Fleming, who maintained an interest in the scheme up to his martyrdom near Prague in 1631, and the Jesuit Stephen White. It was White, for example,

Fig. 3.1. Detail from title-page of Thomas Messingham's *Florilegium* (cat. no. 26) (*opposite*).

who discovered and transcribed the earliest known manuscript copy of the Life of an Irish saint, the early eighth-century copy of Adomnán's Life of Colum Cille, then in the Reichenau, now in Schaffhausen (Stadtbibliothek, MS Generalia 1). Many other friars were enlisted in the project, with the approval of the Franciscan authorities, and a substantial library of relevant materials soon began to be assembled at Louvain. The project was first directed by Hugh Ward, whose health deteriorated rapidly in the years before his premature death in 1635, when John Colgan assumed control. From the outset, the Bollandists of Antwerp maintained close contact with the Franciscans of Louvain.

The texts collected or transcribed on the Continent were exclusively in Latin, so that separate provision had to be made for the collection of Irish vernacular materials, many of which were in danger of destruction through the ravages of war or neglect. Mícheál Ó Cléirigh was the man entrusted with the onerous duty of seeking out as much as could still be discovered of the early manuscript remains, transcribing them and forwarding his transcripts to Louvain. Ó Cléirigh belonged to a family skilled in vernacular learning, and the decision taken by Hugh Ward in 1626 to send him to Ireland, with strict instructions that he carry out his work both diligently and faithfully, was arguably the most inspired one of his whole stewardship of the Louvain scheme.

How far the friar travelled in search of suitable documents, where he stayed while collecting or transcribing, and how much time he devoted to carrying out his instructions can be gleaned from the frequent colophons he added to his transcripts. His itinerary for 1629, which in Ó Cléirigh's calendar ran from 25 March 1629 to the following 24 March, was typical of his travels in other years, and may serve here as an example.[2]

By now in the third year of his mission, in late March 1629 Ó Cléirigh was in the house of the friars at Drowes, near the Donegal–Leitrim border, busily preparing clean copies of previous drafts of saints' Lives, among them an 80-page Life of Bréanainn of Clonfert and a fragment of the Life of St Brigit. With the weather doubtless much improved, Ó Cléirigh appears to have left Drowes in April, probably with a predetermined route in mind. He would have known from his contacts with brethren in other parts of the country where other Lives might be preserved, including some in large, late medieval manuscript miscellanies. The course of his travels is not always clear, but it appears that he visited the area about Leighlin, where he transcribed a fragment of a Life of Caoimhghin, and Castlekevin near Glendalough, where he made a copy of the metrical Life of the same saint. He also spent some time in Franciscan houses in Wexford, where he transcribed Lives of Maodhóg and Seanán, and Clonmel, where he made a copy of a Life of Mochaomhóg of Leigh. By 20 June he was in Timoleague, Co. Cork, where, in the house of the Franciscans, the great Book of Mac Carthaigh Riabhach, now better known as the Book of Lismore, was at his disposal. He copied from it some Lives of Munster saints but appears to have had little time to examine or make transcripts of the extensive extraneous materials in the manuscript, for within four days he was in the Franciscan refuge in Cork, where he transcribed a number of Lives, including one of Barra, patron of Cork. This was taken from a vellum manuscript, now lost, in the possession of Domhnall Ó Duinnín, whose own collection of saints' Lives, probably also made on behalf of the Louvain Franciscans, is now preserved in the Royal Irish Academy (RIA MS A iv 1).

Wherever possible, Ó Cléirigh stayed in Franciscan friaries, which appear to have had instructions to procure for him suitable manuscript materials. Thus, having visited Limerick in August to attend the chapter held by his order, he copied there some texts relating to Seanán of Scattery and Éanna of Aran. Thereafter, it would seem, he travelled on to Killaloe, where he made good his previous promise to the vicar-apostolic, Malachy O Queely, to spend some time in Thomond. There also he transcribed, in deference to his instructions from the directors of the project in Louvain but against his own better judgement, a metrical Life of St Caimín of Inishcaltra. All of these places appear to have been visited before he made his way in early October to the friary of Kinalehin

(*Ceinéal Féichín*) in Galway, where the great Book of Dún Doighre, now known as the *Leabhar Breac* (RIA MS 23 P 16), was waiting for him. From this manuscript, which is largely made up of texts of a religious character, he duly copied at least one Life, that of Ceallach, bishop of Killala.

By November, Ó Cléirigh was back in his own community at Drowes, busily making fresh copies of the Lives transcribed during his journey, and adding notes that occasionally reveal something of the character of the man. For example, on 17 November 1629, having completed a fresh copy of the Life of Maodhóg of Ferns, he repeated, credulously, a wild claim made by an earlier copyist that the text had previously been copied from 'old black books from the time of the saints' written from the very mouth of the saint.

Through the winter of 1629, when travel would have been difficult, Ó Cléirigh remained at or near the refuge of the friars on the River Drowes. He took advantage, however, of the colder months to make copies of Lives of saints attached to churches in west Ulster and north-east Connacht that lay within manageable walking distance of his base on the River Drowes. We may assume either that Ó Cléirigh travelled to the churches connected with these saints or, more probably, that manuscripts containing their Lives were brought to him. The former group of saints included Molaise of Devenish, Lasair of Aghavea, and Náile of Inver and Kinawley, all of whom belonged to churches in Fermanagh or Donegal; the latter comprised Bearach of Termonbarry and Greallán of Creeve, both of whose churches lay in north Roscommon, and Forannán of Alternan in Sligo.

Once the conveniently located sources had been exhausted, the ever-industrious friar filled the short days of the winter months by preparing clean copies of transcripts made on previous journeys, so as to bring them up to a standard suitable for dispatch to his colleagues in Louvain. From the colophons attached to these fresh copies, details of his earlier travels often emerge, as is shown by the Lives of Ciarán of Saighir and Déaglán of Ardmore, which are described as having being previously copied at Cashel, no doubt on the occasion when he was met by Malachy O Queely. Similarly, an earlier journey to the Dublin house of friars is revealed by the colophons that accompany his fresh copies of the Lives of Finnian and Beinéan. Clearly there was much work of this kind to be done, and the winter months were generally devoted to such tasks.

Once copied out afresh and brought together, Ó Cléirigh's superiors would have arranged to have his collections transferred to Louvain. Although some of what he copied may since have been lost, we none the less owe to Ó Cléirigh the survival of the contents of two substantial collections of saints' Lives, now Brussels, Bibliothèque Royale, MSS 2324–40 and 4190–200. Of the over 50 vernacular Lives of Irish saints, or recensions of Lives, that have been preserved, Ó Cléirigh supplied almost 40, fifteen of which are now unique copies. Interestingly, however, of the similar number of copies of vernacular Lives of non-Irish saints that have been preserved, not one is in Ó Cléirigh's hand. Apparently, the instructions given to him by Hugh Ward were to transcribe Lives of Irish saints only. Furthermore, no copy of the vernacular Life of Colum Cille, Ó Cléirigh's Donegal patron and favourite saint, survives in his hand, but this may be due to the fact that Maghnus Ó Domhnaill's Life of this saint (**7**), now UCD-OFM MS A 8, was probably already in the possession of the Franciscans.

The esteem in which Ó Cléirigh held Colum Cille is reflected in the extraordinary length of the entry for his feast-day in the Martyrology of Donegal, which extends to six and a half printed pages and is thus perhaps the most extensive account ever given of a saint in a text of this kind. Ó Cléirigh's contribution to the Irish martyrological tradition equals, or even surpasses, his role in ensuring the survival of saints' Lives. The contents of no fewer than three of his manuscripts, formerly in the library of St Anthony's in Louvain, now Bibliothèque Royale, Brussels, MSS 4369, 5100–4 and 5095–6, bear witness to his concern with transcribing martyrologies— again, no doubt, in line with the instructions he had received from Hugh Ward. The second of these manuscripts contains copies of no fewer than three martyrologies: a transcript of the Martyrology of Óengus made from a source now lost; a copy of the entries relating to Irish saints in the Martyrology of Tallaght (**2**), based on the version otherwise preserved in the Book of Leinster (**1**) but containing much material since lost from the original source; and, finally, the unique surviving copy of the martyrology compiled about 1170 by Maol Muire Ua Gormáin at Knock Abbey, Co. Louth, complete with the author's important prologue. The two other Brussels manuscripts contain copies, one of which is annotated, of the martyrology compiled by Ó Cléirigh himself, in collaboration with his cousin Cú Choigcríche.

The production of a new martyrology seems to have been one of the first tasks to which Ó Cléirigh applied himself after his return to Ireland from Louvain in 1626. Moreover, while based mainly on the Martyrology of Gorman, Ó Cléirigh's version, the first recension of which had been completed by 1628, reflects the progress of his labours in other fields. By then, for example, he had at his disposal a number of individual saints' Lives, and the increase in the availability of this kind of source between 1628 and 1630 can be gauged from the extensive notes added during this period. Among other sources used by him were the hagiographical part of the twelfth-century Book of Leinster, a copy of at least one set of annals, a draft of *Genealogiae Regum et Sanctorum Hiberniae*, a copy of *Náemhsheanchas Náemh nÉireann* [**Fig. 3.2**] and a version of *Liber Hymnorum* (**3**). Clearly, the Donegal refuge of the Franciscans could boast at this time of a substantial library, much of which was later transferred to Louvain.

Unlike previous Irish martyrologies, Ó Cléirigh's Martyrology of Donegal (**38**), as it was dubbed by John Colgan [**Fig. 3.3**], was compiled neither to form part of a chapter book nor to be used in a liturgical context. As is shown by its focus on native Irish saints only, it was to form part of the Louvain scheme for providing a *Thesaurus Antiquitatum Hiberniae*, to be placed alongside the new histories then being written all over Europe. To this end, once in Louvain, the text of the martyrology, as of the saints' Lives supplied by Ó Cléirigh, was first to be translated into Latin and then published. Latin translations of his transcripts of saints' Lives are featured among the texts edited by John Colgan in his two monumental volumes, *Acta Sanctorum Hiberniae* and *Triadis Thaumaturgae* (**28**). No Latin translation of Ó Cléirigh's martyrology has survived. The Bollandists, however, appear to have possessed either a full or a fragmentary Latin copy, which is occasionally quoted in their *Acta Sanctorum*.

Of all those who collaborated in the Louvain scheme, more is perhaps owed by posterity to Ó Cléirigh than to any other, not least because of the many texts transcribed by him whose sources have since perished. His was a truly remarkable achievement and, in composing the *praefatio ad lectorem* of his *Acta Sanctorum Hiberniae* 'a few months' after Ó Cléirigh's death in 1643, John Colgan paid due tribute to his confrère. Placing him third after Ward and Fleming, Colgan devoted more space to outlining Ó Cléirigh's contribution than to any other, describing him as 'a man exceedingly well versed in the antiquities of his country, to whose pious labours over many years, this, and the other works we are printing, owe most of all'.[3] Alas, Colgan's *Acta* was the only published volume of four, covering the saints of the whole year, planned for publication. His other published work, *Triadis Thaumaturgae*, was concerned with Ireland's three principal saints, Patrick, Brigit and Colum Cille (**28**). Despite their involvement in an organised scheme, and unlike the Bollandists of Antwerp, the Irish Franciscans at Louvain did not allow for the need to put their arrangements on a permanent footing, designed to last well beyond the lifetimes of the originators. What remained after the collapse of the scheme, however, was a huge collection of mainly hagiographical manuscripts, many of them in the hand of Mícheál Ó Cléirigh. Moreover, despite the dispersal of the library at Louvain in the wake of the French Revolution, the greater part of the collection has survived and is now divided between the Bibliothèque Royale in Brussels and the Franciscan Collection in University College Dublin.

FURTHER READING: Brendan Jennings, *Michael Ó Cléirigh, chief of the Four Masters and his associates* (Dublin and Cork, 1936). Tomás Ó Cléirigh, *Aodh Mac Aingil agus an scoil Nua-Ghaedhilge i Lobháin* (Baile Átha Cliath, [1936]), 11–17. Pádraig Ó Riain, 'John Colgan's *Trias Thaumaturga*', in reprint of J. Colgan, *Triadis thaumaturgae seu divorum Patricii, Columbae et Brigidae, trium veteris et maioris Scotiae seu Hiberniae, ... acta* (Louvain, 1647; repr. Dublin, 1997). Pádraig Ó Riain, *Feastdays of the saints: a history of Irish martyrologies*, Subsidia Hagiographica 86 (Brussels, 2006), 281–313. Charles Plummer, *Miscellanea Hagiographica Hibernica*, Subsidia Hagiographica 15 (Brussels, 1925), 184. Richard Sharpe, *Medieval Irish Saints' Lives* (Oxford, 1991), 39–74. Paul Walsh, 'The travels of Michael Ó Cléirigh', *Catholic Bulletin* 27 (1937), 123–32, reprinted in Paul Walsh, *Irish leaders and learning through the ages*, ed. Nollaig Ó Muraíle (Dublin, 2003), 350–61. Robert Welch, *The Oxford companion to Irish literature* (Oxford, 1996), 410–11.

1    Brendan Jennings, 'Documents from the archives of St Isidore's College, Rome', *Analecta Hibernica* 6 (1934), 218.

2    This chronology is explained in Paul Walsh, 'The work of a winter', *Catholic Bulletin* 28 (1938), 226–34, reprinted in Paul Walsh, *Irish leaders and learning through the ages*, ed. Nollaig Ó Muraíle (Dublin, 2003), 361–70.

3    John Colgan, *Acta Sanctorum ... Hiberniae* (Louvain, 1647; repr. Dublin, 1948), *praefatio ad lectorem*, sig. b 3.

# SEANCHAS MOR ERENN

Ap na leannam zo ambuanaz ofpe moib
dccap an apnzp plo catch z ach
pi diobh aceeannap, iv
Al ccumacht abhhhh
Erenn pia
pizhe

# GENEALUIGH NA NAOIM NER

eannach amail fpi pao alleabh
poibh na peann nz dap ap na
ccup por pia pleaic tan aib
amail z do zablaiz
peao ap upo
aib zepe

Do chum zloipe de, onopa na naoim z na
pozhaichce iv do tabhdht apchne z collap
ap na netcib pempaice, iv fop z na hnzh
tapaib plo comeo peanchap epenn pia ceisto
eamh, iv iap cepe deamh
Ap na ccpiochnucció acconten bpacaip
ob fennantice mainip tpeach Xialnam
an ga bacc opo each

Clearname nop
·1 6 30·

Fig. 3.2. Genealogies of the Saints and Kings. UCD-OFM A16, f. viii r (cat. no. 23) (*opposite*).

Fig. 3.3. Fresco of John Colgan OFM, from aula of St Isidore's, Rome (*above*).

## Aois Cr. 1395.

Aois Criost. mīle, trīched, nochatt, a cūic.

Archidiacoñ in Branan Olfinia occisꝗ a Concho=
varo O Flanagan. in x̄b.

[Irish text]

[Irish text]

O Neill buide do ecc, & a adnacul pr̄ Ardmaca

[Irish text]

[Irish text] dragesima. m. s. l.

[Irish text]

[Irish text]

[Irish text]

& a ecc da er inz hmhel

[Irish text]

[Irish text]

in Donn mctaidg in brian m andasa in brias lyzne omer,

[Irish text]

beos o ghab porrle do ecc iccayst ghce peccmaz pra nodlыcc

in Catal in Don,
[Irish text]

O Briain i. Brian mc ... do dul go tech ruig sax̃ & honorificè re=
ceptꝰ. in x̄b.

Niall occ m̃ neill mc āda Ꝉ neill do dul tegh ruig sax̃ vbi honorificè habi=
tus. 1603.

[Irish text]
a mayyrt na brlle & m. s. l.

[Irish text]

[Irish text]

[Irish text]

Rodericꝰ o Moelbrenañ futurꝰ dynasta de clāconor obīt.
    Mac-Altair (i. f˴ svalt̃) Rex Scotiæ obijt. in x̄b.

Magnus f. Joāñis o Duvegan insignis Antiquariꝰ obijt. 1603.

Nix magna in festo S. Patricij: bou̇ & pecorū intit̄q. 1603.

Dẽaldꝰ f. Diermitij o Donell obijt. ib̃3.

Lochluñiꝗ o Higgin insignis Poeta obijt. 1603.

Donaldus f. Henr: o Neill cū copijs Brianū f̄ Nielli
O Neill cepit, & spoliavit. ib̃3 Idꝰ Donaldꝰ vxorē D̄ni o Neill
& alios captivos abduxit a

# Chapter 4
# The Ó Cléirigh manuscripts in context

Raymond Gillespie

Writing an overview in the 1970s of Irish-language scholarship in the early modern period, Brian Ó Cuív found himself 'immediately struck by the amount of literary and scribal activity [in the early seventeenth century] despite the unsettled state of the times'.[1] Ó Cuív's observation becomes even more paradoxical if the views of the literati from the seventeenth century itself are also considered. The professional poets claimed, with much justification, that the practice of poetry was dying and the old literary order collapsing. Gaelic lawyers too saw clearly that English common law had superseded older brehon texts. But as the older literary order became more irrelevant to daily life, paradoxically it became much easier to obtain a copy of a literary or a legal text than it had been before. A resurgence in scribal activity and an interest in collecting and lending older manuscripts in the seventeenth century meant that Irish-language manuscripts, both old and new, were common features of life for descendants of settlers such as James Ware (**29**), James Ussher (**30**, **31**) and Arthur Brownlow, as well as for Gaelic families such as those of Conall Mageoghegan in Westmeath and Tadgh Ó Rodaigh in Leitrim. Of the more than 4,000 extant manuscripts in the Irish language, about 250 were written before 1600, and of these 40 pre-date 1400. By contrast, over 200 Irish-language manuscripts written in the seventeenth century survive.[2] At least some of these were the product of professional scribes, such as Dubhaltach Mac Fhirbhisigh (d. 1671) or the Connacht scribe Dáibhí Ó Duibhgeannáin (d. 1696), who now found their services in demand.

By far the largest single body of work produced by a group of scribes working together were the thousands of folios of texts copied or compiled by the Franciscan lay brother Mícheál Ó Cléirigh or by those working under his direction in the late 1620s and early 1630s. The scale and range of this scribal activity was considerable, and some of its best-known products, including the Annals of the Four Masters, retain their value as important compilations of historical evidence. The sheer volume of this material allows us to have at least a glimpse into the making of manuscripts in the early seventeenth century. [Fig. 4.1]

Given the size of the Ó Cléirigh corpus of manuscripts, it is worth stressing the range of subjects covered. Mícheál and his associates included in their work prose Lives of Irish saints, verse and other material said to have been composed by saints, liturgical litanies, genealogies, secular prose tales, secular poetry, annalistic compilations (both contemporary and older texts such as the Annals of Roscrea) and martyrologies. It is also worth noting the range of treatments that the existing texts were given at the hands of the scribes. In some cases Ó Cléirigh simply copied the texts without amendment, according to the instructions given by his patrons in Louvain. He deviated from this mechanical task only to insert chapter divisions into each of the saint's Lives after he had copied them. He wrote chapter numbers in the margins of his text preceded by 'c', 'cap' or 'capituli', using Roman rather than Irish letter forms. This was an innovation since the chapter numbers do not conform to the paragraphing of the text, chapter divisions sometimes appearing in the middle of a line of text. Ó Cléirigh used these chapter divisions for scholarly convenience, citing them in his later Martyrology of Donegal.

In general, the task of transcribing was not an intellectually challenging one, and the exemplars with which he was working were not always of the best quality and the lives not the most edifying. Thus in the case of some

Fig. 4.1. Annals of the Four Masters. TCD 1301, f. 693r (*opposite*).

of the saints' Lives he complained that although they were not to his taste he made faithful copies. When he copied the metrical Life of St Caimín of Inishcaltra in 1629, he commented in a colophon that he found it 'very corrupt, sad, too short in some verses and too long in others and a great deal of utter nonsense. But I make my excuse that it was enjoined on me to follow the track of the old books'.[3] In other cases, too, he was not slow to insert colophons on the deficiencies of his exemplars, as warnings to later copyists, but in the main he appears to have copied faithfully, preserving the older linguistic forms of the exemplars.[4]

This was not always the case. Ó Cléirigh's version of the prose tale *Fled Dúin na nGéd* is only about a quarter of the length of the other known versions of the tale, suggesting that he edited it heavily, and his copy of *Buile Shuibhne* received similar treatment.[5] Thus his methodical transcripts of saints' Lives destined for Louvain to be translated into Latin as part of a large hagiographical project contrast with his treatment of many secular sources copied for other purposes and funded by other patrons. The Ó Cléirigh scribes were not averse to improving a text that they were copying. The copy of the late twelfth-century Martyrology of Gorman made by Mícheál Ó Cléirigh contains a large number of topographical, linguistic and genealogical glosses that appear to be much later than the main text of the martyrology and are almost certainly by Ó Cléirigh himself. Finally, the scribes created new texts on the basis of the copies of the older ones that had been made. Most famously the Genealogies of the Saints and Kings (**23**), the Martyrology of Donegal (**37**) (in its two recensions) and the Annals of the Four Masters (**18, 19, 20, 21, 22**) fit this description. Clearly, scribes such as Mícheál Ó Cléirigh and his associates had a range of skills at their disposal, most particularly a knowledge of the working methods of *seanchas* or the recording of the past, as well as their technical expertise in preparing usable manuscripts. Not all scribes were of equal learning and authority. For instance, of the six or more scribes who worked on the Annals only two, Mícheál and Cú Choigcríche Ó Cléirigh, made systematic corrections to the text, suggesting that they were regarded as the most learned, with sufficient authority among the group to make final decisions on content or difficult or variant readings.

It would be tempting to regard what we can glean from this corpus of Ó Cléirigh material concerning the role and practices of the scribe in the early seventeenth century as exceptional, yet all the indications are that it is not. The few scribal notes that describe the conditions of the making of the manuscripts are remarkably similar to notes that had appeared in manuscripts for generations. Even Mícheál Ó Cléirigh's extensive travels in order to make copies of manuscripts do not appear to have been unusual among fifteenth-century scribes. Members of the Connacht scribal family of Ó Maoil Chonaire can be found far from home in Athboy, Co. Meath, copying a manuscript about the year 1500, and another scribe from that family was at work in the house of Sir John Plunkett, Baron Dunsany, also in County Meath, about the same date. Sioghraidh Ó Maoil Chonaire can be traced in the early sixteenth century working in places as far apart as County Limerick and south Ulster, as well as in unidentified locations.[6] Medical families similarly moved around the country in search of new texts to copy, and Mayo families can be found in Ossory in the 1590s.[7] Again, the ways in which at least some of the scribes laid out their page with lines and borders in dry point ruling—clear in RIA C iii 3 and UCD-OFM A 13—were thoroughly traditional (**18, 20**), although Mícheál Ó Cléirigh was rather less careful than his associates in the way he laid out the page, not always troubling to ensure that the lines of text were quite straight.

There were, of course, changes in Ó Cléirigh scribal practice from that of the fifteenth-century scribes. Some of these were technical. Mícheál Ó Cléirigh, for example, used a pointed pen rather than an edged quill, which reduced the serifs on letters to simple lines at some points. Again, the Ó Cléirigh scribes abandoned the normal late medieval practice of laying out manuscripts in double columns and used long lines instead, in the same way as the compilers of the late sixteenth-century Annals of Loch Cé had done. More importantly, the replacement of parchment or vellum, which had been the normal medium for writing manuscripts, with paper during the sixteenth century meant that the Ó Cléirigh scribes almost never resorted to vellum. Paper was less durable but lighter (and hence more portable) and cheaper. This meant that the Annals of the Four Masters and other Ó Cléirigh texts do not have the cramped appearance of their earlier vellum counterparts. It was feasible, for instance, to leave a half-page or more blank to incorporate new material as it became available. This would have been too costly a practice to contemplate had vellum been used. Paper could not be made locally, however, but had to be purchased from merchants in markets. Despite this, paper was not in short supply, and when copying the Lives of the saints Ó Cléirigh usually made a rough copy of the text on which he was working and later prepared a fair copy to be sent to the house at Louvain. It does at least suggest that he had a familiarity with features of modern commercial life, such as buying and selling, that some other literati condemned. Openness to the outside world is also suggested by the occasional use of Roman letter forms instead of Irish ones in the text.

Familiarity with recent developments in other spheres of life is also suggested by the structure of the Annals. Aping the emerging printed book, the annalists addressed their patron, Fearghal Ó Gadhra, in a preface that would not have been normal practice in late medieval Irish manuscripts. Such preliminary matter was becoming more common by the seventeenth century. The Westmeath scholar Conall Mageoghegan added a preface to his manuscript Annals of Clonmacnoise in the 1620s, and Geoffrey Keating even more daringly addressed his reader, rather than a patron, in his *Foras feasa ar Éirinn* (**25**) in the 1630s.

All this suggests that the output of the Ó Cléirigh scribal group was very much the product of their own time rather than simply a perpetuation of older traditions. This further suggests that while modern historians and literary scholars have concentrated on the literary families (particularly the poets, with their specialist training in the composition of verse), who were usually associated with lordly courts and who acted as conservators of tradition, the regular scribe may have been of even greater importance in shaping contemporary perceptions of life. Indeed, with the collapse of the system of lordship in the seventeenth century the scribe may have come to the fore as the reshaper of tradition in a new context. The power of the scribe in this context came from the main attributes of manuscripts. Most importantly, they were physical objects and hence could be moved about the countryside. By following the movements not only of the manuscripts that the Ó Cléirighs made but also of those that they used as exemplars and sources, it is possible to reconstruct something of the emerging intellectual networks of early modern Ireland.

First, and most obviously, the ultimate destination of the manuscripts in Louvain points to the Franciscans as a patronage network that enabled Ó Cléirigh and his associates to function. At the simplest level they provided an Irish base for the project and a network of houses in which Ó Cléirigh could stay while collecting and compiling material. Some late medieval Franciscan houses did have scriptoria for the production of liturgical and other books, although book production was not a central element of the friars' role (**9**). The fifteenth-century Book of Lismore is thought to have been written in the Franciscan house at Timoleague, but more clearly Bodleian Library MS Rawlinson C 320, which included a Franciscan rule, was written in a Franciscan house at Adare in 1482.[8] The late sixteenth-century *Seanchas Búrcach* (**8**) can be tentatively linked with the Franciscan house at Moyne, Co. Mayo. Individual Franciscans also compiled books for their own use, such as TCD MS 667, apparently written by a Franciscan comfortable with both English and Irish script.[9] By the early seventeenth century the effects of the dissolution of the religious houses meant that the Irish Franciscans had few manuscripts of their own. What was distinctive about the Franciscan pastoral style in the early seventeenth century, however, was their close links with the local lay community, reflected, for instance, in the large numbers of chalices presented to them by lay patrons. As a result, local Franciscan communities almost certainly knew the whereabouts of manuscripts in lay hands. Even before Mícheál Ó Cléirigh began his travels, other Irish Franciscans had displayed curiosity about local manuscripts and had made copies of saints' Lives from locally available material.[10] In the same way, they could have arranged access for Ó Cléirigh to locally held manuscripts.[11] A case in point may be the Book of Lismore, from which Ó Cléirigh copied the life of St Findchú at Timoleague friary in 1629. The evidence indicates that both before and after this the manuscript was in the hands of the Mac Cárthaigh Riabhach family, suggesting that it was lent by them to the friary for the specific purpose of allowing the Lives of the saints to be examined and copied.[12]

The evidence of the exemplars suggests that Ó Cléirigh had a second network on which to rely—that of learned men who had interests similar to his own. Some, but not many, of these were the traditional learned families. Men such as Flann Mac Aodhagáin provided both source texts and approbations for Ó Cléirigh's work. The book belonging to Brian Óg Ó Maoil Chonaire (who was probably a descendant of the early sixteenth-century scribe Muirgheas Ó Maoil Chonaire) probably came from that family's own collection of exemplars which Muirgheas had used and which the Four Masters also consulted for their redaction of the *Leabhar Gabhála*. While a few of these manuscripts were undoubtedly old they were not all necessarily so. Some, such as the Life of Náile or the long Irish Life of Maodhóg, may have only been compiled recently, and many were sixteenth-century copies of lost older works. Thus Ó Cléirigh's exemplars for his copies of the Lives of SS Declan and Mac Creiche had only been made in 1582 and 1524 respectively.[13]

Of more importance was a third network then evolving. Many of the key texts that Ó Cléirigh used for his work did not come from the learned families who had owned them in the Middle Ages. Texts such as the Book of Lecan, the Annals of Ulster (5) or the Book of Leinster (1) came to the Ó Cléirigh scribes from New English collectors of manuscripts such as Sir James Ware and James Ussher, archbishop of Armagh. The trade in texts was not all one way, for among Ware's papers are lists of saints and their families, with their churches and their feast-days, in Mícheál Ó Cléirigh's hand.[14] It was also presumably through this network that Ware received news of the work that John Colgan was undertaking in Louvain, and among Ware's papers are lists of texts that Colgan intended to publish.[15] A further volume among Ware's papers contains a fair copy of extracts from the Annals of the Four Masters, possibly made for him before they were sent to Louvain.[16] The network is clearly seen in the case of the manuscript Psalter of St Caimín. Ó Cléirigh acquired this manuscript from the Mac Bruaideadha family, who lived on the termon lands of Caimín, and by 1645 it was in Louvain bearing a note, possibly by Colgan, that it was 'ex libris Conventus de Dunnagall'. [Fig. 4.3] By 1639, however, both James Ussher and James Ware had seen the same manuscript or a copy, Ware noting that it was 'among the books of the convent of Franciscans at Donegal'.[17] Clearly there was a reciprocal process of ongoing lending and returning of manuscripts along this network, also seen in the history of the Franciscan *Liber Hymnorum* (3), which had also been made available to Ussher and Ware.

Precisely how these networks evolved is unclear, but it is known that the Franciscans Fr Thomas Strange and Fr Francis Matthews had both gained access to Ussher's library before Mícheál Ó Cléirigh did so. Another important contact was the Westmeath collector Conall Mageoghegan, who acted as intermediary between Ussher, Ó Cléirigh and, indeed, Geoffrey Keating in arranging access to manuscripts such as the Book of Lecan. In addition, both Ó Cléirigh and Mageoghegan had access to the annals of Maoilín Óg Mac Bruaideadha, and an entry from this source was copied into a manuscript owned by Mageoghegan.[18] In return Mageoghegan received copies of works by Ó Cléirigh, possibly including the first recension of the Martyrology of Donegal.[19]

Conall Mageoghegan was not descended from the older learned families. He was English-speaking, had an interest in the Irish past and was part of the new political and social order as a small Westmeath landowner. As such he resembles the other patrons on whose support Mícheál Ó Cléirigh drew in Ireland. Fearghal Ó Gadhra, who funded the Donegal annals project, was an MP in the Irish parliament of 1634—a fact recorded by Ó Cléirigh—while Turlough MacCoghlan, the patron of the Genealogies of the Saints and Kings (**23**), was also an MP in that parliament and that of 1640–1. [**Fig. 4.4**] MacCoghlan may also have been the means by which Ó Cléirigh obtained his copy of the Life of St Colman Ela in 1629 from a book of Eachraidhe Ó Siaghail in Fir Cell, since the Ó Siaghail family were hereditary physicians to the MacCoghlans.[20]

We know little of the politics of these men, but it seems clear that the idea of a kingdom of Ireland, as they saw it revealed in the older texts, was of great importance to them in reflecting on society in their own day in the aftermath of the Nine Years' War. This scribal project was reflecting new ideas about the status and condition of Ireland, first formulated by the Anglo-Irish in the 1541 Act for the Kingly Title but now being developed in a different context, as well as remembering the past.[21] Different patrons required different products, and while the Franciscan interest was in the accurate transcription of holy lives, secular patrons of other parts of the Ó Cléirigh enterprise sponsored a more innovative approach to the sources. In understanding the form and function of manuscripts in their own world, as in the writing of history generally, context is still king.

1    Brian Ó Cuív, 'The Irish language in the early modern period', in T. W. Moody, F. X. Martin and F. J. Byrne (eds), *A new history of Ireland: iii. Early modern Ireland* (Oxford, 1976), 529.

2    Brian Ó Cuív, 'Ireland's manuscript heritage', *Éire-Ireland* 19 (1984), 87–110. Problems with composite manuscripts and what were single items that have now been split mean that these numbers should be regarded as orders of magnitude rather than statistically precise counts.

3    Brendan Jennings, *Micheal Ó Cléirigh, chief of the Four Masters, and his associates* (Dublin, 1936), 87.

4    For instance see Charles Plummer (ed.), *Bethada náem nÉrenn* (2 vols) (Oxford, 1922), vol. 1, 154, 182, 289–90.

5    See Ruth Lehmann (ed.), *Fled Dúin na nGéd*, Medieval and Modern Irish Series 21 (Dublin, 1964), 31–7; J. G. O'Keeffe (ed.), *Buile Shuibhne*, Medieval and Modern Irish Series 1 (Dublin, 1931), 92–6.

6    Brian Ó Cuív, *Catalogue of Irish language manuscripts in the Bodleian Library at Oxford* (2 vols) (Dublin, 2001–3), vol. 1, 63, 233, 234; Jennings, *Michael Ó Cléirigh*, 77, 95.

7    John Bannerman, *The Beatons* (Edinburgh, 1986), 104; Ó Cuív, 'Ireland's manuscript heritage', 95–6.

8    On Lismore see R. A. S. Macalister (ed.), *The Book of Mac Carthaigh Riabhach* (Dublin, 1950), xii.

9    Alan J. Fletcher, 'Preaching in late medieval Ireland: the Latin and English traditions', in Alan J. Fletcher and Raymond Gillespie (eds), *Irish preaching, 700–1700* (Dublin, 2001), 58–9.

10   For example FLK MS F1 and RIA MS A iv 1, ff 122–60, contain Lives copied on the instructions of the Franciscan Fr Francis Matthews.

11   See Jennings, *Michael Ó Cléirigh*, 219–20.

12   Macalister (ed.), *Book of Mac Carthaigh Riabhach*, xii.

13   Charles Plummer, *Miscellanea hagiographia Hibernia* (Brussels, 1925), 90; Patrick Power (ed.), *Life of St Declan of Ardmore and Life of St Mochuda of Lismore*, Irish Texts Society 16 (London, 1914), 73.

14   Bodleian Library, Oxford, Rawlinson MS B 484, ff 86–7; Rawlinson B 487, f. 74v.

15   Bodleian Library, Oxford, Rawlinson MS B 487, ff 68, 74. The list of works for publication is edited in Charles McNeill, 'Reports on the Rawlinson collection of manuscripts in the Bodleian Library, Oxford', *Analecta Hibernica* **1** (1930), 143–6.

16    British Library, Add MS 4784, ff 36–86.

17    Myles Dillon, Canice Mooney and Pádraig de Brún, *Catalogue of Irish manuscripts in the Franciscan library, Killiney* (Dublin, 1969), 1–2. The text was certainly known in Ulster in the 1620s; see Lambert McKenna (ed.), *Iomarbhágh na bhFileadh* (2 vols), Irish Texts Society 20–21 (London, 1916–18), vol. 1, 137.

18    S.H. O'Grady and Robin Flower, *Catalogue of Irish manuscripts in the British Library* (3 vols) (Dublin, 1992), ii, 472–3.

19    Bernadette Cunningham and Raymond Gillespie, 'James Ussher and his Irish manuscripts', *Studia Hibernica* 33 (2004–5), 88–95; Pádraig Ó Riain, *Feastdays of the saints*, Subsidia Hagiographica 86 (Brussels, 2006), 311.

20    Paul Walsh, *Irish leaders and learning through the ages,* ed. Nollaig Ó Muraíle (Dublin, 2003), 362, 368. Two O'Sheils witnessed the will of Sir John MacCoghlan in 1590: Lord Walter Fitzgerald, 'Notes on Sir John MacCoghlan, knight, of Cloghan, chief of Delvin-MacCoghlan, who died in 1590', *Journal of the Royal Society of Antiquaries of Ireland* 43 (1913), 229–31.

21    Breandán Ó Buachalla, *The crown of Ireland* (Galway, 2006), 18–23.

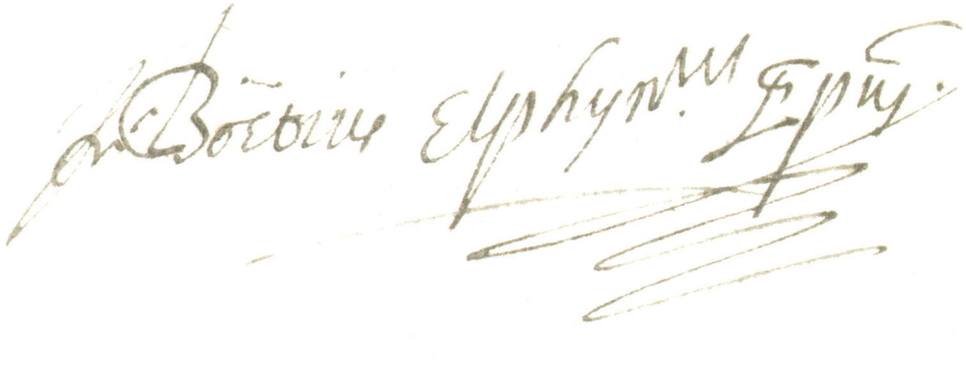

**Fig**. 4.2.  Rule of St Francis. TCD 97, f. 178r (cat. no. 9), the earliest Irish copy of the Rule of St Francis, compiled for the Victorine Canons of St Thomas's Abbey, Dublin (*opposite*).

punctata impia sponti de cęro omnes uni
ouib; fratris suis omni caritate et tolle
rendine obediant. Quod si quis contensio sue
reprtur corripiatur. Si quis aut frater
pro quauis minima causa ab abbate uel a quo
cumque fratre suo corripitur quolibet modo uel
si leuiter senserit animum fratris cuiuscumque
contra se matum uel motum ex modice mor
sene mora tam diu prostratus iaceat ante
pedes eius iaceat satisfaciens. usque dum
benedictione sanet illa commotio. Quod si
quis contempserit facere: aut corpo
rali uindicte subiaceat aut si contumax
fuerit: de monasterio expellatur. De zelo

Siue est zelus bono quem monachi de
amaritudinis malus bene habere.
qui separat a deo et ducit ad infernum. ita
est zelus bonus qui separat auitiis et du
cit ad deum et ad uitam eternam. hunc ergo ze
lum feruentissimo amore exerceant mo
nachi. id est ut honore se inuicem preuen
iant infirmitates suas siue corporum
siue morum patientissime tollerent obe
dientiam sibi certatim impendant. Nullus
quod sibi utile iudicat sequatur. Sz quod ma
gis alio. Caritate fraternitatis casto impen
dant amore. Deum timeant. abbatem
suum sincera et humili caritate diligant.
Christo omnino nichil preponant. qui De eo quod
Regulam aut totius iustitie obseruatio in
hac describimus hec regula sit constit
ut hanc obseruantes in monasteriis constituta
riis aliquatenus uel honestate morum
aut initium uisitationis nos demon
stremus hanc. Ceterum ad perfectionem usque
tionis qui festinat sunt doctrine sanc
torum patrum. quorum obseruatio perducit ho
minem ad celsitudinem perfectionis. Que
enim pagina aut quis sermo diuine
auctoritatis ueteris ac noui testamenti
nest rectissima norma uite humane: hu
mane. aut quis liber sanctorum catholicorum
patrum hoc non resonat ut recto cursu
perueniamus ad creatorem nostrum. et non
collationes patrum. et instituta uite eorum.
Sz regula sancti patris nostri basilii si quid

aliud sunt et bene uiuentium et obedienti
um monachorum instrumenta uirtutum.
Nobis aut desidiosis et male uiuentibz
atque negligentibz rubor et confusionis est.
Quisquis ergo ad patriam celestem festinas. hanc
minimam inchoationis regulam descriptam
adiuuante xpisto et perfice. et tunc demum ad maio
ra que supra commemorauimus: doctrine
uirtutumque culmina deo pergente per
uenies. Explicit regula sancti benedicti.

Honorius episcopus ser Incipit regula
uus seruorum dei dilec beati fran
tis filiis fratri francisco et cisci
aliis fratribus de ordine fratrum mi
norum salutem et apostolicam benedictionem. So
let annuere sedes apostolica piis uotis. tho
nestis petentium desideriis fauorem beni
uolum impertiri. Ea propter dilectissimi in dno
filii. uestris piis precibus inclinati. ordinis
uestri regulam a bone memorie innocentio
papa predecessore uestro approbatam annotinis
presentibz. uobis nouis apostolica confirma
mus. et presentis scripti proemio communi
que talis est. Incipit regula fratrum minorum.

Regula et uita fratrum minorum hec est. dominum
nostrum iesum et euangelium obseruare. uiuendo
in obedientia sine proprio et in castitate. frater
franciscus promittit obedientiam domino pape
honorio ac successoribz eius canonice intran
tibus et ecclesie romane. et alii fratres teneantur frater reuerentiam
franciscus et successoribz obedire. De recipiendis hanc uitam testi
ficari debeant.

Si qui uoluerint hanc uitam et eam accipe
re uenerint ad fratres nostros mittant eos ad suos
ministros prouinciales. quibus solum et non
aliis recipiendi fratres licentia concedatur.
ministri uero diligenter examinent eos de
fide catholica. et ecclesie sacramentis. et si
hec omnia credant. et uelint ea fideliter confi
teri. et usque in finem firmiter obseruare.
et uxores non habent. uel si habent iam mona
sterium feceruntque uxores. uel licentiam eis
dederint auctoritate diocesani episcopi uoto et contine
rie iam emisso. uelut iuxta sint etatis uxo
res. et ut possit de eis oriri suspicio: dicant il
lis uerbum sancti euangelii: quod uadant et
uendant omnia sua et ea studeant paupribz

Beati immaculati in uia qui
ambulant in lege domini.

Beati qui scrutantur testimonia
eius in toto corde exquirunt eum.

Non enim qui operantur iniquitatem in
uiis eius ambulauerunt.

Tu mandasti mandata
tua custodiri nimis.

Utinam dirigantur uie mee ad
custodiendas iustificationes tuas.

Tunc non confundar cum perspe-
xero in omnibus mandatis tuis.

Confitebor tibi in directione cordis
mei quod didici iudicia iustitie tue.

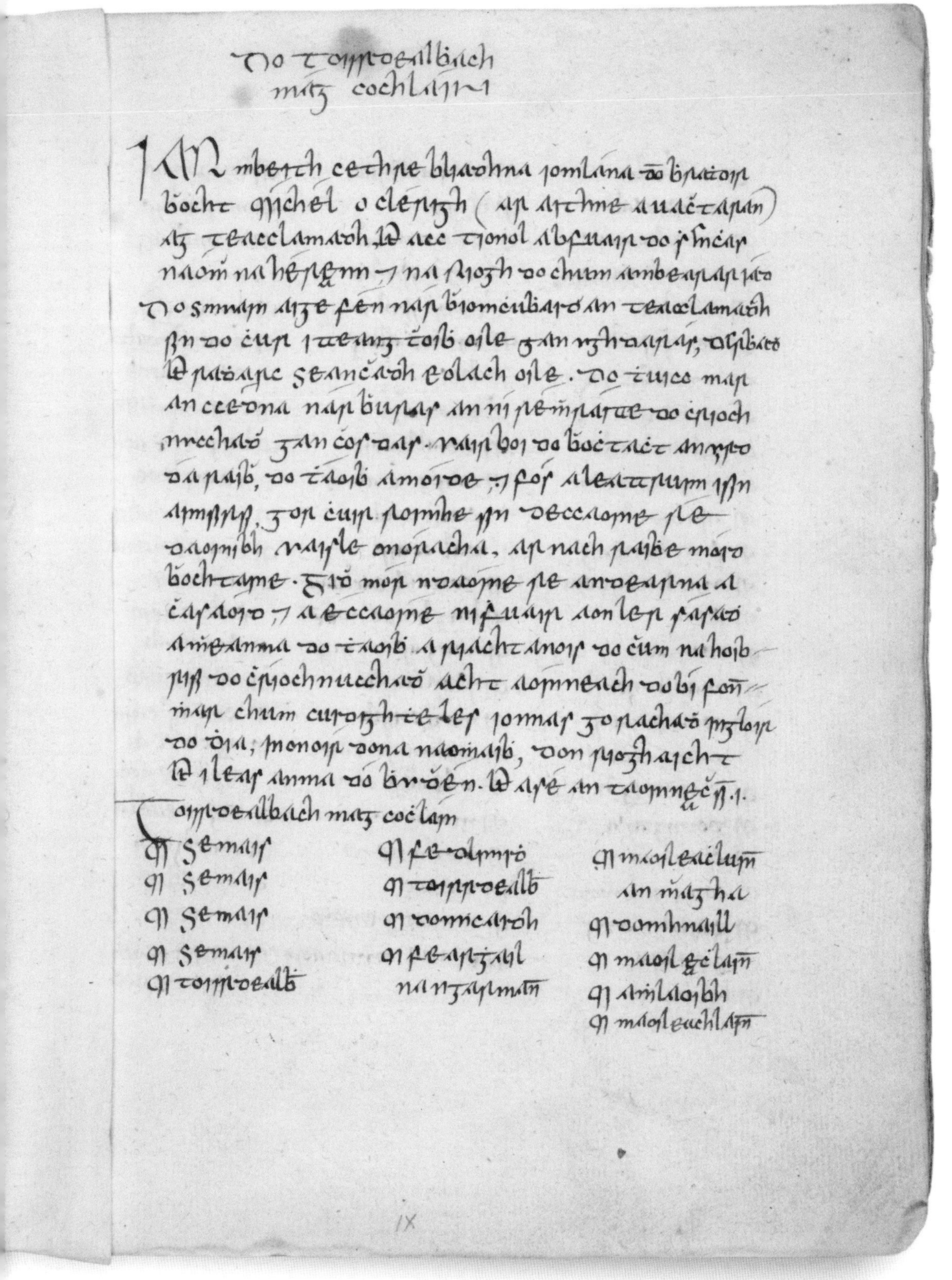

**Fig. 4.3.** Psalter of Caimín of Iniscealtra. UCD-OFM A1, p. 1 (*above*).

**Fig. 4.4.** Genealogies of Saints and Kings. Dedication page to patron Toirdhealbhach Mac Cochláin. UCD-OFM A 16, f. ix (*opposite*).

SIR JAMES WARE K.<sup>t</sup>

NAT. 26 Nov. 1594 - OB. 1<sup>mo</sup> Dec. 1666

HANLON

# Chapter 5
# Seventeenth-century historians of Ireland

Bernadette Cunningham

In Ireland, as throughout western Europe, in the age of the Reformation and Counter-Reformation many scholars turned their attention to writing ecclesiastical history. The encounter between the existing *seanchas* tradition, European national histories and the emerging religious tensions of the age provided the inspiration for new ways of interpreting the past. The debate over which was the true Christian church had a strong historical element. Each side of the confessional divide was keen to demonstrate that theirs was the true successor of the church of Christ. The study of the lives of saints, bishops and others whose careers formed part of the story of the evolution of the Christian church became an important element of historical writing. In Ireland, for example, scholars from both the Catholic and Protestant traditions sought out sources that could be used to shed light on the story of St Patrick, Ireland's national apostle. Writing from a Catholic perspective, Richard Stanihurst's Life of Patrick was published in Antwerp in 1587, Robert Rochford's English adaptation of Jocelyn's Life of Patrick, together with lives of Brigit and Colum Cille, was published at Louvain in 1625, while Thomas Messingham's compilation of Irish saints' Lives (**26**), with its particular emphasis on Patrick, Brigit and Colum Cille, was published at Paris in 1624.[1] Similarly, collections of saints' Lives compiled in Ireland by the Franciscans Mícheál Ó Cléirigh, Thomas Strange, John Goolde and others during the 1620s were used by John Colgan in his Latin editions of Lives of Irish saints (**28**), published in Louvain in the 1640s.[2] From a Protestant perspective, James Ussher wrote extensively on the sources for the life and work of St Patrick in his 1639 ecclesiastical history of Ireland, and Sir James Ware's Latin Life of Patrick was published in London in 1656.[3] [Fig. 5.1]

For others, the objective was to write a comprehensive account of the story of Ireland, beginning with the creation of the world and continuing down to modern times. The example of other European nations was an important influence here. Nations such as Scotland and France had their own historical narratives available in print, whereas Ireland did not. For those concerned with the potential political messages of the Irish past, telling the story of the kings of Ireland was no less important an objective than telling the story of Irish saints and the early Irish church. The two most ambitious seventeenth-century undertakings in this context were the Annals of the Four Masters, compiled by Mícheál Ó Cléirigh and his associates in the 1630s, and *Foras feasa ar Éirinn* by Geoffrey Keating (Seathrún Céitinn), completed in the same decade (**25**). Both works were influenced to some extent by European trends in the writing of history while also drawing on the rich store of historical knowledge preserved in manuscript form in Ireland.

Keating's history was written in modern Irish prose. It was an elegant flowing narrative that gained wide popularity not just among his contemporaries but also among later generations. Keating's work, like that of the Four Masters, took as its framework the *Leabhar Gabhála* (Book of Invasions) and the succession of kings of Ireland. He continued his history down to the coming of the Normans in the late twelfth century, and his version of the Irish origin-myth culminated in this last invasion of Ireland. He carefully avoided contemporary history, and was silent about the new waves of English, Welsh and Scottish settlers who had come to Ireland in his own lifetime as part of schemes such as the late sixteenth-century plantation of Munster or the early

Fig. 5.1. Sir James Ware. Detail from published version of the *Martyrology of Donegal* (1864) (cat. no. 38) (*opposite*).

seventeenth-century Ulster plantation. Instead, Keating focused on the elements of the Irish past that were important to him. Like the Four Masters he was writing primarily for his own community, but each in their own way was broadening the scope of historical writing when compared with what had gone before. Thus, whereas the late sixteenth-century compiler of the *Seanchas Búrcach*[4] focused on the history and propaganda of just one north Mayo lordship (**8**), these new seventeenth-century 'national' histories were conceived as histories of Ireland as a whole and consciously drew on a wide range of manuscript sources.

Although Geoffrey Keating was of Anglo-Norman descent, he had specialist knowledge of the Irish language, having grown up in the most strongly Irish-speaking part of south Tipperary. He understood the complexities of the historical language and had sufficient connections with others within the Gaelic scholarly community to allow him access to many key manuscript sources for the early history of Ireland. While rooted in the historical sources, Keating's history of Ireland was an innovative one, informed by contemporary political concerns and written in the modern Irish language of his day. It told the story of all *Éireannaigh* (Irish people), whom Keating defined as Irish-born and Catholic. In taking this approach he was combining the history of the Old English descendants of the twelfth-century Anglo-Norman settlers with the history of the Gaelic peoples whose much earlier origins had been the subject of the *Leabhar Gabhála* origin-legend. While Keating's history was inclusive in so far as it combined Gaelic and Anglo-Norman histories into one prose narrative, it was also an essay in exclusion. Those who were not Catholic or had only recently arrived in Ireland as new settlers in the late sixteenth or early seventeenth century did not qualify as 'Irish' under his definition. Nevertheless his history was more consciously inclusive than that of the Four Masters, for whom the origin of the Old English Catholics was of very marginal concern. In ecclesiastical terms, too, there was a difference of emphasis between Keating and the Four Masters. Keating, a diocesan priest, paid special attention to the history of the formation of Irish dioceses, whereas the Four Masters concentrated instead on the role of religious orders, most especially the Franciscans. Thus the histories that were written in seventeenth-century Ireland reflected the divisions and preoccupations of contemporary society, and secular and ecclesiastical histories were interlinked, just as secular and religious matters were intertwined in everyday life. [**Fig. 5.2**]

In the early seventeenth century it was not just those with specialist knowledge of the Irish manuscript sources, such as Keating or Ó Cléirigh, who were inspired to write new versions of the Irish past. Old English Protestant writers, no less than Catholic ones, were keen to narrate the story of the Irish past from their own political and religious perspective. The most prolific and influential Irish Protestant historian and theologian of this period was James Ussher, bishop of Meath and later archbishop of Armagh. He undertook to research and write comprehensive accounts of the ecclesiastical history of Ireland. His polemical *Discourse of the religion anciently professed by the Irish and British* (**30**) was first published in 1622 and reissued in 1631, while his *Britannicarum Ecclesiarum Antiquitates*, a comprehensive scholarly account of Irish church history, was published in Latin in 1639. [**Fig. 5.3**]

As a church historian genuinely interested in the earliest and most authentic sources for the history of Christianity, Ussher maintained a network of contacts with other scholars throughout western Europe who could assist him. The picture that emerges is of a prominent Protestant clergyman who took the risk of engaging in correspondence with Catholic historians both at home and abroad as a means of gaining access to the historical source documents he needed. In theological matters, Ussher was a strong opponent of Catholicism and devoted much effort to refuting Catholic doctrine, yet he maintained personal contacts with some prominent Irish Catholics. Fascinating evidence has survived among his unpublished papers about some of his contacts in respect of sources relating to Irish church history. Some of his correspondence with David Rothe, Catholic bishop of Ossory from 1620, can be found among his papers in Trinity College Dublin.[5] Rothe was a prominent figure in the Counter-Reformation Irish church. He had once served as secretary to Peter Lombard, a former professor of theology and philosophy at the University of Louvain, who became the leading Irish official in the Roman Curia and mastermind of papal policy on Ireland in the early seventeenth century. Though nominally appointed to the position of Catholic archbishop of Armagh, Lombard remained in Rome, and Rothe was effectively in charge of the Irish church at home. As well as discussing historical matters, Ussher was able to borrow books and manuscripts from Rothe, and he acknowledged his help in his publications. Not surprisingly, given his position, Rothe was cautious about these contacts, and writing to William Malone as intermediary in 1619 he pleaded, 'I pray you in all Curtasie let mee not bee named at all in any correspondence that should pace [pass] between you both either by letter or message'.[6] Ussher also made contact, through intermediaries, with Luke Wadding, a leading Irish Franciscan based in Rome. [**Fig.** 5.4] Wadding was equally cautious and never corresponded directly with Ussher. Nevertheless he was able to obtain extracts of manuscripts in Ussher's possession while in turn providing Ussher with transcripts of some documents held in the Vatican.[7] Though divided by their circumstances, these men shared an interest in the Irish past and particularly in the origins and early history of Christianity in Ireland.

Ussher continued to research early Irish ecclesiastical history and sought out not just Latin sources, such as the Book of Armagh, but those in the Irish language also. He had made contacts before 1619 with Gaelic scholars who owned historical annals and other medieval Irish manuscript sources, and was able to purchase or borrow material in this way. Among the Irish manuscripts he was able to cite in his published work were the Book of Ballymote, the Book of Lecan, the copy of the *Liber Hymnorum* that had been in the Franciscan friary at Donegal (**3**), the Annals of Ulster (**5**), the Annals of Tigernach and the Annals of Innisfallen.[9] His use of these manuscripts was largely confined to sections that were in Latin rather than in Irish, such as the early part of the Annals of Ulster, or to material from those sources that he employed others to translate from Irish into Latin for his use. His lack of special expertise in the Irish language did not deter him. Rather it prompted him to increase his circle of scholarly contacts so that he could obtain the assistance of Irish scholars as necessary. Thus, for example, a miscellaneous collection of Ussher's historical notes (**31**) includes translated extracts from the Annals of Ulster alongside a transcript of the Irish text.

Sir James Ware, who had been a student of Ussher's at Trinity College, likewise needed to draw on a wide range of manuscript sources in Irish and Latin for his research into the Irish past. Ware's historical endeavours made an impact in two ways. His dictionaries of Irish writers and Irish bishops, published in Latin, were significant compilations of biographical data for the Christian era in Ireland (**29**), and were successfully reissued in translation through the eighteenth century.[9] His 1633 edition of the work of four other writers on Ireland, most notably Edmund Spenser, brought an immediate response from Geoffrey Keating, whose *Foras feasa ar Éirinn* (**25**) was presented as a refutation of all that Spenser represented. Ware's other original historical compilations generally took the form of annals, and in these his concern was with the recent past.[10] His biographical lists and annals provide a clear contrast in style with Ussher's interpretive and polemical essays, and indeed these two divergent approaches to historical writing existed in parallel among their contemporaries throughout western Europe.

Irish writers of all denominations were anxious to reach as wide an audience as possible by getting their works into print. For Ussher and Ware this was a relatively straightforward, if expensive, undertaking. Given Ussher's standing as an archbishop in the established church, he could publish freely in Ireland under his own name. Ware, a government administrator, could do likewise. Catholic authors had to be much more circumspect.

David Rothe was the author of two influential tracts on the Irish church, *Analecta sacra* and *Hibernia resurgens*, published in Europe between 1616 and 1621, though to protect his identity he did not publish under his own name.[11] Peter Lombard, too, had written a polemical account of Irish history. His treatise was designed to persuade European powers to support the Catholics of Ireland, and circulated in manuscript prior to its publication in Latin in 1632.[12]

For those who wrote in Irish rather than Latin, matters were more complicated still. There was no printing press with an Irish font available in Ireland, and though the Irish Franciscans at Louvain had acquired such a font by the second decade of the seventeenth century, it was used only for catechisms and devotional works. For authors such as Geoffrey Keating, scribal publication was still the most efficient way of disseminating his writings. Indeed, Keating's *Foras feasa ar Éirinn* proved to be a 'best-seller' in manuscript through the seventeenth and eighteenth centuries. Having been written in the language of the people, it was more influential in the long term in shaping modern perceptions of Ireland and Irishness than were the Latin published works of Ussher, Wadding or Rothe. The Annals of the Four Masters likewise circulated in manuscript only until the mid-nineteenth century, and almost exclusively in an antiquarian context. The work of the Four Masters was not forgotten, however, and in the long term the annals proved fundamental to the version of the Irish past that was adopted as the basis for twentieth-century accounts of early and medieval Irish history.

1    Richard Stanihurst, *De vita S. Patricii Hiberniae apostoli* (Antwerp, 1587); [Robert Rochford], *The life of the glorious bishop St Patricke . . . together with the lives of the holy virgin S. Bridgit and of the glorious abbot Saint Columbe*, English Recusant Literature 210 (St Omer, 1625; repr. London, 1974).

2    Brussels, Bibliothèque Royale, MSS 2324–2340, 4190–4200, 5100–5104; RIA MS A iv 1; FLK MS F 1. John Colgan, *Acta sanctorum . . . Scotiae seu Hiberniae* (Louvain, 1645; repr., Dublin, 1948); *Triadis thaumaturgae, seu divorum Patricii, Columbae, et Brigidae . . . acta* (Louvain, 1647; repr. Dublin, 1997).

3    James Ussher, *Britannicarum ecclesiarum antiquitates* (Dublin, 1639); James Ware, *S. Patricio, qui Hibernos ad fidem Christi convertit Adscripta opuscula quorum aliqua nunc primùm, ex antiquis MSS. codicibus in lucem emissa sunt, reliqua, recognita : omnia, notis ad rem historicam & antiquariam spectantibus, illustrata* (London, 1656).

4    TCD MS 1440; Bernadette Cunningham, 'Politics and power in sixteenth-century Connacht', *Irish Arts Review* 21 (Winter 2004), 116–21.

5    William O'Sullivan (ed.), 'Correspondence of David Rothe and James Ussher, 1619–23', *Collectanea Hibernica* **36–7** (1995), 8–49.

6    David Rothe to William Malone, April 1619, printed in O'Sullivan (ed.), 'Correspondence', 15.

7    Brendan Jennings (ed.), *Wadding papers, 1614–1638* (Dublin, 1953), 280, 289, 304, 319, 349, 551, 606.

8    Bernadette Cunningham and Raymond Gillespie, 'James Ussher and his Irish manuscripts', *Studia Hibernica* **33** (2004–5), 87–8.

9    Sir James Ware, *Archiepiscoporum Casseliensium & Tuamensium vitae* (Dublin, 1626); *De praesulibus Lageniae, sive provinciae Dubliniensis* (Dublin, 1628); *De praesulibus Hiberniae, commentarius. A prima gentis Hibernicae ad fidem Christianam conversione, ad nostra usque tempora* (Dublin, 1665).

10   Sir James Ware, *Rerum Hibernicarum Henrico Octavo regnante annales* (Dublin, 1662); *Rerum Hibernicarum annales, regnantibus Henrico VII, Henrico VIII, Edwardo VI, et Maria, ab anno scil. Domini MCCCCLXXXV ad annum MDLVIII* (Dublin, 1664).

11   *Analecta sacra nova et mira. De rebus catholicorum in Hibernia pro fide et religione gestis* ([Paris], 1616); *Hibernia resurgens sive refrigerium antidotale* (Rouen, 1621).

12   *De regno Hiberniae, sanctorum insula commentarius* (Louvain, 1632).

Fig. 5.2.   Geoffrey Keating's *Foras Feasa ar Éirinn*. UCD-OFM A14, f. 59v (cat. no. 25) *(opposite)*.

oilizech dona heaspocaib ḟin ⁊en nos nḃi znáiad e bi rinal do do pḣp pompla am e doo crpaoib
doḃrar an oilen nac paibe na eaxprec pa paicep ⁊ na manac. ⁊ ap eolz ⁊ab o colymcille an croceip
rap an ppepleco apez an i moal ndḣp Beda pm 10 ca dan 5 leaḃz don fanp c ni **Columba erat**
**primus doctor fidei Catholico transmontanis pictis ad Aquilonem, primusque fundator**
**Monasterij ghod in Hu Jnsula multis diu sctorum, pseloca[n]que populis, dencabile**
**monsit.** Ddḃe colim appe e doo crp an operom catoḣca dona proiṡ pan apo moga gna pleaḣ
 td an e arne do coceiṡ manap em moṡlen ⁊ ob cadzad oan arppz nec ion do poppbeniad na Scot
td na bpior. 2ls na bppicipaliṡ **Beda** ap iompz ccc zpiab e colymcille e doo crp do enaro oo
ṡod an opṡrom dona proiṡb ronap od alt te zpiab zme zn ⁊ hi ainab do z abaṡz na
paccip ⁊ namṁ opa ḟm bhi inal do colymcille te oaṡb i da exp ⁊ pop do zabaṡ na hḣppte opa
ḟm e oobpiz ⁊ npiab e colymcille ncc pola an opṡrom ap oz rdib. Ddap zme ṡ canzac eapprec a
ccompcep colymcille zo heṡ zo mopiaṡl opomactd. IS ani canpicc colymcille zoheṡ te
bṗro crapca caṡpna apapphṡh zanc eacpb zepp opp dobi apach ap zam npep opiopm
an epac do crp molappd dobṗbe nanz ⁊ol malte zanpon nahep op epcp zo bap ionzz
ccapmec depn z canpd an bṗro crapca apapphṡh an peal dobi meṡ zo edlt malte do zoṁd
nec apnṡ an comṡell apammbṗr em do pṗre molaṡ anpṁo.

ze canpicc colim anoip an tez zam mopṁz ⁊ pacaro z meṡ am iap doodeṡ ṁ mopiaṡl

Se dobz ṁ papree molapṡ dobṗr ⁊ colymcille onl malte ma canpicc do colymcille meaton
do ddp ṁep mrca cae exle opṡmme, cae exle pacappṁ ⁊ cae exle p bdṁ. ISe ndḃz enae exle
opṡmme do phṡp an eṡhnleaḣz oanzopṡe zṁp crapapṁ ṡ hṡ chinze do pṁe oiṡm me eḣzapa
eḣṁbeoil ṁ epṁ. ⁊ do maṡb oarne napal apanpeltṁoṡh le crṁnan me dooad me encḣ coprṁoṁm
Ddap zme do maṁ crapṁ an Crṁnampo, epe inz do maṁ peṡpon an oarne napal apanbeṡp amṁ
ailz td eḣmaṁ na tlṡp, td pṁl do maṁb crṁnan do enaro ⁊ comṡce oa mac eṁcu ⁊ p hṁz
td ooimall, td crppa ṁ ap comṡce colymcille e td ep comṡce colṁm meṡb. ṁe crapṁ e e call
pema na eṁṁz, td canpicc oe epn z cronaṡl colymcille clamaneṡll an onapop (epe nadṁe

ḟm ⁊ comṡce clome carṁca do papṁoe) z ṁpenṁ cae exle opṡmme ap orapṁ, td ep ddppṁb

**Bapeacap** ⁊ z bṁṁ oob e z do colymcille. crppo leaṁb anb molaza ndbz oṁe ṁṁ pṁ
nce cae exle opṡmme, mrcae epe pan eclaopṡbṗpe pṁce crapṁ maṁṁ colymcille an oṁ

po pṁb an onṡeel a leaṁb ⁊ zonzz zṁpop. Ddconbe ḟon aṁz zṁpab liṁpṁm an manelḃz
do pzṁb apa leaṁb ḟm ṁme zn do cozaṡo lṁeaṁplṁ crapṁ na bṗreṁ ṁ lcoṁpa, td apṡbṗr ṁce
orapṁ z npiab lep zach bopn abopṁm td zṁb lṁṗ zach leaṁz amacleaḃz, z onedeṁ an
crapṁ hndḃz p aṁce cae exle opṡmme. ISe ndḃz pa cnce colymcille p aoḣpa cae exle p bdṁ
pacappṁ do cabe ap oal naṁpe, td ap nṁce, do cnce an mṡlṁm caṡla e colymcille ⁊ coḣppṁ

mo camp be nac oal napapoe ⁊ ollcaṁz iooṗ ḟm lecpomac maṁṁ colymcille pm mpṗpapṁ
ISe ndḃz pa cnce colymcille p aoḣpa cae exle p bdṁ do cabe ap colṁ me onṗna anṁal a
papapṁ e p pa bṁo oam me npṗoa ṁ epṁ do maṡb le conam me colmaṁ nce lṗm an epe ⁊
comṡce colymcille. ⁊ mallap colymcille z ona mapmelṁm ahalte (amaṁl aondpaṡ) z heṡ
td an cae do bṁ nce epṁ anzapṁ na coṁ adla aoanbe an mṗz bṁ doad le nemac ⁊ oll zṁ crṁz
do cabe don compelepṗce maṁ oal bṁoṁm td ap peazṁanl p ṁ el appṁ do colṁm pṗb pṁapṁec an
licaṗ ap bṁh aoopbe. IS cdo hompṁ an mṗz da hṗle do bhṁ appṗo oa copp accṗon anaṗo
epaṗ zo al aṁbarṁ. nce po ohṡmmep na hampa, az apeṁ poeal bṗpaṁz colymcille pm papṗo
IS cdo oṁ bhṁ na copp zam eliṁz zo polomṁ. pap cdo oal hṡpṗe zo chepe bhṁ na copp na comṁ nce doṁ
Ddap zme do opeo an pṗle do bhṁ na copp napapon pṡṡ mṗz do bṗṁz zab i canpicc nce appṗm
on mṗz za oaill oal pṁoal pṗp zam caṡoṡ do cabe do coppellṁṗ. td do elṗṗm ona lam do onapṗo
zo ppeaṗce oal copp do znce apaṁmaṗc ceoalaṗmle oṁm ṁeoo opṗoṁ ciile. Dola colymcille ⁊ papṗope

na coṁ adla do apṗe oippṗ conaṡll me doẃa me dpṁṁṁ bamḃpdoo don conoaṡl. td ṁ do 2napṗo
conaṗll na cleṗpa, z pḣpṗ oaopz ḟi anopṗepaṗp ṁ pcaṗb, epṁ miloṁbz ahoṁ, z z abaṗo do
caobaṡb cppṁo oppa ⁊ ṁ bṗeoz do naclepṗz leo, td pṁapṗe colymcille cṁa do bi aza mbnaṗl
amil em. do enaṗ colymcille z npṗbe conṁll me doẃa do bi azamzhṗp ṁe oeṁ an zpoṁ
ḟm. td crppṗ colṁm p aoḣpa ⁊ naṗz coelaṗm do bnaṡm an epaṗpm ap conaṡll, z heṁpocampṗo
le colṁm e. td z npṗbli pṗze td appeacḣz caill ⁊ crṁnne td a pṁ elenṗo oe. td ona eloceaṗpṁ

USHER ARCH BISHOP of ARMAGH

Fig. 5.3. James Ussher, engraved by G. Vertue (1738) from a painting by Sir P. Lely (*above*).

Fig. 5.4. Luke Wadding OFM, engraving from an eighteenth-century edition of the *Annales Minorum* (*opposite*).

Aois dom. 4528

A oir dom cheile mile, cuig cet, fich, ahos, an tug bl do ciomb.

Aois dom 4529.

A oir dom. cheile mile cuig cet, fich, anai. acteig do. ciom.

Aois dom. 4530.

A oir dom cheile mile, cuig ced, tochat. acing do ciomboc

Aois dom. 4531.

A oir dom cheile mile, cuig ced, tochat ahan. age do. ciom.

Aois dom. 4532. R 48 blin iar cemna righe chomcais.

A oir dom. cheile mile, cuig cet, tochat, ado. Iarmbliia peact
mbliaona h righe nen do ciomboc an ts peacht Romao
macha righi cohu pnaioh mc haoigin bale peal ahaig
don righe itebhit oiochonbu, R ciombioch na ciohai oan
righe do mnioi, feachair cach leoipia, brizir macha fuu
go nor ioraib oiochonbu da clain h cconucheizh co cirei
iccorain doblgit iiiri ciomboc cuicee do ceili oi, R do
bliii in righe do dochoroir iiin nahiaong h cconucheic, R cug
clem oiochonbale in doioipchizul co hileoib ahos anihic
R doblgit iiro io cimoione go io chaioirt iiat eaminu oi
go muio R buo iiom catairi nt do gnes

5199
4532
6 67

## Chapter 6

# The manuscripts of the Annals of the Four Masters since 1636 [1]

Nollaig Ó Muraíle

When in August 1636 the work that we know as the Annals of the Four Masters was completed by Mícheál Ó Cléirigh and his small band of assistants, there seem to have been two complete copies. Each of them was divided into two manuscript volumes (i.e. four volumes in all), written on paper by a number of scribes, most notably Brother Mícheál himself and his cousin Cú Choigcríche Ó Cléirigh. It has been suggested that one of these two-volume sets was a working copy and the other a clean copy. The latter, it has been assumed, was intended to be sent back to Louvain, where it would in due course be published. (It may be, though, that—as with the saints' Lives—what was to appear in print was a Latin translation rather than the original Irish text.) It has also been suggested that the other copy, the supposed working copy, was to be presented to Fearghal Ó Gadhra, MP for County Sligo, in return for his patronage of Ó Cléirigh and his team; without that patronage, the work would almost certainly not have been compiled in the first place.

Recent research by Bernadette Cunningham has shown, however, that the situation with regard to the various copies may not be quite as simple as had been thought: the supposed 'Louvain copy', for example, is not as clean and free of revision and insertions as had been believed,[2] while there is no clear evidence that the other copy ever reached Ó Gadhra's hands. The matter is clearly deserving of further study.

In this chapter we will look briefly at each of the four volumes in turn. These may be designated, respectively, by the letters C, H, A and P. (The reason for using the letters will become apparent presently.) The two copies, or sets of volumes, are represented respectively—according to the most generally accepted assessment—by the combinations CH and AP.

### Manuscript C
522 folios, covering the period AM 2242–AD 1171
[Fig. 6.1]

This volume (**18**) now forms part of the collection of the Royal Irish Academy, Dawson Street, Dublin—the largest collection of Irish-language manuscripts in the world—where its designation is C iii 3. It was used by the Sligo scholar Dubhaltach Mac Fhirbhisigh when compiling his great Book of Genealogies in Galway city in August 1649—he refers to it (perhaps significantly) as 'The History Book of Fearghal Ó Gadhra' (*Leabhar Airision Fhearghail Uí Ghadhra*)—and a few years later it was in the hands of one Henry Bourke in County Galway. It was in Bourke's possession between 1651 and 1658, but he may well have had it for some time prior to the former date—perhaps as early as 1647—and for some time after the latter date. Later in the seventeenth century it may for a time have been held by the Galway scholar—and protégé of Mac Fhirbhisigh's—Ruaidhrí Ó Flaithbheartaigh, alias Roderic O'Flaherty, who has numerous citations from the Four Masters (which he terms 'Annales Dungallenses', the Annals of Donegal) in his principal work, *Ogygia*, published in 1685 (**32**). Thereafter nothing more is heard of C until 1724, when it was reported as being in the possession of a certain

Fig. 6.1. Annals of the Four Masters, MS 'C'. RIA C iii 3, f. 107r (cat. no. 18) (*opposite*).

John Conry, owner of an extensive library in Dublin. It was one of two volumes of the Four Masters in the Conry collection, described as 'two thick Volumes in *Quarto*'; of this volume it is said: '[it] begins AM 2527, and ends AC 1171' (AM = *Anno Mundi*, 'the year of the world'; AC = *Anno Christi*, 'the year of Christ').

In 1731 C seems to have been purchased at the sale of Conry's library by, or on behalf of, Archbishop Brian (or Bernard) O'Gara of Tuam, apparently a grandson of Fearghal's. Three years later the archbishop presented the volume to the noted antiquary Charles O'Conor of Bellanagare, with whom he had family connections—the presentation may have been at the suggestion of O'Conor's grand-uncle, Tadhg Ó Ruairc OFM, bishop of Killala. (There are some questions, which need not concern us here, as to the possible migrations of this manuscript— or arguably, but less probably, P—to and from the Continent in the seventeenth and eighteenth centuries.) After Charles O'Conor's death in 1791, many of his manuscripts—including this volume—were transferred to Stowe in southern England, the seat of the marquis of Buckingham, by O'Conor's grandson, Fr Charles O'Conor DD, who was employed as librarian at Stowe and as chaplain to the marchioness. While at Stowe, C was used by the younger O'Conor to produce an edition of the portion of the Annals of the Four Masters from the beginning down to the year 1171. This edition—which was accompanied by a Latin translation but was, in textual terms, woefully inadequate—appeared in the third volume of Dr O'Conor's substantial four-volume work *Rerum Hibernicarum scriptores veteres* (1826) (**34**).

In 1849, following the bankruptcy of the second duke of Buckingham and Chandos, the Stowe manuscripts were sold at auction at Sotheby's, London; they were purchased by the earl of Ashburnham, who promptly locked them away in his London home and denied scholars—and anyone else—access to them for over three decades. On Ashburnham's death, the collection was purchased by the British government, and in 1883 the Irish manuscripts that were formerly at Stowe—including this volume, C, of the Four Masters—were transferred to the Royal Irish Academy, where they remain.

It may be noted that after MS C became the property of the elder Charles O'Conor, no fewer than three transcripts were commissioned from scribes of the period. As early as 1734–5 a copy of the manuscript was executed by Aodh Ó Maolmhuaidh on behalf of Dr John Fergus, a Mayo-born, Dublin-based medical doctor who was a close friend of O'Conor's and also a noted collector of books and manuscripts. Ó Maolmhuaidh's copy is now TCD MS 1300 (formerly H.2.9–10). Another copy of C was made, on the orders of Charles O'Conor, for the Chevalier Thomas O'Gorman in 1781, apparently by a young scribe named Martin Hughes, whom O'Conor himself had trained; this is now RIA MS 23 F 2 and 23 F 3. A third copy of C, the work of the well-known Monaghan-born scribe Muiris Ó Gormáin, is now TCD MS 1279 (formerly H.I.3–5).

When in the middle of the nineteenth century John O'Donovan was completing his monumental seven-volume edition of the Annals of the Four Masters (**37**), which appeared in 1851 (the post-Norman portion from P, discussed below, having already been published in 1848), he was handicapped by the unavailability of C. He was forced to base his text on the version of C published by Dr O'Conor in 1826 (**34**), but sought to correct 'the errors with which it abounds' by collating it with two of the manuscript copies then available to him in Dublin— that in TCD made by Ó Maolmhuaidh and that in the Royal Irish Academy made 'under the inspection of Charles O'Conor, and by his own scribe' (i.e. MS 23 F 2–3).

## Manuscript H
466 folios, covering AD 1334–1605
[Fig. 6.2]

This volume (**19**), which is now incomplete (lacking more than 160 years' material at the beginning), is preserved in the library of Trinity College Dublin, where its traditional designation was H.2.11; under the system now in operation it is known as MS 1301. Towards the end of the seventeenth century and/or early in the eighteenth century it was (as C may have been) in the hands of Roderic O'Flaherty (**32**), who made numerous marginal additions in this volume—most of them taken from a variety of now-lost annalistic collections, such as the Annals of Lecan. (The two principal sources of marginalia down to the year 1430 are works designated 'MS L' and 'McFirb.'—the former probably representing 'MS *Lecan*'.) It seems arguable that H had earlier been in the hands of Mac Fhirbhisigh, from whom it may well have passed to O'Flaherty. It may also, like C, have been in the hands of Henry Bourke (mentioned above) in County Galway for at least the greater part of the 1650s.

O'Flaherty died in 1718 (or possibly 1716), but as he had lost most of his manuscripts towards the end of his life H seems likely to have passed into the collection of John Conry some considerable time before that date. In 1724 it was described as 'having been rob'd of the Transactions of more than a whole Century of Years', with the addition that 'we find nothing here before 1335, whence the Thread is afterwards spun out to the year 1609'. (The actual dates—given above—are slightly different: 1334 and 1605.)

The volume was bought by Dr John Fergus at the sale of Conry's manuscripts in 1731 and he had it bound in 1739. Following Fergus's death in 1760 or 1761, his extensive library was auctioned in 1766, when it was acquired for the library of Trinity College Dublin. There it has rested ever since.

## Manuscript A
551 folios, covering the period AM 2242–AD 1169
[Fig. 6.3]

This volume—designated A 13—was continuously in Franciscan hands from the time it was penned some 370 years ago until it was transferred to University College Dublin in 2000 (**20**). It seems highly likely to have been brought to Louvain by Mícheál Ó Cléirigh on his return there from Ireland in 1637. It was used by, among others, the great Franciscan hagiographer Fr John Colgan OFM, notes in whose hand appear throughout the volume. It is almost certainly one of a number of volumes described as having been at Louvain around the year 1673. It was clearly among the Franciscan documents that were removed, about the time of the French Revolution, to the Irish Franciscan College of St Isidore, Rome. There it remained until 1872, when—owing to fears that the government of the newly united Italy might suppress St Isidore's—the Franciscan manuscripts of Irish interest were (with the assistance of the British government) returned to Ireland. Initially kept in the Franciscan library at Merchant's Quay, Dublin, in the 1940s, they were transferred to the newly founded Franciscan House of Studies (Dún Mhuire), Killiney, Co. Dublin, and in recent years the collection has found a home in University College Dublin (under the auspices of the Mícheál Ó Cléirigh Institute).

A new edition of the Annals of the Four Masters undertaken around 1940 by Paul Walsh was to be based on this manuscript and on P, below, while C and H were 'to be used as comparative and supplemental MSS'. The work, however, was never completed, being cut short by Fr Walsh's untimely death in 1941.

## Manuscript P
580 folios, covering the period AD 1170–1616
[Fig. 6.4]

This volume (**21**, **22**), like C, is preserved in the Royal Irish Academy, where it is now in two parts, designated (since being rebound in the 1830s) 23 P 6 and 23 P 7. (The new volumes contain 287 and 293 folios and cover the years AD 1170–1499 and 1500–1616 respectively.) Strangely, nothing whatever appears to be known of the history of P until about the year 1778, when it was in the possession of Charles O'Conor. In March of that year a transcript of it was completed for O'Conor by Muiris Ó Gormáin; this is now RIA MSS 23 F 4–6. One wonders if, perhaps, it spent some time on the Continent—even in Louvain, as one might expect, given the suggestion that it and MS A constituted the 'Louvain set'. If so, when, how and why did it return to Ireland?

At some stage, and in circumstances that are now uncertain, the volume passed from Charles O'Conor into the hands of his friend William Burton Conyngham. When the latter died intestate in 1796, the manuscript came into the possession of one Austin Cooper, whose books were sold after his own death around 1831, P being then acquired by George Petrie on behalf of the Royal Irish Academy. The volume at the time was described as being 'a mere unbound roll; its margins worn away by damp'. John O'Donovan's edition (in three volumes) of the latter portion of the Annals of the Four Masters—covering the period 1172–1616 and published in 1848—was based on this manuscript, with some cross-references to H (described as 'the College copy') (**37**). As mentioned above, this manuscript and A were intended to furnish the text of the re-edition of the Annals of the Four Masters planned, but never completed, by Fr Paul Walsh in the early 1940s.

All of the original manuscripts that together comprise almost two complete sets of the Annals of the Four Masters have been brought together in 2007 for the 'Louvain 400' collaborative exhibition at Trinity College Dublin. The manuscripts have thus been reunited for the first time since they were completed by Mícheál Ó Cléirigh and his assistants in the Donegal friary at Drowes in the summer of 1636.

1  This article is based largely on Nollaig Ó Muraíle, 'The autograph manuscripts of the Annals of the Four Masters', *Celtica* 19 (1987), 75–95, especially pp 88–95, where details of a wide range of relevant sources will be found. I am also indebted to an article by Maura O'Gara-O'Riordan, 'A mystery revisited—Charles O'Conor and the Annals of the Four Masters' (to appear in a forthcoming book on Charles O'Conor edited by Kieran O'Conor), which corrects or clarifies some points in the abovementioned article.

2  Bernadette Cunningham, 'The making of the Annals of the Four Masters' (unpublished PhD thesis, University College Dublin, 2005), chap. 4.

# O G Y G I A,
## OR, A
### CHRONOLOGICAL ACCOUNT
#### OF
### IRISH EVENTS:

Fig. 6.2. Annals of the Four Masters, MS 'H'. TCD 1301, f. 767r (cat. no. 19) (*opposite*).

# Aois Cr. 1438:

Aois Criost, mile, cethre ced, tocatt, a hoct

Abb cille na manach & mocol o nján brocht capt in deobayn robcc marbh do plaig

An tepiscob o gall cob̄. .i. lochlayn decc, episcop juvta bot epide

Priojr cille may̅ nerin decc mac nery iayla cille vayn epide

Pilyb may rom vo zabayl la may rom

Donoch na coyll o domnaill vo myrbeoh la concobayr roon o rān

In tejr enva jarrnaeach don ē.ē.

Catrayr o vachayreargh decc

Concob in giohsit y orbroa etrna clome conch y orbroa roimyb la abrafli pein irrill .i. la zaychleach in coyom in conch y orbroa y la rurays mac rayct la lochlym mm lochlym y orbroa y la heny bayro y ran mac roct de romayl b anoroch myalle pin. Villzm in rivarojn y orbroa vo bcc

ez ez rru cconcobayr rayle e re zallap in ojorayl y domnayll (nell bcop de mez platich .i. enp bull roimyb la epm oplit mew mib e byry ryro qmyr bne put in enan abmyr vo bcc vo zalr byeue. Nyem bayorn .i. vilyem bayro vo bcc villam in reay abyre vo bcc mary rein. Smyrean in reay in oyrell vo bcc fe vo enam vra vob rayle f acub brachayr cathiop o veobayr bryayn .i. rwor in bryayn y bryayn vo are roz la acobbyrcheayr rein .i. la ryacc zayham y obryayn vo zaylm vo rhachrum ep in fcoryr .i. rayr oboo vo bcc chrinayn ollam y eaz rie rrzan vo bcc.

Donch mac syoon y crrayn gaoy le semicz

O out breyrne .i. wo olt y razzyll le van

Concob in edozayr ollam clome mocayro le brebmy vecc

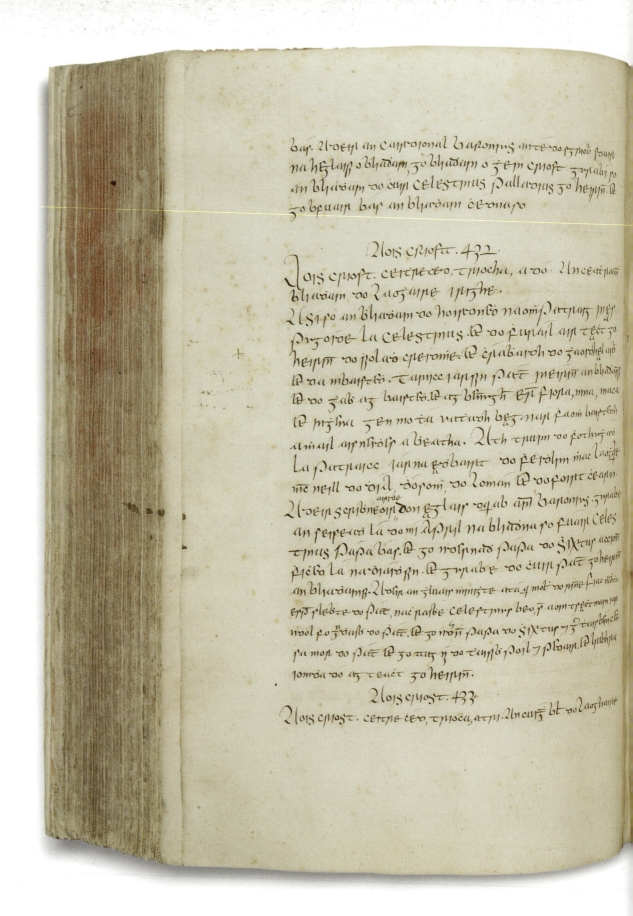

bar. Aodh an caTpojonal Bajonmg arce do fgmob foam
na hEglaip o bhadain go bhadain o gein cpiost grialai po
an bhadain do cain CELESTINUS Pallacipuf go heipin. Wc
go bfuain bar an bhadain cecmairo

## Aois crioft. 432

Aois cpiost. cecepecco, cpiocha, a do. Un ceacipam
bhadain do Laozaipe ipizhe.

Asipo an bhadain do honronto naoim Pacpaig meg
Pizoroe La celestinus. Wc do fuipail aip teet go
heipin do ipolad cpepome. Wc cpiabaincoh do zaozhelaib
Wc da mbaipfcio. Taipnec paippn Pate meipin an bhadain
Wc do gaib ag baipcio. Wc ag blingh Efi fipia, nnia, maca
Wc pizlinc gen mo ca vitcaoh bez naip faoin baipcioh
ainail aip ntraip a Beatha. Ach cpipin do pochng do
La Pacpaice paipma gobaipt do ferolin mac Laoyfi
me neill do oia, doporn, do Loman Wc do foipt ceain.
Aoein scpibneoipn don Eglaip Wc gab aipi Bajonmg grialbe
an feipecio La do in Appil na bhadona po fuaim Celes
cinus Papa bar. Wc go noipinacio Papa do SIXTUS accipin
pfelo La nardipo gn. Wc grialb E do cuip Pate go heipin
an bhadaing. Aloip an fluaip imnigce acai g mok do nime fiuc noch
Epi plebte do Pate, nac paibe celescinup beo, g aoin cgeet main paip
ivel pogoaib do Pate. Wc go noin Papa do SIXTUS 7 g caipbigneii
pa moip do Pate Wc go cuig n do caing poil 7 Ploaiin. Wc fiubhpia
iomoai do ag teeet go heipin.

### Aois cpiost. 433

Aois cpiost. cecepe ceo, cpiocha, acpi. Un cuig bt do Laozhaine

## Aoiser 1394·

Aoisriost, mile tricheo, nochatt, acethar

...

## Aoiser 1395·

Aoisen mile, tricheo, nochatt, acuice

...

135

# Chapter 7

# The nineteenth-century legacy: publishing the Annals of the Four Masters

Bernadette Cunningham

The story of the publication of John O'Donovan's edition of the Annals of the Four Masters is a fascinating one.[1] It could be said to begin at the sale of Austin Cooper's books in 1831, when George Petrie bought the original autograph manuscript of the second part of the Annals (**21**, **22**), the section covering the years 1171 to 1616. He paid £53 for the manuscript, and he then sold it to the Royal Irish Academy for the price he had paid for it. At the time of purchase the manuscript was described as being a damp roll, and the considerable sum that Petrie was prepared to pay was an indication of the special regard in which this work was held. On Petrie's initiative, the manuscript was conserved and bound in two volumes (RIA 23 P 6–23 P 7), by George Mullen of Dublin, in 1837. [Fig. 7.1]

From the time he purchased the manuscript for the Academy, Petrie was anxious that it should be published. He stressed

> the necessity of giving durability, while yet in our power, to the surviving historical remains of our country, and thereby placing them beyond the reach of a fate otherwise inevitable. To me it appears a sacred duty on all cultivated minds to do so.[2]

Petrie had a clear idea of the kind of edition required, and was particularly keen that the Irish text should be printed using an appropriate Gaelic font. By 1835 he had designed a new Gaelic type for this purpose (**37**). Funded by Hodges and Smith, the type was modelled on the lettering in the Book of Kells.[3] The design and physical appearance of the Irish text of the Annals was clearly regarded as important. While the use of a Gaelic script was readily justifiable on scholarly grounds, as necessary for the accurate representation of the written text, its significance transcended those technicalities. Through the medium of print, the Gaelic texts that were central to Irish antiquarian research were being brought into the public sphere. Their Gaelic character was what defined the authenticity of these texts, and it was thought necessary to preserve the essence of that character in the print medium. Parallel Irish and English texts on facing pages were adopted as a means of visibly demonstrating the authenticity of texts while making them accessible to those who could not read Irish.[4] It was all part of the process of Gaelicising the memory of the past.

There had been two earlier attempts to print versions of these same annals. In 1826 the librarian at Stowe, Revd Charles O'Conor, edited the pre-1172 section of the Annals of the Four Masters, based on the autograph manuscript (now RIA C iii 3) for which he provided a Latin translation (**34**).[5] Some years later Bryan Geraghty published Owen Connellan's English translation (**35**) of the annals for the years 1171 to 1616. Appearing in the 1840s, this was seen by some as a cheap rival to O'Donovan's work. Planned as a periodical publication, it was designed to reach a general audience. [Fig. 7.2] There was little comparison between the two, however,

Fig. 7.1. Annals of the Four Masters, nineteenth-century binding of MS 'P'. RIA 23 P 6 (inside front board) (*opposite*).

O'Donovan's edition being far superior in both form and content. The existence of these other editions nevertheless illustrates the huge cultural significance attaching to the Annals of the Four Masters in early nineteenth-century Ireland.

The belief in the national importance of publishing Irish manuscripts such as the Annals of the Four Masters led to the formation of the Irish Archaeological Society, founded on St Patrick's Day 1840, under the leadership of J.H. Todd. Over the previous half-century the acquisitions policy of the Royal Irish Academy had brought many Irish manuscripts into public ownership for the first time. Neither the Irish Archaeological Society nor the Royal Irish Academy had the financial resources necessary to publish the annals, however, and it was the publishing firm of Hodges and Smith that financed the project. The publishers did not merely pay for the typesetting, printing and binding. They also paid John O'Donovan for his work of translating and editing, and employed Eugene O'Curry to transcribe the complete Irish text in a form suitable for use by the typesetter.[6]

John O'Donovan commenced work on translating the annals in January 1832, but owing to other demands on his time it was well into the 1840s before the edition was ready for the press. His edition was greatly enhanced by his extensive topographical notes to the text. He assembled the information for these notes between 1833 and 1842 when he was employed as a topographical researcher by the Ordnance Survey. The publishers made a virtue of the fact that O'Donovan had visited virtually every townland in the country in the course of his research.[7]

When the publication of the Annals was first announced by Hodges and Smith in 1844 a two-volume set was envisaged, with a print run of 500 copies. By the time the work was printed in 1848, John O'Donovan's very extensive notes to the text meant that the work had grown to some 2,498 pages, which necessitated its being issued in three volumes. The three-volume set covered the years AD 1172–1616. After that had been published, O'Donovan continued to work on translating the text for AM 2242 to AD 1171, culminating in a seven-volume edition issued in 1851. [Fig. 7.3] The design of the binding in which the de luxe edition of 1851 was issued was modelled on the shrine of St Maodhóg, first bishop of Ferns. This attention to detail is interesting because it reveals the way in which the artistic qualities of Irish antiquities, such as the eleventh-century reliquary of St Maodhóg, were perceived and valued.[8]

The price for the complete edition in 1851 was a very substantial fourteen guineas, a price which the publishers knew 'chiefly confined the sale to public institutions and men of large fortune'.[9] Sales of the seven-volume edition must have been rather less brisk than anticipated, and John O'Donovan reported to John Windele in June 1852 that Hodges and Smith 'have lost so much by this publication that they can hardly bear the sight of me in their shop'.[10] A considerably cheaper edition, priced at four guineas (or twelve shillings a volume for each of the seven volumes),[11] was issued in 1856. The publicity brochure for this reissue included approbations from various Irish bishops, typical of which was the comment of Dr John Ryan, bishop of Limerick, who welcomed the fact that

> the only work which gives a full, impartial, and authentic account of Irish affairs, *before* as well as after
> the English invasion, is at length to be made accessible to Irish students, in the Irish original, with a
> faithful English translation, learnedly illustrated—and that Irish publishers are the spirited originators
> of an enterprise as perilous as patriotic and useful.[12]

Indeed, the general tenor of these episcopal approbations emphasised the desirability that a work of such national importance should be widely disseminated.

The 1856 edition was twice reprinted in the twentieth century, indicating that the work still continued to have appeal. In 1966 an American reprint company made the seven-volume set available once again, still aimed at the library market. A further lavish reprint in 1990 was aimed at the specialist collector, the Irish publisher even adopting the nineteenth-century strategy of printing a formal prospectus. The advertisement cited P. W. Joyce to the effect that the Annals were 'the greatest and most important work ever issued by any Irish publisher', and emphasised that the new 1990 reprint would be 'printed in Ireland'.[13]

While relatively few people in the mid-nineteenth century could afford the high price of a full set of the Annals, the broad interest that the work elicited is evident from the way O'Donovan used extracts from the Annals in articles in the *Dublin Penny Journal* and the *Irish Penny Journal* (**36**). [Fig. 7.4] In the same way, Philip McDermott and Owen Connellan published material from the Annals in the *Nation* newspaper in the late 1840s. Such publicity helped to ensure that the name of Mícheál Ó Cléirigh became enshrined in the national consciousness as Ireland's most significant Gaelic historian.

Reviews praising O'Donovan's edition of the Annals were published in the *Gentleman's Magazine*, the *Irish Quarterly Review*, the *Dublin University Magazine*, the *Irish Ecclesiastical Journal* and the *Dublin Review*. The praise for O'Donovan's work was of the highest order. The enthusiasm of the *Quarterly*'s reviewer was typical:

> Whether we regard the industry and impartiality of the original compilers, the immense learning and extensive researches of the editor, or the exquisite typography of the volumes, it must be admitted that these Annals, as edited by Dr John O'Donovan, form one of the most remarkable works yet produced on the history of any portion of the British Isles. The mass of information which they embody constitutes a collection of national records, the value of which can never be superseded ... Standing thus alone, it must maintain a high place among the great literary monuments of the world, so long as the study of history continues to retain the charms which it has ever possessed for men of cultivated and philosophic minds.[14]

The reviewer for the *Irish Ecclesiastical Journal*, a Church of Ireland publication, portrayed the work as an icon of Irish ability to triumph over adversity: 'In a year of famine and great mercantile depression appeared the work whose title heads this article, as it were an earnest of intellectual propriety, and an omen of national convalescence'.[15]

Although O'Donovan's achievement in editing the Annals of the Four Masters has remained unsurpassed, it must be noted that his edition of the pre-1171 material has long been regarded as unsatisfactory. As Eugene O'Curry was careful to point out in his *Lectures on the manuscript materials of ancient Irish history*, published in 1861, O'Donovan did not have access to either of the known autograph manuscripts of the Annals for the years before 1171, and hence was not in a position to produce a fully accurate edition. At the time, one part of the autograph Annals (now UCD-OFM A 13) was in the Franciscan Irish College of St Isidore in Rome, eventually being brought back to Ireland in 1872, more than ten years after O'Donovan's death (**20**). The other copy (now RIA C iii 3) had also been inaccessible to O'Donovan, being then owned by the earl of Ashburnham in England (**18**). That manuscript was returned to Ireland in 1883, when the manuscripts of Irish interest in the Stowe–Ashburnham collection were purchased by the British government and presented to the Royal Irish Academy. So although all of the surviving autograph copies of the Annals of the Four Masters are now in archives and libraries in Dublin, that was not the case in O'Donovan's day. It was for this reason that O'Curry regarded

O'Donovan's edition merely as the standard edition 'in the present state of our knowledge' in 1861. Despite this caveat, O'Curry was generous in his praise of O'Donovan's scholarship, but reserved his highest praise for the publisher, George Smith:

> I cannot pass from the subject of this lecture without recording the grateful sense which I am sure all of you ... must feel, as I do, of the singular public spirit of Mr George Smith, at whose sole risk and expense this vast publication was undertaken and completed. There is no instance that I know of, in any country, of a work so vast being undertaken, much less of any completed in a style so perfect and so beautiful, by the enterprise of a private publisher ... the example of so much spirit in an Irish publisher—the printing of such a book in a city like Dublin, so long shorn of metropolitan wealth as well as honours—cannot fail to redound abroad to the credit of the whole country, as well as to that of our enterprising fellow-citizen.[16]

O'Curry was here echoing the sentiments of many of his contemporaries, who saw the publication of these volumes as transcending the mere academic achievement of producing a scholarly edition of an important primary source for the history of Ireland.

The history of Ireland and most especially the Irish-language manuscript sources that had survived the ravages of time became the focus of scholarly endeavour in an age of emerging national sentiment. John O'Donovan, Eugene O'Curry and their associates perceived their work on publishing the Annals not merely as an expression of Irish patriotic endeavour but also as a re-enactment in their own day of the scholarly activities of the Four Masters themselves. These nineteenth-century antiquarians viewed their work on Irish manuscripts as a rescue mission, saving these important Irish texts from oblivion. They projected that notion, somewhat anachronistically, onto their seventeenth-century predecessors, thereby propagating the idea that the Four Masters were engaged on a mission to save from destruction the last remnants of the *seanchas* tradition. While the impetus to commit history to paper lest communal memories be lost is a perennial motivation for the writing of history, it is important to realise that the Four Masters were no mere antiquarians. Rather, theirs was a new history for a Catholic Ireland emerging from the religious and political traumas of the age. Their Annals utilised the past as a means of understanding the present and of focusing minds on future objectives.

1    Bernadette Cunningham, '"An honour to the nation": publishing John O'Donovan's edition of the Annals of the Four Masters, 1848–56', in Martin Fanning and Raymond Gillespie (eds), *Print culture and intellectual life in Ireland, 1660–1941* (Dublin, 2006), 116–42.

2    George Petrie, 'Remarks on the history and authenticity of the Annals of the Four Masters', *Transactions of the Royal Irish Academy* 16 (1831), 387.

3    Vincent Kinane, *A history of the Dublin University Press, 1734–1976* (Dublin, 1994), 130–1; Dermot McGuinne, *Irish type design: a history of printing types in the Irish character* (Dublin, 1992), 102–3.

4    Joep Leerssen, *Hidden Ireland, public sphere* (Galway, 2002), 25.

5    Revd Charles O'Conor (ed.), *Quatuor Magistrorum annales Hibernici usque ad annum MCLXXII ex ipso O'Clerii autographo in Bibliotheca Stowense servato*, Rerum Hibernicarum Scriptores Veteres III (Buckingham, 1826).

6    A four-volume transcript of the Annals in O'Curry's hand is now in Derry Museum. I am grateful to Brian Lacey for this information.

7    RIA 12 I 15, p. 311.

8    Described by the reviewer writing for the *Irish Quarterly Review* 1 (1851), 697n.

9    RIA 12 I 15, p. 571.

10   RIA MS 4 B 12/83 i.

11   RIA 12 I 15, p. 571.

12   RIA 12 I 15, p. 574.

13   *The Annals of the Four Masters: prospectus by Eamonn de Burca* (Dublin, 1990).

14   RIA 12 I 15, p. 587.

15   *Irish Ecclesiastical Journal* 5 (1848), 123.

16   Eugene O'Curry, *Lectures on the manuscript materials of ancient Irish history* (Dublin, 1861), 161.

A. D. 1363.

THIS year Manus Eoghanach, son of Conor, son of Hugh, son of Donal Oge O'Donnell; and Hugh Roe Mac Guire, lord of Fermanagh, died.

Manus Mebhlach (the Crafty), son of Hugh O'Donnell, heir presumptive to the lordship of Tirconnell, a man who performed the most noble and enterprising deeds of any in his time, was slain by Manus the son of Cathal Sramach O'Conor.

Teige Mac Consnamha, chief of Muintir Kenny (in Leitrim), was wounded by Cathal, son of Hugh Brefnach (O'Conor), by whom he was after that taken prisoner; and he died in his imprisonment.

The nineteenth-century legacy: publishing the Annals of the Four Masters

Fig. 7.2. Detail of Owen Connellan's edition of the Annals of the Four Masters (cat. no. 35) (*above*).

# AOIS CRIOST, 1537.

Aoir Criort, mile, cúicc céd, triočat, a Seačt.

Coccað etir aoð mbuiðe ó nðoṁnaill ⁊ Maᵹnur ó ðoṁnaill. Clann uí baoiᵹill ðo bḟit aᵹ conᵹnaṁ lá haoð, ⁊ aoð ḟirrin ðo bḟit i ccairlen ðúin na nᵹall. Ro eiriᵹ commbuaiðreað mór hi ccenel cconaill tre ḟraonta cloinne í ðoṁnaill ḟria poile ðia ro marbað ðronᵹ ðo ḟliočt an erruicc uí ᵹallcubair lá cloinn uí baoiᵹill .i. mac toirrðealbaiᵹ óicc mic briain, ⁊ ðiar mac eoččain tallaiᵹ mic briain ⁊ araill ele cenmotat.

O ðomhnaill aoð mac aoða ruaið mic neill ᵹairb mic toirrðealbaiᵹ an ḟíona tiᵹrna tire conaill innri heoččain, cenel moain ḟirmanač, ⁊ iočtair čonnačt, ḟír ᵹur a ttanᵹattar comta, ⁊ cíorčana ó tirib oile čuicce ḟorr mbaoí a rmačt ⁊ a čuṁačta aṁail atá maᵹ luircc, Mačaire connačt clann čonnmaiᵹ, ᵹoirðealbaiᵹ, ᵹailḟnᵹaiᵹ, tir aṁalᵹaið, ⁊ conmaicne čúile ðon taoð

<sub></sub>

ᵖ *Lord Leonard.*—This should be Lord Leonard Gray.—See the year 1535, where he is called Tiᵹard ᵹrai.

ᑫ *Extended his jurisdiction, &c.*, literally, "a man to whom came gifts and tributes from other territories on which his jurisdiction and power was."

ʳ *Moylurg*, i. e. Mac Dermot's country, coextensive with the old barony of Boyle, in the county of Roscommon.

ˢ *Machaire-Chonnacht*, i. e. the plain of Connaught, comprising the countries of O'Conor Roe and O'Conor Don, in the county of Roscommon.

ᵗ *Clann-Conway.*—This was at the period of which we are treating Mac David Burke's country, in the barony of Ballymoe, in the north-east of the county of Galway.

Fig. 7.3. John O'Donovan's *Annals of the Kingdom of Ireland* (1848–51) (cat. no. 37) (*above*).

Fig. 7.4. Image of birthplace of Mícheál Ó Cléirigh at Kilbarron Castle, Co. Donegal, from *The Irish Penny Journal*, 16 January 1841 (cat. no. 36) (*opposite*).

# THE IRISH PENNY JOURNAL.

NUMBER 29.　　　SATURDAY, JANUARY 16, 1841.　　　VOLUME I.

BRANSTON. S.

## KILBARRON CASTLE, COUNTY OF DONEGAL.

WE think our readers generally will concur with us in considering the subject of our prefixed illustration as a very striking and characteristic one—presenting features which, except among the castles of the Scottish highland chiefs, will only be found on the wild shores of our own romantic island. It is indeed a truly Irish scene—poetical and picturesque in the extreme, and its history is equally peculiar, being wholly unlike any thing that could be found relating to any castle out of Ireland.

From the singularity of its situation, seated on a lofty, precipitous, and nearly insulated cliff, exposed to the storms and billows of the western ocean, our readers will naturally conclude that this now sadly dilapidated and time-worn ruin must have owed its origin to some rude and daring chief of old, whose occupation was war and rapine, and whose thoughts were as wild and turbulent as the waves that washed his sea-girt eagle dwelling; and such, in their ignorance of its unpublished history, has been the conclusion drawn by modern topographers, who tell us that it is supposed to have been the habitation of freebooters. But it was not so; and our readers will be surprised when we acquaint them that this lonely, isolated fortress was erected as an abode for peaceful men—a safe and quiet retreat in troubled times for the laborious investigators and preservers of the history, poetry, and antiquities of their country! Yes, reader, this castle was the residence of the ollaves, bards, and antiquaries of the people of Tirconnell—the illustrious family of the O'Clerys, to

whose zealous labours in the preservation of the history and antiquities of Ireland we are chiefly indebted for the information on those subjects with which we so often endeavour to instruct and amuse you. You will pardon us, then, if with a grateful feeling to those benefactors of our country to whose labours we owe so much, we endeavour to do honour to their memory by devoting a few pages of our little national work to their history, as an humble but not unfitting monument to their fame.

We trust, however, that such a sketch as we propose will not be wholly wanting either in interest or instruction. It will throw additional light upon the ancient customs and state of society in Ireland, and exhibit in a striking way a remarkable feature in the character of our countrymen of past ages, which no adverse circumstances were ever able utterly to destroy, and which, we trust, will again distinguish them as of old—their love for literature and learning, and their respect for good and learned men. It will also exhibit another trait in their national character no less peculiar or remarkable, namely, their great anxiety to preserve their family histories—a result of which is, that even to the present day the humblest Irish peasant, as well as the estated gentleman, can not unfrequently trace his descent not only to a more remote period, but also with a greater abundance of historical evidence than most of the princely families of Europe. This is, indeed, a trait in the national character which philosophers, and men like ourselves, usually affect

# Aoḋ Mac Aingil

## aġus an

# Scoil Ṅua-Ġaeḋilġe

# i Loḃáin

### Tomás Ó Cléiriġ, M.A.,
#### do scríoḃ.

## Chapter 8
# Remembering Mícheál Ó Cléirigh

Bernadette Cunningham

The published Annals of the Four Masters (1851) drew their authority from the authenticity of their connection to the late medieval Gaelic manuscript tradition, and it was this that allowed them to form part of the cultural roots of modern Irish identity. For cultural historians and antiquarians, the Annals of the Four Masters were a bridge between an old world and a new one. The work came to be seen as one of the enduring achievements of native Irish scholars before the disappearance of the Gaelic world. The significance of the Four Masters was described in colourful prose by Aodh de Blácam, author of one of the standard histories of Irish literature, who concluded that:

> Nothing, perhaps, in our history is more piteous or more dramatic than the sitting down of these heirs
> of an immemorial tradition to rescue and set in order what could be recovered, in a land of blood and
> ashes, of the names and titles and deeds of the great men of Éire. Their vast compilation is justly famous,
> although it is somewhat fantastically supposed by many folk to be the prime, if not the only, monument
> of Irish letters ... Be it remembered that the Masters laboured in the cold belief that the Irish nation was
> dead, and that nothing remained to be salved save its memory. They succeeded in their task. They saved
> great tracts of the Irish past from oblivion. Were it not for them our knowledge of mediaeval Ireland
> would be largely a picturesque tradition that could not be related easily to fact. In their vast work we
> see an immemorial civilisation, as it were Atlantis with all its towers and temples, looming out of the
> dim backward of time.[1]

At a popular level, in the late 1880s a column in the *Evening Telegraph* contributed by journalist and poet Eugene Davis, on 'Souvenirs of Irish footprints over Europe', romanticised a visit to Louvain by recalling its association with Ó Cléirigh:

> St Anthony's College will live chiefly in history as the institution where Brother O'Clery, the leading light
> of the Four Masters, matured that remarkable talent of his, and that untiring capacity for intellectual
> research, thanks to which we owe the 'Annals'. It was in these cloisters, under the shade of these trees
> in the courtyard, that he paced up and down often and often, dreaming of the 'magnum opus',
> sketching its proportions with his mind's eye, or lost in enthusiasm at its scope and grandeur.[2]

Similarly, Douglas Hyde, writing his survey of Irish literature in 1899, described Mícheál Ó Cléirigh's scholarly endeavours in heroic terms. Commenting on Ó Cléirigh's researches on hagiographical manuscripts, Hyde noted:

Fig. 8.1. Tomás Ó Cléirigh's biography of Aodh Mac Aingil, published in 1936 (cat. no. 40) (*opposite*).

Up and down, high and low, he hunted for the ancient vellum books and time-stained manuscripts whose safety was even then threatened by the ever-thickening political shocks and spasms of that most destructive age. These, whenever he found, he copied in an accurate and beautiful handwriting, and transmitted safely to Louvain ... Before O'Clery ever entered the Franciscan Order he had been by profession an historian or antiquary, and now in his eager quest for ecclesiastical writings and the lives of saints, his trained eye fell upon many other documents which he could not neglect. These were the ancient books and secular annals of the nation, and the historical poems of the ancient bards ... There is no event of Irish history from the birth of Christ to the beginning of the seventeenth century that the first inquiry of the student will not be, 'What do the "Four Masters" say about it?' for the great value of the work consists in this, that we have here in condensed form the pith and substance of the old books of Ireland which were then in existence but which—as the Four Masters foresaw—have long since perished.[3]

In post-1922 Ireland, the emphasis on Irish history was all the more important in view of the decline of the Irish language. An editorial in the *Irish Independent* in August 1924 headed *Uaisleacht na hÉireann* stressed the 'national' value of history:

It is from history will come to us again the confidence and that national hope that were alive in Ireland when the national language was commonly spoken in our country. Let us give our young students accurate knowledge of the golden age of faith and learning, when our native land was respected throughout Europe. For the salvation and the uplifting of the nation today are in the revival of the spirit that was alive in Ireland at that time.[4]

The story of Mícheál Ó Cléirigh and the Four Masters came to have an important role in this new-found emphasis on Ireland's past golden ages. Tomás Ó Cléirigh's 1936 study of Aodh Mac Aingil (**40**) and the Irish College at Louvain incorporated a succinct version of the Ó Cléirigh myth, affirming the Franciscan scholar's status as Ireland's greatest chronicler.[5] [**Fig. 8.1**] The publication marked the tercentenary of the completion of the Annals. In the same year, Brendan Jennings's meticulously researched book on Mícheál Ó Cléirigh and his associates placed the Annals of the Four Masters in the context of the whole corpus of Ó Cléirigh's writings, sifting through prefaces and manuscript colophons for evidence of the environment in which the work was produced. His essays on Ó Cléirigh had been published over a number of years in *Assisi: Irish Franciscan Monthly* (**41**), and were revised for publication in book form (**39**) in 1936. Jennings was keen to stress the status of Ó Cléirigh as one of Ireland's most important historians, concluding:

this humble Brother, who hid himself so completely while accomplishing so much for Ireland, has fulfilled one of the noblest ambitions man can have. He has written his name large across the history of his country, and has left it engraved indelibly on the hearts of all his countrymen.[6]

The degree of adulation traditionally accorded Mícheál Ó Cléirigh is somewhat curious. He was, after all, only a Franciscan lay brother who was following the instructions of his superiors to collect the raw materials for their research project. Earlier generations of annalists and their annalistic compilations, such as the Annals of Ulster (**5**), the Annals of Connacht or the Annals of Loch Cé, have not attracted the same kind of eulogistic comment. The special character of the Annals of the Four Masters is not difficult to discover, however. The Four Masters, and in particular Mícheál Ó Cléirigh, found ready champions in early twentieth-century Ireland in the Franciscan order. This institutional backing certainly did not do Ó Cléirigh's scholarly reputation any harm. Added to this was the local dimension, evident in the admiration for his achievements felt in his native Donegal. An Irish-language second-level school established in 1906 in Letterkenny, Co. Donegal, at the prompting of the Gaelic League, was named Coláiste na gCeithre Máistrí.[7] Some years later, fund-raisers for a new parish church in Donegal town found that the reputation of the Four Masters could be harnessed for benevolent purposes. The new Catholic church was named after the Four Masters. In October 1938 a new monument to the Four Masters was unveiled in the Diamond, Donegal town. The event was noticed by the *London Times*, and under the heading 'The Golden Age of Ireland' the correspondent commented favourably on the commemoration of 'The Annals of the Four Masters, one of the most remarkable monuments in the literary history of Ireland'.[8]

Such was the enthusiasm of County Donegal for its famous son that controversy erupted in the 1930s when a claim was made that the Annals might actually have been written in County Leitrim. A heated debate raged in the pages of the *Irish Independent* newspaper in 1936 and 1937 as rival claims were made concerning the precise geographical location of the temporary accommodation of the Franciscan friars on the banks of the River Drowes on the Donegal–Leitrim border. Indeed, the matter was still being debated in the late 1950s.[9]

Elsewhere, too, the Franciscan order had come to realise the iconic significance of the Four Masters. Thus, for example, when funds were being raised for a new church at Athlone in 1919, the name of Ó Cléirigh was enlisted for publicity purposes. A fund-raising bazaar was held in the town from 10 to 17 August 1919, and the souvenir brochure produced on that occasion had a sketch of the proposed church with the motto '*Do chum glóire Dé agus onóra na hÉireann*' ('to the glory of God and the honour of Ireland') (adapted from the Annals) underneath. The literature explained that the church would be a fitting memorial to the Four Masters, whose Annals could be regarded as 'The most valuable title-deed of Irish nationality'.[10] More recently, the new all-Irish primary school in the town, which opened in 1990, was named 'Scoil na gCeithre Máistrí' in recognition of the association of the Four Masters with the Athlone region.

At a national level, in the newly established Free State, where the Irish language and Irish history were central to its sense of what it meant to be Irish, Mícheál Ó Cléirigh became the focus of official celebrations of Irish national identity. In a collection of essays on Irish saints and scholars published by F. J. Sheed on the occasion of the Eucharistic Congress in Dublin in 1932, an essay on Ó Cléirigh was included. The Assisi Press reissued the same essay as a pamphlet in 1943 as one of the many Franciscan commemorative activities to mark the tercentenary of Ó Cléirigh's death.

In the midst of the Second World War, the Irish state was drawn directly into the commemorative programme for the tercentenary of Ó Cléirigh's death in 1943–4. Thus, for example, specially commissioned postage stamps were issued in 1944 in honour of Ó Cléirigh (**44**). The stamps were designed by an Irish artist, R. J. King, and the Minister for Posts and Telegraphs emphasised that they were being printed in Ireland using Irish paper. It was noted that 'The stamp is a tribute not only to the great chronicler, Michael Ó Cléirigh, but it recalls to the minds of the present generation the very ancient traditions of our Nation and our civilization'.[11] These were not merely commemorative stamps issued for a short period, but formed part of the definitive series that remained in use until 1969.[12] [Fig. 8.2]

Numerous public commemorative events were staged to mark the tercentenary of Ó Cléirigh's death. Many prominent churchmen and politicians, including the then taoiseach, Éamon de Valera, were present at a gala concert held in the Gaiety Theatre in Dublin on Sunday 25 June 1944 to celebrate Ó Cléirigh's life and work (**42**). The concert was broadcast to the nation on Raidio Éireann, and a special souvenir programme was published to mark the occasion. [Fig. 8.3] The Franciscan community masterminded the event to honour the memory of the lay brother 'whose labours in the cause of Irish history, literature, and language, saved our country's records from obliteration and our native tongue from extinction'.[13]

In the same year, 1944, a substantial collection of academic essays (**43**) in memory of Mícheál Ó Cléirigh, edited by Sylvester O'Brien OFM, was published in Dublin.[14] [Fig. 8.4] The volume concluded with an epilogue in verse, in praise of Ó Cléirigh:

Lo! He who saved from deep oblivion
The chronicle of saint and king and bard
Through gathering menaces of war and strife
Went not all unremembered, for upon
One white memorial war hath not marr'd
His name stands written—on the Book of Life.[15]

In short, by the mid-twentieth century Ó Cléirigh had not merely become a cultural icon of Irishness but was hailed as the saviour of the Irish past. Just as in the 1840s, so too in the 1940s a sense of resilience in the face of catastrophe was evident in the commemorative events that focused on the work of the Four Masters. The perspective of those involved in these commemorations has coloured the understanding of the Annals ever since. Thus it is interesting that although it has been clearly demonstrated, using the evidence of the Annals themselves, that the Four Masters did not regard their own work as a salvage exercise, the popular perception clings to a more romantic view.[16] Indeed, this romantic view is an integral part of the afterlife of these annals. The history of the Annals of the Four Masters did not end on 10 August 1636 when the compilers put their names to the manuscripts they had completed. From the late eighteenth century, at least, it has been culturally important to regard these annals as representing what had been salvaged from the Gaelic past. The Annals were seen as a monument to a once-rich heritage, and the professional scholarship of the Four Masters, whose work preserved the memory of generations of lost heroes, came to be regarded as a work of national salvation.

Though the Annals themselves had ended with stories of defeat and loss, ultimately the way the story of the Four Masters has been remembered in later generations is quite different. It is about triumph over adversity, and in the Irish mind, as universally, that may be the sweetest form of success.

1    Aodh de Blácam, *Gaelic literature surveyed: from earliest times to the present* (Dublin, 1929; repr. Dublin, 1973), 233–4.

2    Eugene Davis, *Souvenir of Irish footprints over Europe* (Dublin, 1889), 9.

3    Douglas Hyde, *A literary history of Ireland, from earliest times to the present day* (London, 1899; rev. edn 1967), 574–80.

4    *Irish Independent*, 5 August 1924, cited in Philip O'Leary, *Gaelic prose in the Irish Free State, 1922–1939* (Dublin, 2004), 259.

5    Tomás Ó Cléirigh, *Aodh Mac Aingil agus an scoil Nua-Ghaedhilge i Lobháin* (Dublin, 1936; repr. Dublin, 1985), 10–14.

6    Brendan Jennings, *Michael Ó Cléirigh, chief of the Four Masters, and his associates* (Dublin and Cork, 1936), 174.

7    Nollaig Mac Congáil, 'Bunú Choláiste na gCeithre Máistrí', *An tUltach* **82** (10) (2006), 10–14.

8    *The Times*, 3 October 1938.

9    Paul Walsh, *Irish leaders and learning through the ages*, ed. Nollaig Ó Muraíle (Dublin, 2003), 360n.

10   I owe this reference to Pat Conlon OFM and Mícheál Mac Craith OFM. A copy of the Athlone brochure is preserved in the Franciscan Library, Killiney.

11   *Comóradh i n-onóir Mhichíl Uí Chléirigh, bráthair bocht, ceann na gCeithre Máistrí* (Dublin, 1944), p. [15]. On the importance attached to the promotion of Irish history in the Irish Free State see Philip O'Leary, *Gaelic prose in the Irish Free State*, 245–343.

12   The stamps, issued on 30 June 1944, were in denominations of a halfpenny and one shilling. They remained in general use until 1969. M. Don Buchalter, *Hibernian specialised catalogue of the postage stamps of Ireland, 1922–1972* (Dublin, 1972), 50–1.

13   *Comóradh i n-onóir Mhichíl Uí Chléirigh*, [16].

14   Sylvester O'Brien (ed.), *Measgra i gcuimhne Mhichíl Uí Chléirigh: miscellany of historical and linguistic studies in honour of Brother Michael Ó Cléirigh, OFM, chief of the Four Masters, 1643–1943* (Dublin, 1944).

15   Liam Brophy, 'Epilogue', in O'Brien (ed.), *Measgra i gcuimhne Mhichíl Uí Chléirigh*, [243].

16   Breandán Ó Buachalla, '*Annála Ríoghachta Éireann* is *Foras Feasa ar Éirinn*: an comhthéacs comhaimseartha', *Studia Hibernica* **22–3** (1982–3), 59–105.

Remembering Mícheál Ó Cléirigh

Fig. 8.2.  Design by R.J. King for commemorative postage stamps to mark the 300th anniversary of the death of Mícheál Ó Cléirigh (cat. no. 44) (*above*).

# Comóradh

## i n-onóir

# Mhichíl uí Chléirigh

bráthair bocht

Ceann na gCeithre Máistri

# Gaiety Theatre
## baile Átha Cliath

Dia domhnaigh. 25ú lá de Mhí an Mheithimh. 1944.

# MEASGRA I gCUIMHNE MHICHÍL UÍ CHLÉIRIGH

.1.

MISCELLANY OF HISTORICAL AND LINGUISTIC STUDIES
IN HONOUR OF BROTHER MICHAEL Ó CLÉIRIGH, O.F.M.
CHIEF OF THE FOUR MASTERS
1643-1943

*Edited by*

FATHER SYLVESTER O'BRIEN, O.F.M.

DUBLIN :
ASSISI PRESS
1944

Fig. 8.3. Souvenir brochure for gala concert in the Gaiety Theatre, Dublin, 1944 (cat. no. 42) (*opposite*).

Fig. 8.4. *Measgra i gcuimhne Mhichíl Uí Chléirigh*, edited by Sylvester O'Brien OFM, published in 1944 (cat. no. 43) (*above*).

# Part 2. Manuscript portfolio

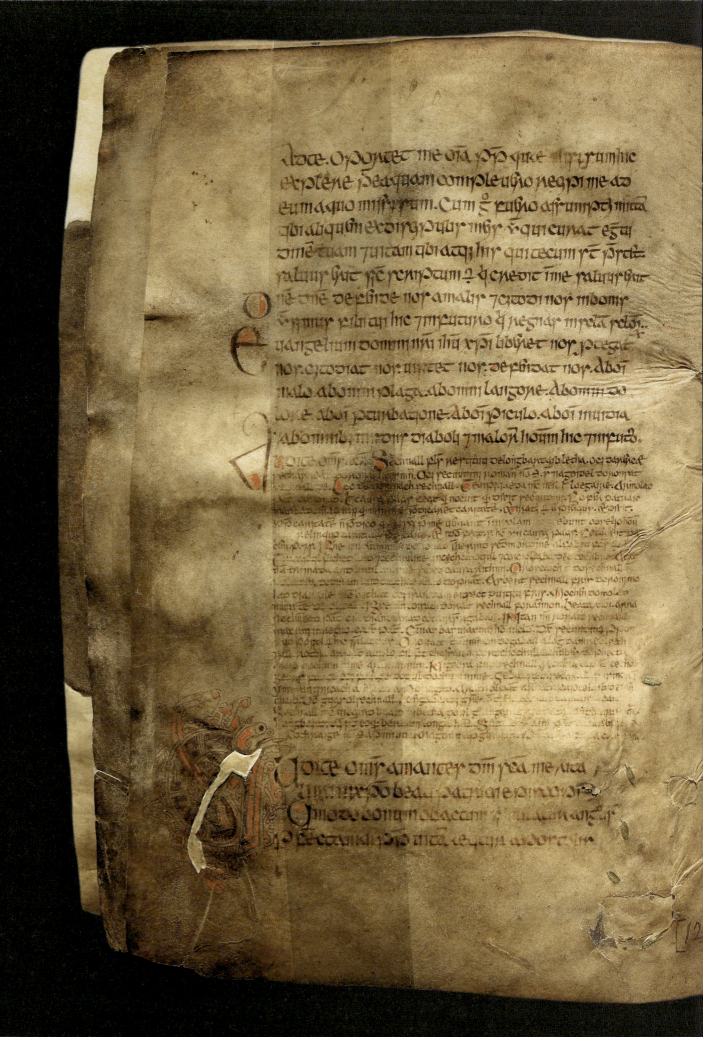

Beati xpi qui custodit mandata monitibus
Et nituntur opa ne fulgent clara inter homines
Sanctumque cum regunt exemplata per pietatem
Ipse docet incelum phylin magnificant dum

Confortantur mot amone et ipse immobilitur
Supra quibus edificatum et petitur ecclesia
Cumque adoportolatum a deo protegitur quia
Inuicunt per onta aduentus imperium signa uisunt

Dominatur illam elegit et docet et bandanar
Pationes et indicauit predocuine nega
Uide recalo credulitur malienet ecclesiam qua
Dominuumque requentibus pede adoctenes

Electa xpi ut ubita uenire et religieus
Ciuitate Inbliunar negligenter cum uisitans exigit
Matugii hoi labonur dum opes uncquam
Cum xpo negin celerur possit ut uni gaudii

Ipse uir di nimitur negmer p ignitur
Aplicam exempla uncommune domus
Esset cum uenit quam et pacatur probicat et
Ut ausin dicetur noncomitat deus p uocem bona

Lorgauit cum xpo honoribus in receculo
Cum abominibz et dei generum in angelus
Quis de impit et plauuls argentes apostolum
Et hominibz uncatum uidebet regno di

Humilitur di obuietam ispiritu et conspone
Supis qui bonum obacui negerat dominus
Cecoz iurta mean ne xpi pontat regmata
Inter pola pertatuur gloriatum me auce

Digit euredentur paratu dolbis celer gio
Ple qui uobiscum cum xpo una pertiant

[13]

recepti

corpus eum. Sed licet non fuerint, fugiant in aliam terram. Ad facienda penitentiam et benedictione dei. Et firmiter volo obedire ministro generali et illi frmciano. et alii guardiano qui ei placuerit in dare. Et ita volo esse captus in manibus eius, ut non possit
ire nec facere ullo modo nisi sua et obediam. qui dominus meus est. Et quamvis sim simplex
frater teneant. ita obedire guardiano suo. et facere officium secundum regulam. Et qui non
essent qui non facerent officium secundum regulam. Et qui invenerit
catholice dicere fratres nec fratres nec fratres pro obedientia teneant. et quicumque invenerint alios propinqui. per
minorem custodem illius loci ubi ipsum invenerint debeant representare. et custos teneat
eum firmiter pro obedientia ipsum fortiter custodire sic hominem in vinculis die noctuque. ita quod non possit elabi de manibus suis. donec ipsa sua propria persona ipsum repre-
senterint. in manibus sui ministri. Et minister teneat pro obedientia firmiter. mittendo ipsum per tales
fratres qui die noctuque custodiant eum sic hominem in vinculis donec representent ipsum
coram domino Hostiensi. qui est dominus protector et corrector fratrum. Et non dicant fratres que
est alia regula quia hoc est recordatio. admonitio. exhortatio. et meum testamentum
quod ego frater franciscus parvulus facio vobis fratribus meis benedictis ut hoc ut regulam
quam domino promisimus melius catholice observemus. Et minister et omnes alii ministri
et custodes pro obedientia teneant in istis verbis non addere ullum minuere. et sic
hoc scriptum habeant iuxta regulam. Et in omnibus capitulis que faciunt quando legunt regulam. le-
gant et ista verba. Et omnibus fratribus meis clericis et laicis precipio firmiter ut
obediam ut non mittant glossas in regulam nec in istis verbis ita dicendo. ita
nolumus intelligi set sicut dedit michi dominus simpliciter et pure dicere et scribere regulam et
ista verba. ita simpliciter et sine glossa intelligatis et cum sancta operatione observetis
in finem Et quicumque hoc observaverint in celo repleantur benedictione altissi-
mi patris. et in terra benedictione dilecti filii sui cum sanctissimo spiritu paraclito
et omnibus virtutibus celorum. et omnibus sanctis. Et ego frater franciscus parvulus vester confirmo vobis quantumcumque possum confirmo vobis istam sanctissimam benedictionem.
Amen. Explicit testamentum beati Francisci.

Prophetia ioachim in maiori volumine de concordanciis anno domini M.
CC. L. convenient nobiles et principes et multi tyranni et potestates in conspectu
paganorum et movebuntur. quia pro nichilo et multa eorum captivabuntur. Et Anno illius
recipiabitur quam constantinopolim et eligent inde imperatorem licuriatum. Anno LVII erunt duo pape. unus lugduni. alter rome. lugduni erit

...ribus et equinis. alr. ii. mil'c' et miq'. et mille se mutuo msultabut. Anno lx.
cui etia et der in tanta utilitate et glulcagone in q n fuerint spe
extantim q feodario ecclie residente ip. siluet. in ecca romana. Anno lxv. redibit tota gra ad obeam romane ecce. et ca audient noua
de predicone anxpi.

Dicat io ioachim q pmi stac sci fuinuo in dilectione in deox. sub
gyro. Scdo e fineni tenent Xminano sub regibz mtat uxtec
ab orieu sol. q filin iplin x. Terca s cpe libtate sub gog. qua dd ad
indiciu uemens indicabit. Silo et exxaim. etam signat q rexbait
dd in siut malicie et erroribz. et destructio xpe est Juda. etam lacmoy q
sub uno tpe destent. q ambe duo prauerunt. Licet pmum orientalis
ecca flagellanda sit a gentibz. Duos ordies fratos. aliqs in pueris ah
quos in iuuembz denotati sn pmi. pdicatorys. sic siu abrahe. Jn
aliis. ioseph. et beniamm. so in messione por ordo sec est. Scdo in col-
lectione. qz colligit uiride. Vide in q iii. dicol metat. als colligat
indifferent boes terre. q ac dc mtanus lig m panem et picilla floy
frum. et xanoy gspiranaum admuato eis pilato infidelium gentiu. et
theode hericoy. Summus pontifex q custiccat in ysaac duos ordies
edet. qz minor ordo eoy festin ad obem. dicos et laicos in differe
nter admissos. extouatos a fris. incorpabit ecclesie. Tande uero
rediens clau. dolebit de pmogenitis dicos sublatis de pfessione
sz pdicagoms et eruditiome eoy. inuidebit alteri. nesciens qd
erunt pmi nouissimi. et no p sed ibit ad alias hech scolasticas
et uialem et seclarem pdenciam exqrant. ip q eum dd odio hebit
.s. cpe dd. qz doctriam suam cu claribz doctine admistet. Unde
caueat is ordo postm ne plequat ab eo. et octeat q et exa
tu magidris gfidenciu in armis disputatois et aublo. et subuerte
ac eum dd. de filiis datis. Anglc dd. cpe dd est. et q lucat in
notte xbuisois fuerit. qz et doctoribz spualibz uis mane don
aurora patis roddica xuscat iacob torentem xbuisois heri
te in bacilo paup. acceptor doctrine. et puemat ad ysaac epos

Canteda. xxv. se uillas. et qs uilla
ip. ae sist mes oaedem pastmos. et
bace ei omioant in qenor aunca
ntta eay xpuabit seliq. Onets nilla
gtmbz. um. chucadas xpe.

GVIDO Bentiuolus Dei & Apostolicæ Sedi
Albertum Archiducem Austriæ, & Isabellam
Comites, nec non ad Comitatum Burgundiæ, &
subiecta Sanctissimi in Christo Patris, & Domini
Sanctæ Sedis cum facultate Legati à latere Nunciu
audituris salutem in Domino sempiternam. Cùm dilectus in

cialis Hibernia, exponi nobis nuper fecerit si nonnullosq. alios eiusdem famil
ipsis aliàs attignatou, ad eam modo inopia esse redactos, ut sese relatrius su
Catholicous Hibernia detrimentu, cum in eam Prouincia ad fidem Cath
Cuemque propterea à Nobis idem Prouincialis humiliter petierit, ut sibi, prædict
uincias circumeundo ee elemosynas petere possint, Nos illaru paupertatim
studyis uacare possint, eisdem Prouinciali et Pribus nras datas eras dedimu
eis omni auxilis, et christianæ charitatis officijs præsto esse uelint. Ro
consfueuas personas, ut eorundem Prium necessitati omni humanitate occ
Datis Bruxellis Mechliñ Diocesis die 24. Januarij. 1606

J. Archiepus Rhod. Nuncius

...ia Archiepiscopus Rhodiensis, Ad Sereniss. Principes
...aniarum Infantem Coniuges, Burgundiæ, & Flandriæ
...rsas Belgicas Diciones, & Dominia eisdem Principibus
...D. Pauli diuina prouidentia Papæ quinti, & eiusdem
...iuersis, & singulis præsentes litteras, inspecturis, lecturis pariter, &

Fr̄ frater Florentius Corryus, ordinis S. francisci de obseruantia, Prouin
cia..., Louanij studiosæ causa commorans, ob defectū nonnullorū redituum,
...nimimè ualeant, uerendumq̄ sit ne studia deserere cogantur in magnum
...prædicandā et administranda sacramenta ijdem Patres hebinde mittere?
...Patribus nr̄as commend. tr̄as concederemus, quibus nr̄æ Legationis Pro
...tum in Nobis & iuuare cupientes, ad hoc præsertim, ut in missionem præd:
...bus ipsos Vniuersis nr̄æ Legat. xr̄i fidelibus in D̄n̄o commendamus quat.
...j insuper Dn̄os Archiep̄os, Ep̄os, Abbates, ceterasq̄ in dignitate ecclēs
...e non dedignentur, omnipotentis manū centuplum rependentis honore.

Ita Bacius Secr.

Aois criost mile, tricc o, nochat, a trī

Seaan mc Seā́n i̅ i̅nat̄zill espdarabreis ne dece
s̄niathana heozin caibellan p̄ris cam dece; Anguet dcles̄ dec
Aṓ mc concōb mc oig̅hna tr̄g hina ma̅t̄s̄ luip̄ dece ia
milinar̄o ṁ́p̄z̄ i nartedhe in catal amac dobhit̄ h iaip̄.
Haolp̄uitṁ mc f̄hag̅ail mc oiarimaoa oo z̄albhal tr̄g̅na is mo
luip̄ce tre nhat̄ i̅t̄ europt̄c t̄omalt̄ mc oenc̄h.
Iongais̄ oo eabt̄ ooelos̄i eloia mc oiap̄ma z̄o eluaim oec
iecal locha tethe i ap̄ince n̄oip̄mua̅a, iombrait̄ oo eib
ooih oiaipone. ṁ́p̄is s̄opelos̄i Aoia. Concōb i Rua̅o vann
Aoia mc oig̅hna oo z̄albhal. f̄hag̅ail mc oenc̄h i̅p̄at̄ oaz̄alb
ṁ́ailte p̄iu i a eluo apa haidile. Domnall vih in oiap̄
ið z̄oct̄ oile oo maip̄t̄ oon tois̄e̅s̄n ma t̄ip̄neell
Brian mc maoile chlam i ceall tanais̄s̄ra mamp̄es̄
f̄hag̅al mez̄ pamp̄aoam taois̄ teall euchō, f̄ṅ z̄o mip̄e i
oo chap̄uibh. l℮

Maz̄ṅg̅ o heaz̄ra tanais̄s̄ luip̄ne dece
Seh oo oenam onais̄libh mot̄s̄e luip̄ce ne p̄ois̄e ṁp̄op̄i
z̄nais̄a i in cōmp̄uap̄ure̅c anz̄all az̄ hiṁlibh
i az̄naile f̄ṁ́ mc f̄ holis̄i i concōb bh oih oealbr̄oa oaoi
ṁ́p̄tip̄ eam mc Ruap̄oip̄i mez̄ eochaz̄am i
Brian mc uilliam oice mceeochaoeam oez̄

Cadam prghin Cataíl oíce ⁊ deabaid bhfídhbaidh me maoílshellaín y céall. Doinnall
le Emand airine muircheachlainn y céall. le Cryst mac Lamacaim adós cróip enghte pata toéce
Annspria chille haémro in efsporéicc éille requi do dénaim do bpaibh. s. pfi la háimcéocéo ffauilge

## Aois Criost 1394.

Aoiscriost, míle trícéd, nochatt, acethaír

i Rychard pi ga x do téf inép f ofeil quidil, uéet rith ls a3e ⁊ adol inf e 3ohait chai

3olla doinnaig na hlo3 am offícel loca hepne, 3fium, ⁊ ashmeth m cam
Mata me 3ollacoffele biocaine claoin m le
Cuéip maz seolo3éce biocaine uchaíp rpchaim do éce

i Ulla omuis do téct inép.

Catos me 3olla jo3a y fl inaccaim crófp cuinté ata doin3b lá clóin oaifeo
y flamaceam ⁊ lá clóin aripchéfe y fl inaccaim, aldós odfo3aip doin3b lazuit inp éjcc
comay na odam stod3 tz hina élopne onaoil Kpla do maybéno lá sédaméní
Mac smpth 3lim me apúohn tz hina baile acallém do múp3b du bpaithh in é ell i.
élon ⁊ 3lim odxéce

Slúaicé lá in3et me impchta lá púéi la3, do púh 3ill 3o nolopéce Rop m tzn duchib
y da émplénuth do púéo op y map fit y bpaith oé lsf.

i Ulla rimm do tíonol 3 a lan3 ml da mill y lo3ce y 3 y un mill 3 uhne dé y céall maze
bemétam y laoiffi rpoud do oua étz h papom fi Rmín me i Rmarém ne ill do múp3b lá clóin empim neill

Mac shetra i. Aple me aiple do dén éoéce ple ih 3a x da mpne 3o nomúp3b poép lmf y adóé fa
élopo do tz im péi la háplaé 3all 3 aoroé y lapin y po 3ax enpoé da iomláé am p pfip.

i Ulla rpimm do líee papt y plo conté o drimp, omoroa 3 a lan o mallam fillaim oja éir.

Mac uilliam buple i. Comar do oul do tíeh in péi, le omaip múp oz y tz bin oé y tzmz y3 uit df
coin me théb na paienn3 y bum do clóin buipuaid do dénaim éoée ap inpe in péi iminain 3ill aip in
le conaié lymmf do loppéuoh y do ancéam do. Camelaana o bonacam do múp3b lá imn y pze 3a x múp éé
Bam me maolph3aím in 3ail in orpima adós ét ma maip lspce doin3b lá maoléei in cleim me ajpm y dochí aupaip
y adós mhéeuch m paof phdam do múp3b lá clóin i inp y oalaz3 in ollaimná é y neill.

## Aois Criost 1395.

Aoiscriost míle, trícéd, nochatt, acuíce

Aín teispeob oée o mocaim oéce ap plá tó na nonia, Ain broéise op lam míle i. broése séene edoaim nadós
Aín compéel o cunía3 y nob biocaine in lon3a é éfen fi tz tíe naoredh oin éée do éce
O neillbrófe do éce le atonaéal in abomaéa fi Dalsp meda mez ypp tz na3 humam, fi hí cmih m
reopam ta aépche, fi hiapílom éfe oueln y oa oifoéz do éce ipi inonanonainp3 he

Comar maz yopp i. Aín 3allavomb me pilp do 3abail tz lá naip fi hmanach
Doinnallna maplé opn lpce do 3abail lá clóin auét mez yopp ne ill pelimon oalbeoéc zachpfl
imbpan3 olnap 3o hína doinnall y uéce on ep pipmol.

135

Ricaipo mic uillicc vo ṁaṗbaö lé cloinn mic uilliam oile .i. clann Riocaipo óicc iaṗ mbṗíṫ ṗoṗṗa a ttoṗaiʒeaċt ⁊ iaṗ ttſlcclamaö cṗeaċ an tíṗe vóiö.

Mac ʒoiṗvealbaiʒ Sſan mac an ʒiolla öuiö, pſṗ vſplaicṫeaċ, vſiʒeiniʒ vſiʒeſnnaiṗ pſona pṗi vénaṁ uaiṗle vo ṁaṗbaö tṗé ċanʒnaċt lá vṗuinʒ via cinſö pſin.

O conċobaiṗ pailʒe, bṗian mac cataoíṗ vionnaṗbaö aṗ a öuṫaiʒ, ⁊ a ċaiṗlém uile vo bṗiṗſö iaṗ maṗbaö ṗocaiöe via ṁuintiṗ aʒá nʒabail laṗ an iuṗtiṗ Saxanaċ .i. loṗv linaṗv, ⁊ tṗia ṗoṗmat, ⁊ tṗia imveall veaṗbṗátaṗ uí concobaiṗ pſin .i. catal ṗuaö vo ṗónaö innṗin.

Donnċaö ua cſṗbaill vaiṫṗíoccaö pipʒanainm, ⁊ uaiṫne ċaṗṗaiʒh a öſṗbṗataiṗ pſin, ⁊ tiʒſṗnaṗ vo öſin víö aṗaon.

## AOIS CRIOST, 1537.

Aoiſ Cṗioṗt, mile, cúicc céö, tṗioċat, a Seaċt.

Coccaö etiṗ aoö mbuiöe ó noóṁnaill ⁊ Maʒnuṗ ó voṁnaill. Clann uí baoiʒill vo bſiṫ aʒ conʒnaṁ lá haoö, ⁊ aoö pſiṗṗin vo bſiṫ i ccaiṗſlen öúin na nʒall. Ro eiṗiʒ commbuaiöṗeaö móṗ hi ccenel cconaill tṗe ſṗaonta cloinne í voṁnaill pṗia ṗoile via ṗo maṗbaö vṗonʒ vo ṗſlioċt an eṗpuicc uí ʒallċubaiṗ lá cloinn uí baoiʒill .i. mac toiṗṗvealbaiʒ óicc mic bṗiain, ⁊ viaṗ mac eoccain ſtallaiʒ m'c bṗiain ⁊ aṗaill ele cenmoṫat.

O voṁnaill aoö mac aoöa ṗuaiö mic neill ʒaiṗb mic toiṗṗvealbaiʒ an ṗíona tiʒſṗna tiṗe conaill innṗi heoccain, cenel moain pſṗmanaċ, ⁊ ioċtaiṗ ċonnaċt, pſi ʒuṗ a ttanʒattaṗ coṁċa, ⁊ cíoṗċana ó tiṗiö oile cuicce ṗoṗſ mbaoí a ſmaċt ⁊ a ċuṁaċta aṁail atá maʒ luiṗcc, Maċaiṗe connaċt clann ċonnmaiʒ, ʒoiṗvealbaiʒ, ʒaillſnʒaiʒ, tiṗ aṁalʒaiö, ⁊ conmaicne cúile von taoö

⁹ *Lord Leonard.*—This should be Lord Leonard Gray.—See the year 1535, where he is called Ⱡinaṗv ʒṗai.

⁴ *Extended his jurisdiction, &c.,* literally, "a man to whom came gifts and tributes from other territories on which his jurisdiction and power was."

ʳ *Moylurg,* i. e. Mac Dermot's country, coextensive with the old barony of Boyle, in the county of Roscommon.

ˢ *Machaire-Chonnacht,* i. e. the plain of Connaught, comprising the countries of O'Conor Roe and O'Conor Don, in the county of Roscommon.

ᵗ *Clann-Conway.*—This was at the period of which we are treating Mac David Burke's country, in the barony of Ballymoe, in the north-east of the county of Galway.

two sons of Rickard, son of Ulick, were slain by the sons of the other Mac William, namely, the sons of Rickard Oge, they being overtaken in a pursuit, after they had gathered the preys of the country.

Mac Costello (John, son of Gilla-Duv), a bountiful and truly hospitable man, a captain distinguished for noble feats, was treacherously slain by a party of his own tribe.

O'Conor Faly (Brian, the son of Cahir) was banished from his country, and all his castles were demolished; and numbers of his people were slain, during the taking of them, by the English Lord Justice, i. e. Lord Leonard[p]. And this was done through the envy and machinations of Cathal Roe, O'Conor's own brother.

Donough O'Carroll deposed Ferganainm, and Owny Carragh, his own brother, and deprived both of the lordship.

### THE AGE OF CHRIST, 1537.

*The Age of Christ, one thousand five hundred thirty-seven.*

A war [broke out] between Hugh Boy O'Donnell and Manus O'Donnell. The sons of O'Boyle sided with Hugh, who was in the castle of Donegal. In consequence of this dissension between the sons of O'Donnell, a great commotion arose in Tirconnell, during which a party of the descendants of the Bishop O'Gallagher were slain by the sons of O'Boyle, namely, the son of Turlough Oge, son of Brian, and the two sons of Owen Ballagh, the son of Brian, and others besides these.

O'Donnell (Hugh, the son of Hugh Roe, son of Niall Garv, son of Turlough of the Wine, Lord of Tirconnell, Inishowen, Kinel-Moen, Fermanagh, and Lower Connaught), [died; he was] a man to whom rents and tributes were paid by other territories over which he had extended his jurisdiction and power[q], such as Moylurg[r], Machaire-Chonnacht[s], Clann-Conway[t], Costello[u], Galleanga[w], Ti-

---

[u] *Costello*, a barony in the south-east of the county of Mayo, taking its name from the family of Mac Costello, who were at this period the proprietors of it.

[w] *Galleanga*.—This was the tribe name of the O'Haras and O'Garas, in the county of Sligo; but it was applied, at the period of which we are now treating, to Mac Jordan's country, or the present barony of Gallen, in the east of the county of Mayo.

# Part 3. Catalogue

## one

Section 1

# The medieval sources

Many of the surviving medieval Irish manuscripts were known to Mícheál Ó Cléirigh and others of the Four Masters and were used by them in the early seventeenth century during their researches into the sacred and secular history of Ireland. Among the great medieval Irish source books of *seanchas* was the Book of Leinster, and Ó Cléirigh and his associates made extensive use of this compilation. Ó Cléirigh also obtained the manuscript containing the Martyrology of Tallaght (**2**), which had originally been part of the Book of Leinster (**1**). They are seen together in this exhibition for the first time since the seventeenth century.

The work of the Four Masters drew its authority from being rooted in the older manuscript tradition. They emphasised the value and authenticity of their history by naming the older sources on which they relied. These included a 'Book of Clonmacnoise', a 'historical Book of Lecan Mic Firbisigh' and a 'Book of the Island of Saints', as well as older historical annals belonging to the Ó Maoil Chonaire, Ó Duibhgeannáin and Ó Cléirigh families. These are typical of the sources mentioned by other contemporaries. In a poem of the 1620s, as part of the poetic dispute known as *Iomarbhágh na bhFileadh*, Aodh Ó Domhnaill listed the Book of Armagh, the Book of Clonmacnoise, the Psalter of Cashel, the *Dinnsheanchas* and the Book of Glendalough among his sources. In another poem of the 1650s, *Aiste Dháibhí Cundún*, the poet repeated many of these and added the *Réim Ríoghraighe*, the *Amra Colaim Cille* and the Speckled Book of Moling, all material of a kind well known to the Four Masters. Geoffrey Keating cited a similar range of manuscript sources in his history of Ireland (**25**) compiled in the 1630s. All of this testifies to a vibrant world in which medieval Irish manuscripts were shared among the learned during the seventeenth century.

The immediacy of the connection between the medieval sources and the work of Mícheál Ó Cléirigh is illustrated by a notebook dating from the late 1620s that preserves some of the transcripts made by Ó Cléirigh (**6**) from the twelfth-century Book of Leinster (**1**). The Annals of Ulster were used extensively by the Four Masters, and indeed are generally regarded as the most reliable surviving source for the history of early medieval Ireland. The texts on Irish saints preserved in the *Liber Hymnorum* (**3**, **4**) were among the sources transcribed for inclusion in John Colgan's published editions of Lives of Irish saints (**28**). Less typical of the medieval tradition were two sixteenth-century works emanating from Gaelic and Gaelicised lordships. They are included here as examples of hagiographical and historical texts dating from the last phase of vellum manuscript production in Ireland. One is a lavish manuscript containing a newly composed Life of St Colum Cille (**7**), while the other is a genealogical and propagandist history of the MacWilliam Burkes. The *Seanchas Búrcach* (**8**) is a unique example of an illustrated secular text from a Gaelicised lordship and provides a rare local example of the nature of historical prose writing in late sixteenth-century Ireland.

History of the Burkes, *Seanchas Búrcach*. TCD 1440, f. 19r (cat. no. 8) (*opposite*).

*1.*

BOOK OF LEINSTER
*Leabhar na Núachongbhála*

TCD 1339 (H.2.18). Twelfth century. Vellum. 32cm x 23cm. 354 pages. [Fig. 1.1]

The Book of Leinster is the largest surviving compendium of early Irish learning dating from before the Anglo-Norman conquest. Up to six scribes worked on the manuscript, most notably Áed Ua Crimthainn, *coarb* of Terryglass, Co. Tipperary, who was active in the mid-twelfth century. He was described in the margins of f. 206 as the 'foremost historian of Leinster for his wisdom and learning and knowledge of books'. There is a considerable amount of decoration, with some human-headed initials as well as an abundance of animal-headed letters. The principal colours used are red, green, yellow and purple.

The Book of Leinster contains an important selection of medieval Irish texts in prose or verse, notably *Leabhar Gabhála*, *Cogadh Gaedhel re Gallaibh*, *Sanas Chormaic*, *Teagasc Chormaic* and the great medieval corpus of topographical lore *Dinnsheanchas Éireann*. There are also numerous Heroic Cycle sagas, including *Táin Bó Cúailnge*, *Scéla Mucce meic Da Thó*, *Táin Bó Flidhais*, and a range of historical poems. The manuscript also includes one of the earliest and most extensive collections of genealogies of early medieval Irish dynasties and saints.

This manuscript was used by many later scholars and is mentioned as a source in late medieval compilations such as the Book of Lecan and the Book of Ballymote. The Book of Leinster was formerly known as *Leabhar na Núachongbhála*, taking its name from Oughavall, Co. Laois. It was in the hands of the O'Mores of County Laois in the seventeenth century. Mícheál Ó Cléirigh transcribed nine poems (RIA B iv 2) and probably the Martyrology of Tallaght from it, or from a copy, in the friary of Kildare in 1627. He may have copied more extensively from this source. According to his preface to the *Leabhar Gabhála*, the Four Masters had before them a copy of that text from the Book of Leinster, and they used the Book of Leinster genealogies when compiling their Genealogies of Saints and Kings (**23**). They also utilised the hagiographical material in it when compiling the Martyrology of Donegal (**38**), where it is referred to as 'a very old venerable vellum book'.

The Book of Leinster was acquired by the Welsh antiquary Edward Lhuyd in 1700. Trinity College Library obtained the manuscript from Sir John Sebright in 1786. EB/BC

Display: p. 159. A decorated capital opens the medieval prose description of the monuments at Tara. The names given to each monument at Tara were devised by medieval historians, who associated the visible and important monuments at the site with heroic characters such as Cormac mac Airt and Cú Chulainn and with saints such as Brendan.

Further reading: Best *et al.* 1954–67; Bhreathnach 2002; Ní Bhrolcháin 2005; A. O'Sullivan 1983; W. O'Sullivan 1966.

*2.*

MARTYROLOGY OF TALLAGHT

UCD-OFM A 3. Twelfth century. Vellum. 32cm x 23.5cm. 10 folios.

The ten surviving leaves containing the Martyrology of Tallaght were once part of the Book of Leinster (**1**). The prose text, which details the feast-days of saints arranged according to the day of the year on which they died, was compiled at Tallaght, Co. Dublin. This, the earliest surviving manuscript, is of twelfth-century date, but the compilation was first made in the early ninth century, based on a universal martyrology of Christian saints that originated at Lindisfarne. There are 3–8 columns per page, and *c.* 60 lines per column. The coloured initials are mostly in red, yellow and green. The manuscript is now enclosed in a vellum cover with the title '*Martyrol. Tamlactense et opuscula S. Aengusi Keledei*' written in a seventeenth-century hand.

Mícheál Ó Cléirigh acquired these leaves from James Ussher, Church of Ireland archbishop of Armagh, possibly during his 1627 visit to Leinster. They were probably already separated from the remainder of the Book of Leinster at that point. The manuscript was used by Mícheál and Cú Choigcríche Ó Cléirigh in Donegal when compiling both recensions of the Martyrology of Donegal (1628, 1630) (**38**). It was then taken to Louvain, where it was used by John Colgan in his *Acta Sanctorum* (1645). Among the marginal annotations in Colgan's hand is that on p.1 which reads '*Ex libris Conventus Dungallensis*'. The manuscript 'Martyrologium Tamlachtensa' was in Colgan's room in Louvain at the time of his death in 1658. It remained in Franciscan hands and was returned to Dublin in 1872, was moved to the Franciscan Library, Killiney, in 1946, and was transferred to University College Dublin in 2000. EB/BC

Display: pp 8–9. These pages contain the end of the Martyrology of Tallaght and part of a text listing the names of the bishops of Ireland, beginning with St Patrick. The feast-days listed in this section of the martyrology fall in December and January. Each kalend begins with saints of the universal church and they are followed by lists of Irish saints.

Further reading: *Cat. Ir. MSS FLK*, 5–10; Best and Lawlor 1931; Ó Riain 2006.

*3.*

BOOK OF HYMNS
*Liber Hymnorum*

UCD-OFM A 2. Late eleventh–early twelfth century. Vellum. 29.5cm x 21cm. 23 folios.

The *Liber Hymnorum*, a compilation of hymns and other devotional texts, is partly in Irish and partly in Latin. Books of hymns are known from the earliest period of the Irish church, the most significant being the late seventh-century Antiphonary of Bangor. The collection here is essentially antiquarian rather than a liturgical work, and each text is accompanied by explanatory notes. Each hymn is preceded by a preface and accompanied by interlinear and marginal glosses. In most cases, antiphons and collects are also attached to the texts. The manuscript contains some of the earliest hymns (without musical notation) dedicated to Patrick, Brigit and Colum Cille, dating from as early as the sixth century. The main texts are written in a large minuscule hand, with the prefaces and annotations in a similar but much smaller hand. The manuscript was formerly in the Franciscan friary at Donegal, and was used by Mícheál Ó Cléirigh in the second recension of the Martyrology of Donegal. The text was also cited in the seventeenth century by James Ussher and James Ware, who evidently borrowed the manuscript from the Donegal Franciscans and later returned it. It was taken to Louvain, probably by Mícheál Ó Cléirigh. John Colgan published extracts from it, including verses on the life of St Patrick, which he printed in Irish with a Latin translation in *Triadis Thaumaturgae* (1647) (**28**).

The manuscript was in John Colgan's room at the time of his death in 1658 and remained in Franciscan hands on the Continent until 1872, when it was returned to Ireland. It was transferred to University College Dublin in 2000. EB/BC

Display: pp 12–13. The hymn dedicated to St Patrick in Latin, *Audite omnes*, was reputedly composed by his disciple Secundinus, the Irish version (Sechnall) of whose name is preserved in the place-name Dunshaughlin, Co. Meath (*Domnach Sechnaill*). It has been argued, however, that the hymn was actually composed by Colmán of Lann Elo (Lynally, Co. Westmeath) in the late sixth century and is the first manifestation of the cult of St Patrick in Ireland.

Further reading: *Cat. Ir. MSS FLK*, 2–5; Bernard and Atkinson 1898; Bieler 1948; Doherty 1991; Kenney 1929, 716–18; O'Neill 1984, 24.

1    2

3

1

## 4.
## BOOK OF HYMNS
*Liber Hymnorum*

TCD 1441 (E.4.2). Late eleventh–early twelfth century.
Vellum. 27cm x 20cm. 34 folios.

This compilation of hymns and other devotional texts
is closely related to the other surviving copy of the *Liber
Hymnorum* (**3**), now UCD-OFM A 2, and is of similar date.
It is written in an elegant script with decorated initial
letters as far as f. 31. The final pages may be of later
date and are of inferior quality. The first folio is missing.

The Latin texts are written in a rounded majuscule,
while the Irish texts are in an angular minuscule. The
prefaces, glosses and marginal notes are in similar but
much smaller script.

This manuscript of the *Liber Hymnorum* has been
in TCD since the seventeenth century, and is believed to
have been formerly in the possession of James Ussher,
archbishop of Armagh. It is clear, however, that Ussher
had access to more than one copy of this work. His copy
of the hymn of Secundinus in honour of Patrick, found
in the Franciscan *Liber Hymnorum*, was taken from the
book of Master Cusack of Gerrardstown, in Meath, which
he copied in 1632.

This manuscript was rebound in modern oak
boards with white calfskin by Roger Powell in 1961, when
a comprehensive repair and rebinding was undertaken
following the practice adopted for the Book of Durrow
in 1954. EB/BC

Display: ff 16v–17r. The poem *Ní car Brigit buadach bith*
'Victorious Brigit loved not the world' is a metrical version of
the Life of St Brigit possibly written in the ninth century. It is
attributed to Broccán Clóen of Clonmore, Co. Carlow, and is
one of a series of hymns dedicated to St Brigit in the *Liber
Hymnorum*. The text begins with a large decorated initial 'N',
coloured in yellow, red and green, which occupies much of
the margin of f. 17. A decorated capital 'B' for Brigit can be
seen on the lower part of f.16v. Colgan printed the Irish text
of the poem, as preserved in the *Liber Hymnorum*, as his first
Life of St Brigit in his *Triadis thaumaturgae . . . acta* (1647),
supplying a Latin translation (**28**).

Further reading: Bernard and Atkinson 1898; Colker 1991,
1245–8; Kenney 1929, 716–18; O'Neill 1984, 24.

## 5.
## ANNALS OF ULSTER
*Annála Uladh*

TCD 1282 (H.1.8). Sixteenth century. Vellum. 31cm x 22cm.
121 folios extant. 10 folios. [Figs. 1.2; 1.4]

This manuscript contains a set of Irish annals for the
years AD 431–1504, with some missing years. The
Annals of Ulster were known to the Four Masters as
*Leabhar Seanaidh Mec Maghnusa for Loch Érne* ('The
book of Seanadh Mhic Mhaghnusa on Lough Erne'), a
reference to the place where the annals were compiled
in County Fermanagh. The principal scribe was Ruaidhrí
Ó Luinín, a member of a hereditary learned family who
were traditionally historians to the Maguires of
Fermanagh.

The Annals of Ulster were prepared under the
direction of Cathal Óg Mac Maghnusa, archdeacon of

Clogher. The text is carefully written on vellum, with
many decorated initial letters. The contents of this
manuscript differ in several respects from another set
of the Annals of Ulster preserved in Oxford, Bodleian
Library MS Rawlinson B 489. Where differences occur,
it appears that the text available to the Four Masters
corresponds more closely to the TCD 1282 text than to
Bodleian Rawlinson B 489. The matter is not clear-cut,
however, and they included some material from the
Annals of Ulster not now contained in TCD 1282. It is
possible that they had access to another copy no
longer extant.

The Annals of Ulster are generally regarded as the
most important annals to survive for the early medieval
period. Annals were compiled in major churches such
as Armagh, Clonmacnoise, Emly, Iona and Kildare to
record the deaths of important churchmen, the reigns of
kings and events associated with the particular churches.
The first entries were in Latin but from the eighth
century onwards the entries tended to be recorded in
Irish. The records were expanded from simple headlines
to include extensive details about particular individuals
and events. Calendar dates were calculated in
accordance with the computation of the date of Easter.
Since there were disagreements in the early church,
including the church in Ireland, as to which Easter table
to follow, this led to a series of readjustments of annalistic
kalends (dates), particularly in the sixth and seventh
centuries. The Four Masters did not simply transcribe
material from the Ulster annals. Instead they selected,
adapted and revised entries as they judged appropriate.
Whereas the Annals of Ulster generally display an
O'Neill bias, this was changed in the Annals of the Four
Masters so that special emphasis was placed instead
on the activities of the O'Donnells of Donegal.

James Ussher had the use of this manuscript of the
Annals of Ulster by 1619, but it did not remain in his
library. The early seventeenth-century foliation added by
James Ware in the top right-hand corner is still in use,
but some folios have been lost since that time. The
manuscript was purchased by Trinity College Dublin in
1766 at the sale of the books and manuscripts of John
Fergus. EB/BC

Display: ff 21v–22r. The Annals of Ulster for the years 589–612
can be seen here. Each initial letter 'K' of 'Kalends' has
rudimentary red decoration. The entry for AD 594 is the last
full entry on col. A of f. 21v. It records the death of Colum Cille
on the fifth Ides of June in his 76th year. The likely year of the
saint's death was 597, but owing to various adjustments in
calculations it was entered at this point in the Annals of Ulster.
Entries prior to and after 594 record the deaths of major
kings, important ecclesiastics and decisive battles.

Further reading: Hennessy and MacCarthy 1887–1901; Mac
Airt and Mac Niocaill 1983; Ó Muraíle 1998.

## 6.
## Ó CLÉIRIGH MISCELLANY

RIA B iv 2. Paper. Seventeenth century. 19cm x 15cm. 304
pages.

This manuscript contains a miscellaneous collection of
texts, including many poems with historical themes. It
is unsigned, but it is in the distinctive hand of Mícheál

Ó Cléirigh and was transcribed by him in 1627 and 1628. The compilation contains nine poems transcribed by Ó Cléirigh from the Book of Leinster in October 1627 when he was in the Franciscan friary at Kildare. This manuscript was copied during the years when Ó Cléirigh's main duties involved transcribing the Lives of Irish saints. It provides clear evidence that Ó Cléirigh was collecting material on the secular history of Ireland several years before he and his collaborators commenced their task of compiling a new set of Annals of the Kingdom of Ireland.

In contrast to another annalist's notebook of the sixteenth century, that of Pilib Ballach Ó Duibhgeannáin (NLI G 1), which contains stories of wonders, rumours and extracts from administrative documents, Ó Cléirigh's notebook concentrates exclusively on primary manuscript sources.

By 1672 the manuscript was in the possession of Roderic O'Flaherty, the Connacht antiquary (**32**), who added many marginal notes. In the mid-eighteenth century it came into the ownership of Charles O'Conor of Belanagare (**33**), who added further notes to the text. The manuscript was later transferred to the collection of the duke of Buckingham at Stowe. It was returned to Ireland in 1883 and placed in the Royal Irish Academy. BC/RG

Display f. 123v. The colophon at the end of f. 123v states that the material translated was taken from the Book of Leinster in October 1627: 'As leabhar na hUa Chóngbála i cCill Dara i Máinistir na mbratar do scriobadh na naoi nduanta sin a mí October na bliadna sa 1627'.

**Further reading:** *Cat. Ir. MSS RIA*, no. 1080, pp 3021–9.

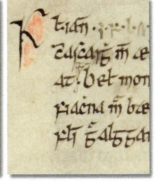

6

6

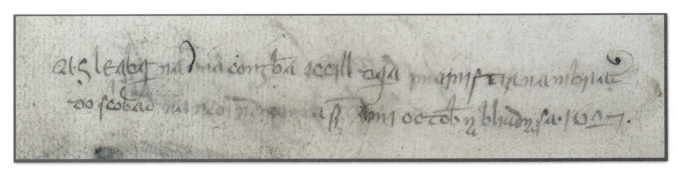

**7.**

## LIFE OF ST COLUM CILLE
*Beatha Cholm Cille*

UCD-OFM A 8. Sixteenth century. Vellum. 32.5cm x 24cm. 68 folios.

This sixteenth-century Life of St Colum Cille was compiled on the instructions of Maghnus Ó Domhnaill in 1532. The manuscript was written by Eoghan Carrach Ó Siaghail for Maghnus Ó Domhnaill's son-in-law, Niall Óg Ó Néill. Ó Siaghail's hand is also found adding items to an early sixteenth-century collection of poems on Colum Cille (Laud 615, p.129) and in another early sixteenth-century volume of verse (NLS, Advocates MS 72.1.29, f. 5). The family were traditional physicians to the MacCoghlans but were also active as scribes in the sixteenth century. Another copy of the same text, written by Giolla Riabhach Mór Ó Cléirigh and once owned by James Ware, is now preserved at Oxford, Bodleian Library, Rawlinson MS B. 514. Scholars differ over which is the older of the two sixteenth-century manuscripts of the Life of St Colum Cille. Paul Walsh argued that UCD-OFM A 8 was older, while more recently Brian Ó Cuív expressed the view that the Rawlinson copy was probably earlier in date. Another seventeenth-century copy made by Brian Mac Niallghuis of Glencolumcille with frequent marginal notes by John Colgan also survives (UCD-OFM A 19). Both this and A 8 were in Colgan's room at the time of his death. The text of A 8 is written in double columns, with a decorated initial T on the opening folio and some colour added to capital letters in later parts of the manuscript. The volume is bound in embossed leather.

This Irish Life of the saint is partly derived from Adomnán's Latin Life of St Colum Cille. To this were added Irish stories about the saint that were in circulation at the time of compilation, so that the Life reflects aspects of contemporary religious perspectives in early sixteenth-century Ireland. Maghnus Ó Domhnaill had a clear sense of the significance of St Colum Cille in the life of his community. Local stories, associated in particular with monuments in Gartan and Glencolumbkille, Co. Donegal, appear in the Life.

The patron of this work, Maghnus Ó Domhnaill, has been described as an Irish 'Renaissance prince'. He succeeded to the O'Donnell lordship on the death of his father in 1537, and according to the Four Masters he was inaugurated 'by the successors of Colum Cille, with the permission and by the advice of the nobles of Cenél Conaill, both lay and ecclesiastical'. He features prominently in the Annals of the Four Masters, where the military exploits of his youth are narrated in detail. Scholars from the Ó Cléirigh family of historians enjoyed his patronage. EB/BC

Display: binding. The Life of Colum Cille is in its original embossed leather binding, dating from the early sixteenth century. The binding is made from oak-tanned cattlehide, stained a dark colour. The decoration was applied using a technique known as *cuir bouilli*, whereby the leather was soaked in cold water, modelled using moulds of sand or clay, and dried using heat. The design resembles that on the leather satchel associated with the Shrine of St Maedhóg in the National Museum of Ireland.

Further reading: *Cat. Ir. MSS FLK*, 16–17; Bradshaw 1979; Lacey 1998; 2006; McDonnell 1997, cat. 1; Ó Cuív 2001–3, vol. 1, 261–74; O'Kelleher and Schoepperle 1918; Stokes 1871; Walsh 1929.

*8.*

## HISTORY OF THE BURKES
*Seanchas Búrcach*

TCD 1440 (F.4.13). Sixteenth century. Vellum. 24cm x 15cm.

The *Seanchas Búrcach* was compiled in the 1570s for Seán Mac Oliverus Burke, who held the title of MacWilliam from 1571 until his death in 1580. The manuscript was apparently commissioned by the 'great prince' Seán Mac Oliverus to demonstrate his civility and his honourable ancestry as a means of bolstering his status as head of the MacWilliam Burkes. It contains an account of the rights and properties of the MacWilliam Burkes of Mayo and asserts their claim to a shared ancestry with Queen Elizabeth I of England. The opening section of the text is in Irish, and this is followed by broadly similar historical and genealogical material in Latin. Two praise poems on the MacWilliam Burkes are also included. One of these, *Fearond chloidhemh críoch Bhanbha* ('The land of Banba is but swordland') by Tadhg Dall Ó hUiginn, explicitly supports the claims of MacWilliam to territorial overlordship in north Connacht by recognising the legitimacy of the right of conquest.

The principal significance of this manuscript history of the Burkes is the unique sequence of fourteen political portraits and religious images that it contains. There are four religious images depicting scenes from the Passion of Christ: Christ before Pilate, the Scourging at the Pillar, Christ carrying the Cross, and a scene depicting the Five Wounds of Christ. Whereas the religious scenes are crowd scenes, reminiscent of the Passion woodcuts of Albrecht Dürer, the political images are individual portraits, all clearly the work of the same artist. They depict the influential ancestors of Seán Mac Oliverus Burke, from the thirteenth to the sixteenth century. The first of these is a portrait of Richard Mór Burke (d. 1243), who is shown in armour, carrying a sword and a heraldic shield. He is wearing a large-brimmed felt hat with a feather of a kind that became fashionable in England in the 1570s, a feature that helps to date the paintings. The last image in the sequence is that of Seán Mac Oliverus Burke himself, shown in a full suit of armour and riding a white horse.

The *Seanchas Búrcach* is a rare survival of a propagandist text in which the history of a Gaelicised lordship over an extended period was documented in prose. The secular material owes much to the earlier tradition of *seanchas*, while the religious element suggests that the manuscript may have been connected to the Franciscan community at nearby Moyne, in north Mayo, where a friary had been established under the patronage of Thomas Burke in 1458.

The manuscript was acquired by TCD in 1741 as part of the Stearne-Madden bequest. BC

Display: ff 18v–19r. These two pages contain religious and secular images on facing pages: on the left-hand page is a crowd scene depicting Christ carrying the Cross, reminiscent of Albrecht Dürer's woodcuts of the early fifteenth century, and on the right is a portrait of Riocard Mór Mac Uilliam (d. 1243), anachronistically dressed in a fashionable late sixteenth-century Tudor style.

**Further reading**: Cunningham 2004; 2006b; Ó Raghallaigh 1927–9.

7    8

7

pro nobis deus. Alle

Petrus apostolus et paulus doctor gentium

ipsi nos docuerunt legem tuam domine.

Salue sancte pater patrie lux forma minorum

virtutis speculum recti via regula morum carnis

ab exilio duc nos ad regna

## two

Section 2

# The Franciscans in Ireland and Europe

The Order of Friars Minor (or Franciscans) was founded in the early thirteenth century by St Francis of Assisi. As the number of followers grew, a formal 'Rule of the Friars Minor' was approved by Pope Honorius III in 1224, and this set out the basic guidelines for Franciscan life (**9**). Members of the order took vows of obedience, poverty and chastity. The order quickly established a presence in Ireland during the thirteenth and early fourteenth centuries, mainly in areas of Anglo-Norman settlement (**10**). In the early fifteenth century, a reform movement led to the establishment of the Observants, who followed the Franciscan rule more strictly (**11**). A new wave of Franciscan houses developed in Gaelic parts of Ireland during the fifteenth century, and many of these foundations are recorded in the Annals of the Four Masters. There was a serious decline in the sixteenth century following the enforced closure of monastic houses in Ireland as part of government efforts to impose the Protestant Reformation. Not all Franciscan houses were forced to close, however, and those in places like Donegal continued to function.

By the early seventeenth century there was a revival in the number of Franciscans at work in Ireland. The Poor Clare nuns (**12, 13**) were likewise encouraged to establish a community in Ireland by 1629, and they moved from Bethlehem in Lough Ree to Galway in the late 1640s. The revival in the fortunes of the religious orders in Ireland owed much to the success of the Continental Irish colleges, including Louvain, and St Isidore's, Rome, which provided training for Catholic clergy and established important links between Catholics in Ireland and in mainland Europe. Irish Franciscans in Europe were engaged in scholarship at many levels, catechetical, devotional, theological, hagiographical, historical and philosophical, their influence extending far beyond Ireland itself (**14, 15, 16**). In Spain and the Spanish Netherlands, Florence Conry (Flaithrí Ó Maoil Chonaire) was active as a politician on the international ecclesiastical stage, and his network of contacts was vital to the success of the College of St Anthony at Louvain in its early years (**17**). At Rome another Irish Franciscan, Luke Wadding (**27**), became historian to the Franciscan order, an indication of the high standing of Irish Franciscans at the centre of the Catholic world.

Irish Observant Franciscan antiphonary. TCD 109, f. 94v (cat. no. 11) (*opposite*).

*9.*
## RULE OF ST FRANCIS

TCD 97. Thirteenth–fourteenth century. Vellum. 28cm x
20cm. 276 folios. [Fig. 4.2]

The Franciscan friars were one of the most influential
religious, cultural and intellectual forces in medieval and
early modern Ireland. The Irish Franciscan province was
established in 1230, and by 1325 they had established
32 friaries, mostly in the towns and boroughs of the
Anglo-Norman colony. Despite the idealism of their
founder, St Francis of Assisi (1180–1226), racial tension
between Gaelic and Anglo-Norman members of the
order was a recurrent problem.

The oldest surviving Irish copy of the 1224 Rule of
St Francis is contained in TCD MS 97, a late thirteenth–
fourteenth-century manuscript from St Thomas's
Abbey in Dublin, a wealthy house of Victorine Canons.
The rule is contained in the bull *Solet annuere*, which
begins on f. 178. It is a relatively plain working
manuscript with occasional rubrication and decoration.
The manuscript also contains a number of other
monastic rules and liturgical texts. CÓC

Display: f. 178. The Rule of St Francis is contained in the bull
*Solet annuere*. The initial letter H of Honorius is ornamented
with red and blue decoration.
**Further reading:** Colker 1991, 183–95; Ó Clabaigh 2006.

*10.*
## FRANCISCAN VADE-MECUM

TCD 347. Late thirteenth century. Vellum. 16cm x 11cm. 407
folios.

The Franciscans were principally noted for their
activities as confessors and preachers, and organised a
comprehensive educational network to provide the
intellectual training necessary for this work. They also
produced a variety of texts and reference works to assist
friars and other clerics in their pastoral activities, and
the manuscript on display is a good example of the
compact, portable commonplace or vade-mecum book
associated with the mendicant friars. The volume has
attracted attention primarily because it contains the
Annals of Multyfarnham, but it is also important because
it contains the earliest surviving copies of some of the
writings of St Francis of Assisi. Stylised hands in the
margin of the manuscript draw attention to passages in
the saint's Testament and to a prophecy of the Calabrian
Abbot Joachim of Fiore. These indicate that the divisions
over the observance of poverty experienced throughout
the Franciscan order were also felt in Ireland. The other
texts in the manuscript consist principally of model
sermons and other material for the use of preachers.
CÓC

Display: ff 388v–389. Selected prophecies of Joachim of Fiore.
**Further reading:** Colker 1991, 710–40; Fletcher 2001; Ó
Clabaigh 2006.

*11.*
## IRISH OBSERVANT FRANCISCAN ANTIPHONARY

TCD 109. Fifteenth century. Vellum. 47cm x 33cm. 134
folios.

The Irish Franciscans underwent a period of expansion
in the fifteenth century with the establishment of ten
new houses. This expansion was closely associated
with the austere Observant reform movement, which
sought to follow the Franciscan rule with greater fidelity.
The reform was adopted by a number of the older
foundations as well, so that 38 out of Ireland's 60 friaries
were Observant houses by 1540. The new foundations
were generally established in Gaelic territories, which
enabled a number of houses to survive the initial
dissolution of the monasteries. Their close links with
their reformed brethren on the Continent facilitated the
transmission of texts and ideas and enabled them to
establish a number of Irish friaries on the Continent,
such as the one in Louvain, in the early seventeenth
century. They were particularly effective as preachers
and confessors, and were highly regarded as spiritual
and moral authorities.

This large-format service-book or antiphonary
contains the texts and music used by the Irish Observant
friars for their daily celebration of the Divine Office. It
contains a number of liturgical texts relating to St Francis
and other Franciscan saints. CÓC

Display: f. 94v. The folio on display includes the antiphon *Salve
Sancte Pater Francisce* ('Hail, Holy Father Francis'), which is
traditionally sung by the friars in honour of their patron.
**Further reading:** Colker 1991, 234–5; Ó Clabaigh 2006.

*12.*
## RULE OF ST CLARE
*Riaghail ar Máthar Náomhtha S. Clara*

RIA D i 2. Seventeenth century. Paper. 10cm x 7.5cm. 9 +
163 folios.

The text of the Rule of St Clare was printed in English in
1621, probably for the use of the English Poor Clare nuns
who had established a convent at Gravelines, close to the
French/Belgian border. Some years later, a translation
from English into Irish was made for the use of the Irish
convent of Poor Clares. The Poor Clares were established
in Ireland in the late 1620s and founded a convent
called Bethlehem on the shores of Lough Ree, near
Athlone, Co. Westmeath. While the early members were
mainly drawn from the Old English community, the
existence of this manuscript demonstrates that Irish
was the preferred language of at least some Irish Poor
Clare nuns.

The translation was the work of two Franciscan
priests, Aodh Ó Raghallaigh and Seamus Ó Siaghail. In
October 1636 Mícheál Ó Cléirigh made a neat transcript
of their Irish translation, and his manuscript is the only
Irish copy of the text that survives. He inserted his own
request for a prayer at the beginning of the manuscript:
'For the love of Jesus Christ and His sweet holy Mother
the blessed Virgin Mary, for the love of St Francis and
St Clare, whose Rule begins here, let there be

remembrance daily in your prayers, Sisters, of your poor brother Michel Ó Cléirigh, in recompense for his labour'. BC

Display: title-page. '*Riaghail ar Máthar Naomhtha S. Clara. Ar na tionntúdh i nGaoidhiloc as Bérla, le toil a nuachtarán, 1636*' 'The rule of our holy Mother S. Clare, translated into Irish from English with the permission of the superior, 1636'. The facing page is endorsed: 'For the use of ye Poor Clares of Gallway, 1647'.

Further reading: *Cat. Ir. MSS RIA*, no. 1221, pp 3282–6; Jennings 1936, 150–2; Knott 1948.

## 13.
## HISTORY OF ST CLARE

*The History of the Angelicall Virgin Glorious S. Clare . . . extracted out of the R. F. Luke Wadding his Annalls of the Freer Minors . . . now donne into English.* Douai, 1635. Printed work.

The text is translated from Francis Hendricq's abridgement of Luke Wadding's Annals of the Friars Minor, but the translator of this work is uncertain. Wadding himself credited the translation to Elizabeth Evelinge (Sr Catharine Magdalen), but it is Catharine Bentley's name (as Sr Magdalen Augustine) that appears on the title-page. This may have been a collaborative venture by two Poor Clare nuns, both members of the recently founded convent at Aire in the province of Artois. Aire was founded in 1619 as an offshoot of the English convent of the Poor Clares at Gravelines. The existence of thriving communities of English-born religious in northern France and Spanish Flanders is, along with very active English-language printing presses at St Omer and Douai, evidence of the vitality of Catholic exiles from all of the Stuart kingdoms in continental Europe.

The exiles were deeply concerned with their countries of origin, and in this case the translation is dedicated 'to the most high and mighty princess Mary Henriette, Queen of Great Britain, France and Ireland and sovereign lady of the isles of the British ocean'. This is Henrietta Maria, the Catholic wife of King Charles I, whose French blood is particularly praised as a preface to a 'life of a saint of feminine sex but masculine virtue'. The book is conveniently divided into 55 short chapters, most likely designed to provide a cycle of daily readings. The translator not only provides a Life of the saint but further edifies the reader with accounts of Franciscan martyrs and missions in the contemporary mission fields of Latin America, Canada, India, China and Japan. JMcC

Display: title-page.

Further reading: Allison 1955; C. O'Brien 1992; Steggle 2004a; 2004b.

9  10

11  12

13

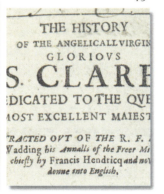

13

*14.*

FOUNDATION LETTER OF ST ANTHONY'S COLLEGE,
LOUVAIN

UCD-OFM C 11. 21 September 1606. Paper. 29cm x 21cm. 1
folio. [Fig. 0.2]

Dated 21 September 1606. From Philip III, king of
Spain, to Albert, archduke of Austria and co-governor
of the Spanish Netherlands with Isabella, Philip's half-
sister. Issued from the royal monastery of San Lorenzo
del Escorial. Original in Spanish.

The support of Albert and Isabella created an
environment in which the University of Louvain and its
associated colleges prospered. Through the diplomatic
negotiations of Florence Conry OFM, the Irish
Franciscan College of St Anthony received both moral
and financial support from the archdukes.

Translation of the Foundation Letter -

Philip III to the Archduke Albert, San Lorenzo, 21
September 1606 (UCD-OFM, MS. C11). Most Serene
Lord, Friar Florence Conry, provincial of the Irish
province of the order of St Francis has explained to
me that, due to the persecution by the heretics, the
order has suffered a great decline in that kingdom.
But despite this, having gone to nothing and become
deserted, they have returned to some monasteries
which have remained, to rebuild and maintain them.
For this reason and as studies are prohibited, the old
preachers that they had have gone. He begs that, in
order that they are not entirely extinguished and to
have the Catholic faith flourish in that kingdom, to
help learned members of the said order by providing
annual alms during the persecution by which a
number of young friars can be supported in their
studies at the University of Louvain.

And by the reasons referred to, and other just
considerations to the service of God, I have shown
them favour and alms to this effect of 1000 ducados
per annum, for as long as I shall wish. Your Highness
will order that from the above date onwards to
provide the rector or person in charge of the said
religious with the said 1000 ducados per annum so
that they can study and support themselves. They
will be paid from the money provided for the army,
punctually. I consider this for good, in spite of orders
to the contrary which I dispense with, remaining in
force and in effect from now onwards. May Our Lord
protect your Highness as I desire. From San Lorenzo,
21 September 1606. Good Brother of your Highness,
I the King. Andrés de Prada [Secretary]. To the most
serene Lord the Archduke Albert my brother. San
Lorenzo His Majesty to his Majesty, 21 September
1606. Franciscan Fathers of Ireland. *Dorso*: Letter of
the king for our alms.

EB/BH

Display: full document.

Further reading: Conlan 1977; Jennings 1968, no. 1; Ó
Cléirigh [*c*.1936].

*15.*

BULL OF FOUNDATION

UCD-OFM G 9 (formerly C 12). 1607. Vellum with papal seal
attached. 22cm x 11cm (folded); 80cm x 50cm (opened).

Papal bull issued by Pope Paul V on 3 April 1607
sanctioning the foundation of St Anthony's College,
Louvain.

The reorganisation of the church in the
Netherlands in the reign of King Philip III of Spain
created a favourable environment for Counter-
Reformation activities there. This included the
foundation of seminaries, such as the Irish Franciscan
college at Louvain, established to train clergy for the
Irish church. The college operated under the
supervision of the archbishop of Malines, in whose
diocese it was located. The University of Louvain was
one of the intellectual powerhouses of Counter-
Reformation Europe, and students from the Irish
colleges could become students of the university.

The Bull of Foundation was a formal
administrative document addressed by the pope to the
archbishop of Malines (Mechelen). It sanctioned the
foundation of St Anthony's College in Louvain, as
sought by Florence Conry OFM (**17**), in order to defend
and promote the Catholic faith in the kingdom of
Ireland, which was under severe pressure from England
and Scotland. As outlined in the foundation letter (**14**)
issued by Philip III, the pope regarded the college's
main function as providing a novitiate and house of
studies for the Franciscans to train friars to return to
their native country. Papal indulgences were granted to
whomever worshipped in the college on the feast-day of
St Anthony of Padua (13 June). A further grant of papal
indulgences was issued from Rome on 26 February
1608 for those who worshipped in the college on 17
March, St Patrick's feast-day. EB/BC

Display: full document (folded).

Further reading: Conlan 1977; Jennings 1968, nos 6 and 14;
Ó Cléirigh [*c*.1936].

*16.*

PERMISSION TO RECEIVE FISH FROM SANT VLIET

UCD-OFM C 11. Paper. 31cm x 21cm. 1 folio.

Letter of permission in French issued on 28 October
1628 and signed by the Archduchess Isabella, allowing
the captains of Irish fishing-boats harboured in Sant
Vliet to send two tonnes of salted fish to St Anthony's
College as alms for the month of November 1628.

The document provides an example of the
practical ways in which the Irish Franciscan
community at Louvain were able to draw support from
those Irish who traded or worked overseas. Irish soldiers
in regiments in Spanish Flanders formed another
important element of the wider Irish community

which contributed to the upkeep of St Anthony's College. EB

Display: full document.

Further reading: Jennings 1968, no. 116.

### 17.
### COMMENDATION FOR FLORENCE CONRY
(Flaithrí Ó Maoil Chonaire)

UCD-OFM C 11, document O.1. Paper (print and manuscript), with seal. 33cm x 21cm. 1 folio.

An official letter of recommendation written on behalf of Florence Conry by the papal nuncio in Brussels, Guido Bentiveglio, titular archbishop of Rhodes and nuncio to Flanders from 1607 to 1615. The letter, issued in Brussels on 24 January 1608, was addressed to the Archdukes Albert and Isabella. It made particular reference to granting the friars permission to seek alms, a subject of contention between the Irish friars and local Belgian friars throughout the early decades of the foundation of the college in Louvain. EB

Display: full document.

Further reading: Jennings 1949; O'Connor 2002.

14    15

16    17

16

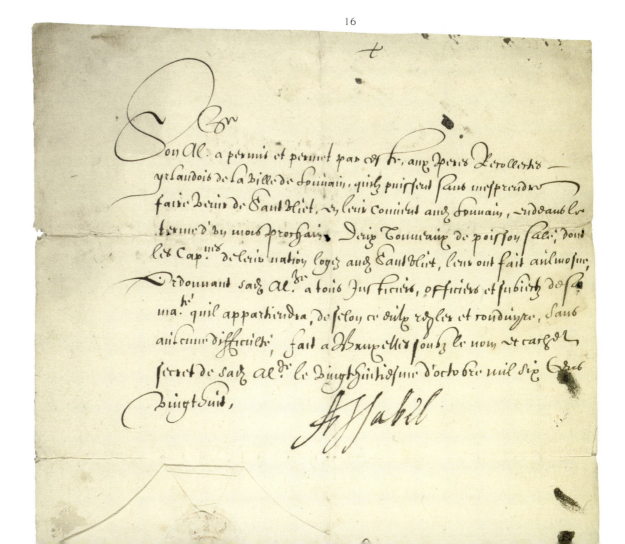

## AOIS CR. 1438.

Aois cr, míle ceithre ched, tochatt, a hochtt.

Airtesprob oꞃ all cobaiꞃ .i. lochlaiñ oꞃ ecc, eꞃꞃ Ratha boi ꞇꞃ oꞃ oꞃ

Pꞃioiꞃ cille maꞃ ñe aiñ oꞃecc Mac meic oꞃ uꞃ la cille oꞃ uꞃ la eꞃꞃoꞃ

Abb cille na manaiꞃ & Mocolomaoiñ bꞃoche ꞇaꞃꞇ mc ꞇcalꞃ oꞃ ecc ꞃa ꞃoiꞃ oꞃ ñ plaꞃꞃ

Doꞃach na coill oꞃ ꞇomnaill oꞃ maꞃ la Concobaꞃ ꞃ oñ oꞃ ꞇomnaill
iñ cciꞃ eꞃaoñ iꞃ na cach oꞃ cꞃꞃ ꞇeꞇa

Eithaoꞃ oꞃ ecaiꞃ caꞃ h oꞃecc ; Piliꞃ maꞃ ꞃoiꞃ oꞃ ꞃ abiꞃ la ꞃꞃaꞃ ꞃoꞃ

Concob mc myꞃ ꞃ oñꞃꞃaꞃ eꞃna cloꞃe ꞇonch ꞃ oñꞃꞃaꞃ oꞃ maꞃ la aꞃꞃ oñ iꞃꞃ aꞃ 4. la
ꞇaꞃꞃ leꞃch mc coꞃꞃbꞃ iñ ꞇonch ꞃ oñbꞃaꞃ lꞃ la Riaꞃꞃ mc ꞇꞃ ꞇꞃ, la Lochlaiñ mc mc Lochlaiñ
ꞃ oñꞃꞃa ꞃ la ñ ampaꞃ baꞃꞃ ꞇꞃ ꞇꞃ mac oꞃ ꞇloꞃ icabꞃ oꞃ myꞃ moꞃ iceꞃ amailꞃ eꞃꞃ
ꞃ llꞃaꞃ mc Rꞃaꞃoꞃ ꞃ oñꞃꞃaꞃ oꞃ ecc.

Cecc aꞃ mc conꞃobꞃaiꞃ ꞃ faꞃꞃ eꞃ ꞃ alliꞃ naꞃ ꞃꞃoꞃ ꞃ oꞃ oꞃ ꞇomnaill bꞃoꞃ
Mac ñeꞃ flaiꞃch .i. eꞃꞃ ballaꞃ oꞃ maꞃ la oꞃꞃ oꞃ ꞇꞃaꞃ ꞃ ꞇꞃ ꞃibaꞃl ꞃ ꞃꞃ ꞃꞃ ꞃꞃ eꞃꞃ
Slꞃaiñ mc ꞇmaꞃꞃ a bꞃꞃ oꞃ ecc oꞃ ꞃ alaꞃ biꞃl ꞃ ; ꞃllꞃaꞃ baꞃꞃ ꞃ iꞃ mc bꞃꞃ oꞃ ecc

ꞃllꞃaꞃ mc ꞃlaiñ albꞃꞃ oꞃ ecc maꞃ ꞃ fꞃñ ; ꞇ oꞃ ꞇꞃ o la icabꞃ faꞃꞃ ꞃ oꞃ ꞇꞃaiñ

o conꞃbꞃ oꞃ oꞃꞃ aꞃꞃaꞃ faꞃoiꞃe

Obꞃꞃꞃ .i. ꞇaoꞃ mc baꞃ ꞃ baꞃ oꞃ aꞃ oꞃ la ꞃ obꞃꞃ .i. la ꞃꞃaꞃꞃaꞃ, Robaꞃ oꞃ ꞃꞃ oꞃ ꞃꞃaꞃꞃaꞃ
Mac meeꞃ boꞃaꞃꞃ .i. Ryꞃ oꞃ oꞃ ecc

Sꞃꞃꞃaꞃ mc ꞃlaiñ mc oꞃ ꞇoꞃlꞃ oꞃ ecc ; Oclꞃmaꞃꞃ ollaiñ ꞃ ꞇꞃ ꞃa ꞃꞃoaꞃ oꞃ ecc

Donch mac Sioꞃ oꞃ ꞃ cꞃꞃeꞃ peꞃ le ꞃeꞃchꞃ

O oꞃ bꞃeꞃꞃe .i. eꞃoꞃ ollaiñ ꞃ Raꞃꞃ le oꞃ

Concob m cobꞃaꞃꞃ ollaiñ cloꞃe Riocaꞃoꞃ le bꞃꞃ ꞃꞃꞃ oꞃ ecc.

# The Annals of the Four Masters

A team of professional historians trained in the Gaelic tradition came together in the 1630s to compile a new set of annals of Irish history that would meet contemporary standards for a history of the Irish nation. The scribes and scholars who became known as the 'Four Masters' wrote their annals in the Irish language, drawing on evidence available to them from older manuscript sources, many of which no longer survive. The Annals of the Four Masters contain a history of Ireland, arranged in chronological order, starting at the time of the biblical Flood and continuing down to the death of Hugh O'Neill, earl of Tyrone, in 1616. The four annalists, Mícheál Ó Cléirigh OFM, Cú Choigcríche Ó Cléirigh, Fearfeasa Ó Maoil Chonaire and Cú Choigcríche Ó Duibhgeannáin, were assisted by two other scribes, Muiris Ó Maoil Chonaire and Conaire Ó Cléirigh. The annals were compiled between January 1632 and August 1636 at the Franciscan house then located at Drowes, near Ballyshannon, Co. Donegal. The entries were arranged by year, hence the name annals. Prior to commencing the annals, the same team had prepared other new texts, including the Genealogies of Saints and Kings (**23**) and a new recension of the *Leabhar Gabhála*, and used these as the basis of their chronology.

The Four Masters made at least two sets of their new annals, each set being divided into two volumes, divided at the years 1207/08. When completed, one set (**20, 21, 22**) was taken to Louvain in 1637 with the intention that it would be used as the basis for a published history of Ireland, probably in Latin translation. The second set of autograph manuscripts (**18, 19**) remained in Ireland, where it was made available to a series of later historians during the seventeenth and early eighteenth centuries. In the early nineteenth century part of that set, too, was taken abroad, and remained inaccessible to Irish historians until 1883, when it was returned to Ireland and deposited in the Royal Irish Academy.

Until now, the autograph manuscripts of the Annals of the Four Masters have never been reunited. They are seen together in this exhibition for the first time since being completed by the Four Masters in August 1636.

Annals of the Four Masters, *Annála Ríoghachta Éireann*. RIA 23 P 6 f. 175r (cat. no. 21) (*opposite*).

*18.*

ANNALS OF THE FOUR MASTERS
*Annála Ríoghachta Éireann*

RIA C iii 3. Seventeenth century. Paper. 30cm x 21cm. 522
folios. [Figs. 2.4; 6.1]

This manuscript contains the autograph Annals of the
Four Masters for the years AM 2242–AD 1171. Written
on laid hand-made rag paper of uniformly good quality,
the text is in a single column with standardised annual
headings. The opening few pages are less formally laid
out, but the scribes soon established a consistent style
for the volume as a whole. The generous margins
allowed the scribes scope to insert additional material
where necessary. The main scribe involved in this
manuscript is believed to be Muiris Ó Maoil Chonaire,
who was employed as an assistant for a relatively short
time. Others of the Four Masters' team also penned
parts of the manuscript.

The early part of the Annals consists primarily of
annual entries recording the early invasions of Ireland
and then itemising the reigns of kings. Even where the
name of the king was the only information available for
a given year, an annal entry was generated nonetheless.
The overall impression thus created is of a kingdom of
great antiquity, which was the essence of the message
the Four Masters sought to convey. Later sections are
more varied and discursive, reflecting the broader range
of source material available to the compilers. The text of
this manuscript corresponds closely to UCD-OFM A 13,
the other autograph manuscript covering the same years.

This manuscript was in Galway in the late 1640s,
when it was used by Dubhaltach Mac Fhirbhisigh. It
was in the hands of Henry Bourke in the 1650s and
was cited by Roderic O'Flaherty in the 1680s. The
manuscript was bound at the expense of Dr John Fergus
in 1735 while owned by Charles O'Conor. It was later
transferred to the collection of the duke of Buckingham
at Stowe, and thence to the earl of Ashburnham. When
John O'Donovan was working on his edition of the
Annals in the 1830s and 1840s he was unable to have
access to this manuscript and had to rely on the
abridged edition published by Revd Charles O'Conor in
1826 (**34**). The manuscript was purchased by the British
government in 1883 and placed in the Royal Irish
Academy. BC

**Display:** ff 106v–107r. These pages contain the entries for AM
4523–4532. Most of the entries for the pre-Christian period
simply itemise the name of the king and the year of his reign.
Events became more interesting, however, in AM 4532, when
it was recorded that a woman, Macha, successfully challenged
for sovereignty, and then established the fort of Eamhain
Macha (Navan Fort).

**Further reading:** *Cat. Ir. MSS RIA*, no. 1220; Giblin 1967;
O'Donovan 1848–51.

*19.*

ANNALS OF THE FOUR MASTERS
*Annála Ríoghachta Éireann*

TCD 1301 (H.2.11). Seventeenth century. Paper. 30cm x
20cm. 466 folios. [Figs. 4.1; 6.2]

This autograph manuscript contains the Annals of the
Four Masters for the years AD 1334–1605. The opening
and closing sections of the manuscript are damaged,
and the text begins part-way through the entry for
1334. Entries for the years AD 1172–1333 have been
lost, together with the post-1605 material. A fragment
of the final entry in the Annals, on the death of Hugh
O'Neill in 1616, is loosely inserted in the volume.

A great deal can be deduced about the working
methods of the annalists from the pages of this
manuscript. After the main scribe, believed to be Conaire
Ó Cléirigh, had written the text of most of the entries in
this volume, others of the Four Masters revised and
amended the work, adding clarifications about personal
names and sometimes inserting additional entries at the
beginning or end of a given year. Five scribes in all
contributed to this manuscript. It is clear, particularly in
the entries for the early fifteenth century, that the
manuscript was a working document rather than a final
'fair copy'.

This manuscript came into the possession of
Roderic O'Flaherty (**32**) in the late seventeenth century,
and he annotated parts of it quite extensively. In
particular, he added material from a set of Lecan annals
that do not correspond to the text now known as the
Annals of Lecan. Later, Charles O'Conor made even
more extensive additions, many of them relating to his
own ancestors (**33**). The efforts of later readers of the
manuscript, such as O'Flaherty, were directed to making
the work more comprehensive, and they inserted
extracts from other source manuscripts where they
judged this to be appropriate. The marginal additions are
such, however, that this manuscript now appears very
untidy in places, particularly in the sections covering the
fourteenth and fifteenth centuries. In one sense,
O'Flaherty and other annotators were continuing a
process that the Four Masters themselves had
commenced, revising and adding to the text as
additional material came to hand. In consequence, this
is a good example of a manuscript that, unlike a printed
book, was never deemed to be quite finished, but evolved
over time as certain readers made it their own by
further contributing to it.

The manuscript was later owned by John Fergus,
and was purchased by Trinity College Dublin at the
auction of his books in 1766. It was consulted by John
O'Donovan in his edition of the Annals, where it is
referred to as the 'college copy'. BC

**Display:** pp 767v–768. The entry for AD 1439–40 illustrates
clearly the nature of the working document, with the text being
edited after the initial entries had been transcribed. There are
entries in the hands of Conaire and Cú Choigcríche Ó Cléirigh,
with interlined additions and genealogical clarifications.

**Further reading:** Nicholls 1990.

## 20.

# ANNALS OF THE FOUR MASTERS
## *Annála Rioghachta Éireann*

UCD-OFM A 13. Seventeenth century. Paper. 28cm x 19cm.
[xvi] + 551 folios. [Figs. 2.1; 2.2; 6.3]

This autograph manuscript contains the opening section
of the Annals of the Four Masters, commencing with
AM 2242 and ending with AD 1169. It is continued by
RIA 23 P 6–7, which opens with the year AD 1170. The
division at the date of the coming of the Normans was
not the Four Masters' doing, however; they had divided
their text at the year 1207, commencing their second
volume with the year 1208. A significant portion of this
manuscript is in the hand of Mícheál Ó Cléirigh himself.

The content of this manuscript parallels RIA C iii 3
(18) so closely that it is extremely difficult to establish
which might be the earlier of the two. One point at
which the two texts differ is in the account of the
coming of Christianity to Ireland. In this manuscript,
the original folio (f. 231) containing the entries for the
years AD 428–433 has been removed and replaced by
a revised text that makes reference to the printed
ecclesiastical annals of Caesare Baronius, published in
1601–8:

> According to a certain ecclesiastical writer, named
> Baronius, it was on the 6th day of the month of April
> in this year that Pope Celestine died. And that Sixtus
> was made pope twenty days after that. And that it
> was he who sent Patrick to Ireland in this year.
> According to an explanatory gloss in a praise poem
> [made] by holy Fiacc bishop of Slebhte, Celestine was
> alive for just one week after Patrick was ordained
> and Sixtus was made pope and showed great
> kindness to Patrick, and gave him relics of Paul and
> Peter and many books at his coming to Ireland [f.
> 231v].

Unlike almost all other corrections in the Annals, this
additional material was not replicated in the other
autograph copy of the text (RIA C iii 3). This indicates
that this particular revision may well have been made
after Mícheál Ó Cléirigh had taken the manuscript to
Louvain.

This manuscript has remained in Franciscan
hands from the time of its first compilation. It was
used by John Colgan in his work on the lives of Irish
saints, published under the title *Acta Sanctorum
Hiberniae* in 1645, and various marginal notes in his
hand can be seen. It was in St Isidore's College, Rome,
during most of the nineteenth century, and John
O'Donovan was unable to consult it for his edition of
the Annals. The manuscript was brought back to
Ireland by the Franciscans in 1872 and transferred to
University College Dublin in 2000. BC

Display: ff 231v–232r. The entries on the coming of St
Patrick to Ireland (AD 431–2) were revised and a
replacement folio inserted.

**Further reading:** *Cat. Ir. MSS FLK*, no. A 13, pp 24–7;
Cunningham 2005, chap. 6.

18   19

20

18

*21.*

## ANNALS OF THE FOUR MASTERS
*Annála Ríoghachta Éireann*

RIA 23 P 6. Seventeenth century. Paper/2 vellum leaves.
23cm x 15cm, inserted into leaves 34cm x 20cm. 287 folios.
[Figs. 6.4; 7.1]

This autograph manuscript continues on from UCD-OFM
A 13 almost without loss of text (the first leaf containing
part of AD 1170 is missing). It contains the Annals of the
Four Masters for the years AD 1170–1499. It is the only
surviving autograph copy of the Annals for the years AD
1172–1334, a section missing from the other autograph
copy (TCD 1301) (19) since the early eighteenth century
at least. Two vellum leaves, measuring 28cm x 18cm,
containing a dedication of the work to the patron,
Fearghal Ó Gadhra, signed by Mícheál Ó Cléirigh, and
the testimonium signed by four Donegal friars, headed
by Mícheál's brother Bernardine, are now bound into
this manuscript. They are placed between AD 1207 and
AD 1208, a point that marked the beginning of the
second volume of the work as originally arranged by the
Four Masters. The text of the Annals as currently bound
is preceded by twelve fragmentary pages written in
double columns that appear to constitute notes towards
an index. Most of the material in this section relates to
the thirteenth to fifteenth centuries, but with some
Early Christian items also included.

Like its companion volume, TCD 1301, this is not
a 'fair copy' of the Annals but a working document
that has been edited and revised by the compilers
themselves. The main scribe responsible is believed to
be Conaire Ó Cléirigh but, as with other sections of the
Annals, others of the Four Masters also contributed,
notably Mícheál and Cú Choigcríche Ó Cléirigh.

George Petrie bought this manuscript and its
continuation, RIA 23 P 7, for the Royal Irish Academy
at the sale of the books of Austin Cooper in 1831.
Cooper had acquired it after the death of William
Burton Conyngham of Slane Castle. Described by John
O'Donovan in the 1830s as 'worn away by damp', it
was expertly conserved and rebound by George Mullen,
a Dublin bookbinder, in 1838 and remains in the
Academy collection. It was used by John O'Donovan as
the basic text for his edition of the Annals. BC

Display: ff 134v–135r. These folios contain the entries for AD
1393, 1394 and the opening part of 1395. Two main hands
are visible here. The entry for 1393 is penned by Mícheál Ó
Cléirigh, while the smaller hand that completes most of the
following page is that of Cú Choigcríche Ó Cléirigh.

Further reading: *Cat. Ir. MSS RIA*, no. 687; O'Sullivan 1999.

*22.*

## ANNALS OF THE FOUR MASTERS
*Annála Ríoghachta Éireann*

RIA 23 P 7. Seventeenth century. Paper. 23cm x 15cm,
inserted into leaves 34cm x 20cm. 293 folios.

This autograph manuscript is the continuation of RIA 23
P 6, and contains the Annals for the years AD 1500–
1616. The penmanship is chiefly the work of Conaire

and Mícheál Ó Cléirigh. Its contents are very similar to
the corresponding portion of TCD 1301, though there are
some minor differences (19). Both sets of manuscripts
are working documents rather than fair copies.

George Petrie bought both 23 P 6 and 23 P 7
unbound for the Royal Irish Academy at the sale of the
books of Austin Cooper in 1831; it was rebound by
George Mullen in 1838 and has remained part of the
RIA collection since that time. It was used by John
O'Donovan as the basic text for the final section of his
edition of the Annals. BC

Display: ff 52v–53r. This section of the Annals is in the hand
of Conaire Ó Cléirigh, an older brother of Mícheál, who was
employed on the project as a scribe but is not usually counted
among the 'Four Masters'. His work was neat, clear and legible,
and his contribution undoubtedly speeded up the production
of the final text. As in other instances, the scribe left blank
spaces for the insertion of new material that might come to
hand at a later stage. In the entry for the year 1537, although
the first item describes a battle between Aodh Buidhe Ó
Domhnaill and Maghnus Ó Domhnaill, it is clear that the
scribe attached special importance to the obituary of Aodh Ó
Domhnaill. The name 'O Domhnaill, Aodh' is written in extra-
large letters to highlight the importance of the man who had
been head of the O'Donnell lordship since 1505. The obituary
draws attention to the extent of his jurisdiction and praises
his special attributes. Aodh Ó Domhnaill was succeeded by
his son, Maghnus Ó Domhnaill, the man responsible for the
manuscript Life of Colum Cille (UCD-OFM A 8) completed in
1532 (7).

Further reading: *Cat. Ir. MSS RIA*, no. 688; W. O'Sullivan 1999.

*23.*

## GENEALOGIES OF SAINTS AND KINGS
*Seanchas Riogh Éreánn 7 Genealuighi na Naomh
nEreannach*

UCD-OFM A 16. Seventeenth century. Paper. 19cm x 15cm.
lv + 125 folios. [Figs. 1.3; 3.2; 4.4]

The autograph manuscript of the Genealogies of Saints
and Kings is partly in the hand of Mícheál Ó Cléirigh,
but there are layers of annotations by other scribes and
scholars, including John Colgan. It was completed in
the Franciscan Observant friary of Athlone in 1630. The
main focus was on the genealogies of saints, and the
reigns of kings were ancillary to the primary purpose of
making the saints of Ireland and their noble ancestry
better known. The tradition of compiling genealogies of
kings and saints formed an essential part of medieval
learning in Ireland. The Irish were keen to trace their
ancestry back to Adam, and therefore created elaborate
pedigrees that fitted them into a biblical chronology and
background. Mícheál Ó Cléirigh used this material to
compile his own genealogical works. The text of A16 is
divided into various parts. Kings of Ireland are classified
as pre-Christian and Christian. The Christian kings of
Ireland are all northern kings who were members of the
various dynasties of the Uí Néill. Exceptions include
Brian Bórama and two later O'Brien kings, Toirdelbach
(d. 1086) and Muirchertach (d. 1119), and two O'Conor
kings, Toirdelbach (d. 1156) and Ruaidrí (d. 1198). The
saints are classified according to the noble dynasties to
which they belonged or to the province from which they
originated. Northern and western saints predominate. EB

Display: f. x v–xi r. Apart from the genealogical and historical content of A16, the manuscript is also valuable for the introductory material included in it. It opens with the approbations in Latin of Malachy O Queely, archbishop of Tuam; Boethius Egan, bishop of Elphin; Thomas Fleming, archbishop of Dublin; and Roch Mac Geoghegan, bishop of Kildare. These are followed by an address to Turlough MacCoghlan, patron of the work (which includes MacCoghlan's genealogy), and a general explanatory introduction addressed to the reader. Both the MacCoghlan address and the one to the reader are signed by the same men who compiled the Annals of the Four Masters—Mícheál Ó Cléirigh, Fearfeasa Ó Maoil Chonaire, Cú Choigcríche Ó Cléirigh and Cú Choigcríche Ó Duibhgheannáin. There are also approbations by George Dillon (guardian of the friary at Athlone) and Conall Mageoghegan, who was Turlough MacCoghlan's brother-in-law, and was among those who provided source material for the Annals of the Four Masters.

Further reading: *Cat. Ir. MSS FLK*, A 16; Walsh 1918.

21 22

23

120|121

22

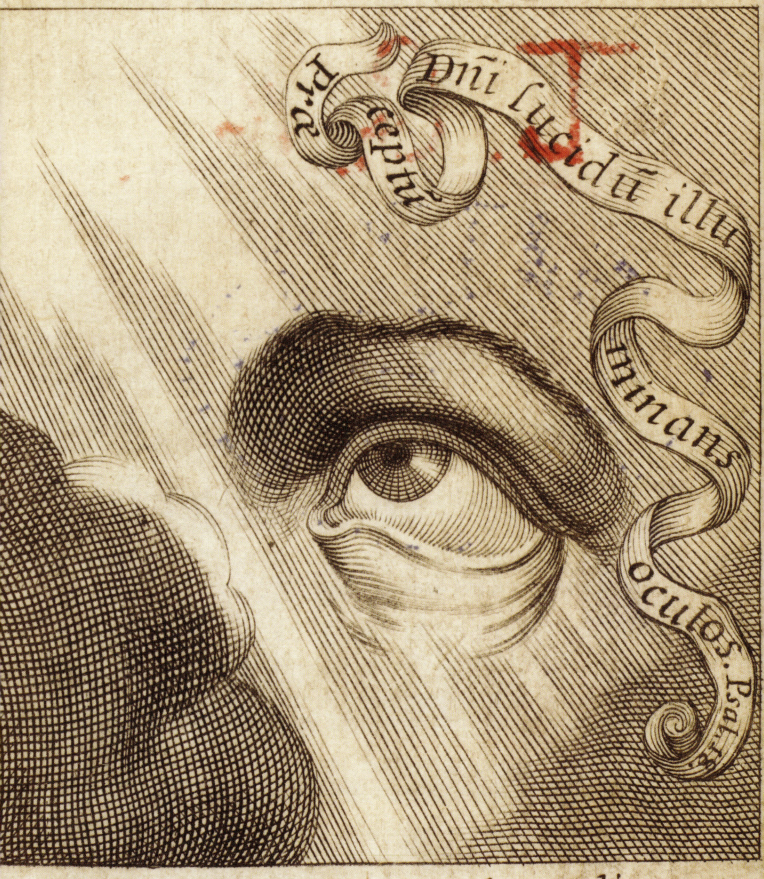

Præcepta Dūi lucidū illūminans oculos. Psal.

vobis Deus illuminatos oculos cordis uestri. Ephes. 1.

# The world of history, scholarship and cultural politics

The Four Masters were not the only Irish historians at work in the early seventeenth century. Their annals were partly based on a biographical narrative of Red Hugh O'Donnell (Aodh Ruadh Ó Domhnaill), one of the Ulster heroes of the Nine Years' War (1594–1603), written by another professional historian, Lughaidh Ó Cléirigh, and composed in a Renaissance style (**24**). Others, too, were writing their own versions of the secular and ecclesiastical history of Ireland, using Irish manuscript sources. Geoffrey Keating's prose narrative history of Ireland, *Foras feasa ar Éirinn*, was written in Irish in the 1630s and proved immensely popular (**25**). Like the Annals of the Four Masters, it began with the *Leabhar Gabhála* and told the story of the successive kings of Ireland as recorded in the early sources. Keating's history had two advantages over the Annals in terms of popular appeal. First, it was written as a story, in flowing Irish prose. Second, it was framed as a defence of Ireland's reputation against the criticisms of all foreign detractors. Keating's polemical preface was designed to persuade readers of the value of telling the story of Ireland's past from an Irish perspective. The Franciscans Mícheál Ó Cléirigh and John Colgan were among the first readers of Keating's history, obtaining a copy of *Foras feasa* almost as soon as it was completed.

From a Protestant perspective, the historical works of James Ussher, the scholarly archbishop of Armagh, were also rooted in the manuscript sources (**30, 31**). Together with Sir James Ware (**29**), he collected manuscripts of Irish historical interest and was in contact with a number of Irish Franciscan scholars for this purpose. In his writings on church history, Ussher insisted that the early church had been corrupted by Roman influence and that the Reformation was necessary to restore the church to its original state. Ussher's achievement was to take a standard argument of European Protestant theologians and present detailed evidence drawn from Irish sources in support of his case. Ecclesiastical history was a central issue of concern in the age of the Reformation and Counter-Reformation, and for Irish Catholic writers the Lives of saints became a particular focus of research. Irish scholars in Europe, not least the Irish Franciscans at Louvain, sought out authentic manuscript sources concerning early Christian saints associated with Ireland, and disseminated this material to contemporary audiences in Latin editions (**26, 28**).

Detail from Luke Wadding's edition of *De oculo morali* (1656) (cat. no. 27) (*opposite*).

*24.*

## LIFE OF RED HUGH O'DONNELL
### *Beatha Aodha Ruaidh Uí Dhomhnaill*

RIA 23 P 24. Seventeenth century. Paper. 18.5cm x 14cm.
85 folios. [Illus. pp 98–9]

The Renaissance-style biography of Red Hugh O'Donnell
(Aodh Ruadh Ó Domhnaill) was composed in the early
seventeenth century. The author was Lughaidh Ó Cléirigh,
a professional historian and third cousin of Mícheál Ó
Cléirigh. This text was referred to by the Four Masters
as the 'Book of Lughaidh Ó Cléirigh', and they relied on
it for much of their account of events during the Nine
Years' War (1594–1603) in Ireland. The autograph
manuscript of the 'Book of Lughaidh Ó Cléirigh' is not
extant, but the text has been preserved in this
seventeenth-century transcript, believed to be in the
hand of Cú Choigcríche Ó Cléirigh, who was one of the
Four Masters. His tiny script can also be seen in the
pages of the Annals. A mid-seventeenth-century abridged
version of this biography also survives (NLI G 488),
which may possibly be the work of the same Cú
Choigcríche Ó Cléirigh.

Red Hugh O'Donnell is eulogised in this biography
and there is a particular emphasis on his heroic exploits
on the battlefield in the course of the Nine Years' War.
As well as recording his actions, the author contextualises
and explains them, using artificially archaic language, as
though he were imitating early Irish heroic literature.
The Four Masters made extensive use of this narrative
in their Annals for the years between 1587 and the
death of Red Hugh in 1602.

The biography ends on a note of lamentation, not
just for the dead hero but for all the Gaeil of Ireland:

> Pitiable, indeed, was the state of the Gaels of Ireland
> after the death of the true prince, for they changed
> their characteristics and dispositions. They gave up
> bravery for cowardice, courage for weakness, pride
> for servility. Their hatred, valour, prowess, heroism,
> triumph, and military glory, vanished after his death.
> They abandoned all hope of relief from any one, so
> that the most of them fled thereafter to the mercy of
> foes and enemies, those who were noblest of them,
> under the guise of peace and friendship. And some
> of them dispersed, not only throughout Ireland, but
> all over Europe in groups and bands, poor and
> miserable, and others as soldiers of fortune in foreign
> lands for pay and hire, so that many of them were
> killed and others died and the graves they are buried
> in are unknown. But indeed it would be tedious to
> recount or relate the great woes which were sown and
> propagated in Ireland as a result of the death of Aodh
> Ó Domhnaill, whose tale thus far we have told.

BC

**Display:** ff 84v–85. The final pages of Lughaidh Ó Cléirigh's
biography of Red Hugh O'Donnell record the death of
O'Donnell at Simancas, Spain, in 1602.

**Further reading:** Breatnach 2002; Ó Riain 2002; Walsh
1948–57.

*25.*

## GEOFFREY KEATING'S HISTORY OF IRELAND
### *Foras feasa ar Éirinn*

UCD-OFM A 14. Seventeenth century. Paper. 31.5cm x
19.5cm (with variations). xvi + 105 folios. [Fig. 5.2]

*Foras feasa ar Éirinn* is a prose history of Ireland,
written in County Tipperary at almost exactly the same
time as the Four Masters were working on their Annals
in Donegal. The author was Geoffrey Keating (Seathrún
Céitinn), an Irish-speaking Catholic priest of Anglo-
Norman descent. The history became a best-seller and
circulated widely in manuscript down to the early
twentieth century, when it was published in a dual-
language edition by the Irish Texts Society.

Keating's autograph manuscript does not survive,
and this present manuscript, which is partly in the hand
of Mícheál Ó Cléirigh, is one of the earliest copies of the
work in existence. This copy and two other extant
manuscripts contain a shorter text than the version that
was normally in circulation, and may have been in the
nature of a preliminary draft. At least some of the
manuscript was transcribed at the Franciscan convent in
Kildare in September of an unspecified year, probably
1636. It seems that as soon as the Four Masters had
completed their Annals in August 1636, Ó Cléirigh came
to know of Keating's work and immediately began to
prepare a transcript. This copy of Keating's history was
taken to Louvain, where John Colgan used it in his work
on the lives of Irish saints. The manuscript includes
marginal notes in Colgan's hand that indicate a
particular interest in identifying the sources used by
Keating. EB/BC

**Display:** f. 59v. This part of the manuscript tells how Colum
Cille was banished from Ireland for his role in various battles,
including the battle of Cúil Dreimhne, and how he returned to
Ireland at the invitation of the king of Tara, Áed mac Ainmirech,
to participate in the Convention of Druim Cett (near Limavady,
Co. Derry) in 575. The folio is of particular interest as the main
hand is likely to be that of Mícheál Ó Cléirigh, while the
marginal annotations and notes in Latin interspersed through
the text are in John Colgan's hand.

**Further reading:** *Cat. Ir. MSS FLK,* no. 14; Comyn and Dinneen
1902–14; Cunningham 2000.

*26.*

## THOMAS MESSINGHAM

Thomas Messingham, *Florilegium insulae sanctorum.* Paris,
1624. Printed work. [Fig. 3.1]

Thomas Messingham's compilation of Irish saints' Lives
placed special emphasis on Ireland's three patrons,
Patrick, Brigit and Colum Cille. He selected and adapted
pre-existing Latin Lives of these three saints from printed
and manuscript sources and published them in one
composite volume. The texts included Jocelin's Life of
Patrick, Adomnán's Life of Colum Cille and two separate
Lives of Brigit, these patrons reflecting the secular priest,
monk and nun as religious vocations. St Bernard's Life
of Malachy of Armagh was also included, together with
material on some Irish saints renowned for their
activities in Europe, notably Columbanus, Fursey, Gall
and Killian.

Messingham believed that these saints' Lives had an important role to play in preserving Ireland—the 'island of saints'—for Catholicism, and in his preface he directly addressed the dilemmas faced by Catholics in Ireland when confronted by anti-Catholic legislation. Arguing for the continuity of the faith from the time of these early Christian saints, he asserted: 'We believe what our Fathers and Patrons believed, the testimony of Patrick, Columba and Brigit; what they taught we teach, what they preached we preach'. The same message was preached by 'BB' [Robert Rochford], an Irish Franciscan friar at Louvain, in his 1625 work *The life of the glorious Bishop S. Patricke*, which printed abridged English translations of the main Lives that Messingham had used. Rochford's book was printed at St Omer and smuggled into Ireland in the 1630s.

James Ussher's copy of Messingham's book, preserved in Trinity College Dublin (TCD DD.d.30), contains Ussher's extensive corrections and marginal annotations to the Life of Colum Cille. BC

Display: title-page. The title-page of Thomas Messingham's *Florilegium* (1624) includes woodcuts of Ireland's three patron saints, Patrick, Brigit and Colum Cille.
Further reading: Messingham 1624; O'Connor 1999.

## 27.
## LUKE WADDING

Pierre de Limoges, *De oculo morali*. Viterbo, 1656. Printed work.

Luke Wadding (1588–1657) was born in Waterford, Ireland, and became the leading historian of the Franciscan order in his day. He spent much of his life in Rome, and established the Irish Franciscan College of St Isidore there in 1625. The work for which Wadding is best known is the *Annales minorum, seu trium Ordinum A. S. Francisco Institutorum*, a history of the Franciscan order, 1208–1540 (8 vols, 1625–54), one of many publications about the work of the Franciscans that he published in his lifetime. His *B. P. Francisci Assisiatis opuscula* was re-issued many times. In 1656 Luke Wadding edited and arranged for the printing of *De oculo morali*, which has been described as 'moral and spiritual applications for prelates and others of the current scientific knowledge of the eye'. Wadding argued that the author was the Franciscan John of Wales, but it is now attributed to Pierre de Limoges (Petrus de Seperia, known to Wadding as La Cepiera).

The book is dedicated to Giulio Rospigliosi, archbishop of Tarsus and former nuncio to the Spanish court. Wadding's own eye for influential contacts was at work here, because while Rospigliosi had been out of favour in the Curia up to 1655, he was to become secretary of state to Pope Alexander VII in 1657. Then in 1677, twenty years after his own death, Wadding's dedicatee was elected pope, taking the title Clement IX. BC/JMcC

Display: title-page.
Further reading: Corish 1957; Fennessy 2004; Franciscan Fathers 1957; Mooney 1958; Spettman 1923.

27

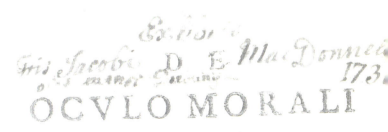

## 28.
## JOHN COLGAN

John Colgan, *Triadis thaumaturgae, seu divorum Patricii, Columbae, et Brigidae . . . acta.* Louvain, 1647. Printed work.

John Colgan's edition of the Lives of Ireland's three patron saints, Patrick, Brigit and Colum Cille, was published by the Irish Franciscans at Louvain in 1647. This collection was printed with the financial backing of Thomas Fleming OFM, archbishop of Dublin. Each of the Lives was accompanied by extensive scholarly footnotes.

Being concerned to make all the available primary source texts accessible in print, Colgan was inclusive rather than selective in his editorial work, printing several Lives of each of these saints rather than merely selecting one text. He used Lives of saints collected by a number of collaborators from printed and manuscript sources. Medieval manuscripts such as the *Liber Hymnorum* (3) had been brought to Louvain from Donegal for this purpose, while the Lives of saints in Irish transcribed by Mícheál Ó Cléirigh were translated into Latin for publication. Colgan also had copies of Latin Lives from a variety of sources.

It was probably because of the sheer volume of material available that the Lives of Patrick, Brigit and Colum Cille were published separately from the others. If they had been included in the main sequence of Colgan's *Acta Sanctorum Hiberniae* (1645), which documented Irish saints whose feast-days occurred in the first three months of the year, the numerous Lives of St Brigit at 1 February and of St Patrick at 17 March would have made that first volume far too large.

In terms of Roman ecclesiastical politics, it was important for the Irish in Europe to publicise their major Christian saints. There was no more effective way of demonstrating Ireland's Catholic pedigree than by publishing these substantial Latin editions of authentic texts documenting the lives and miracles of Ireland's patron saints. BC

Display: title-page.
Further reading: Colgan 1647; O'Donnell 1959; Ó Riain 2006.

## 29.
## JAMES WARE

James Ware, *De Scriptoribus Hiberniae.* Dublin, 1639. Printed work

Sir James Ware's *De Scriptoribus Hiberniae* was first published in Dublin in 1639. This was a biographical encyclopaedia of Irish writers from earliest times down to Ware's own day, arranged chronologically by century. In 1577 Richard Stanihurst had attempted a more modest compilation of 'the names and surnames of the learned men and authors of Ireland' as a chapter of his contribution to *Holinshed's Irish Chronicle*, while in an English context John Bale's *Index Britanniae scriptorum*, first published in 1545, and John Pits's posthumous *Relationum historicarum de rebus Anglicis*, published in 1619, prompted others to attempt similar catalogues of writers and scholars. Ware's volume on Ireland relied in part on Bale and ranged from the writings of many

early Christian saints associated with Ireland to English writers of the fifteenth and sixteenth centuries who wrote about Ireland, men such as Edmund Spenser and Meredith Hanmer. In 1633 Ware had been responsible for publishing the first edition of Edmund Spenser's *View of the present state of Ireland*. Spenser's provocative interpretation of the Irish received a swift reply from Geoffrey Keating in his *Foras feasa ar Éirinn* (25), which was issued shortly after Spenser's work was first made available in print. Among the historical works that Ware compiled himself were several books on recent Irish history, presented in the form of annals, as well as a catalogue of Irish bishops.

Ware's family had been settled in Ireland for some time. He was a graduate of Trinity College Dublin, and as holder of the office of auditor-general was an active Irish politician as well as being an antiquary and historian. While a student at TCD he was taught by James Ussher, and the two men shared a life-long interest in Irish history (30, 31). Ware, like Ussher, was an assiduous collector of Irish manuscripts as well as being an author in his own right. He was in contact with the Donegal Franciscans and was able to borrow certain manuscripts from them, which he cited in his historical works. BC

Display: final page of address to the reader and p. 1 of text.
Further reading: O'Sullivan 1997; Parry 2004.

## 30.
## JAMES USSHER

James Ussher, *A discourse of the religion anciently professed by the Irish and Brittish.* London, 1631. Printed work.

James Ussher, a Dubliner, was Church of Ireland archbishop of Armagh, and an ecclesiastical historian and theologian. He devoted much time to arguing the case that the Protestant church was the true successor of the church of St Patrick in Ireland. His *Discourse of the religion anciently professed by the Irish and Brittish*, his most coherent statement on the theological implications of the history of the church in Ireland, was originally published in Dublin in 1622 as an appendix to Sir Christopher Sibthorp's *A friendly advertisement to the pretended Catholickes of Ireland* and reprinted the following year. Sibthorp's work was an attempt to persuade Catholics to take the Oath of Supremacy and generated a pamphlet war in 1620s Dublin. Ussher's *Discourse* was also issued as an appendix to a 1631 edition of his *An answer to a challenge made by a Jesuit*, first published in 1629. This locates Ussher's work firmly in the context of religious controversy rather than of history. In his address 'To the reader' of his *Discourse of the religion anciently professed by the Irish and Brittish*, Ussher explained that:

> my principal intention in this discourse was to produce such evidences as might shew the agreement that was betwixt our ancestors and us in matter of Religion, and to leave the influences which might bee alledged for the contrary to them unto whom the maintaining of that part did properly belong; yet I

have upon occasion touched upon that part also, and brought to light some things which I met withall in such hidden antiquities, as in all likelihood would not have come unto their notice without my discovery.

The argument of the *Discourse* was that the Reformation of the sixteenth century had not produced a new Protestant church separate from the 'true' church of earlier times. As such, it followed the standard Anglican view of history established by John Jewel, bishop of Salisbury, in his *Apologia ecclesiae Anglicanae* (1562) and subsequently developed by others. Ussher argued, rather, that the early church had become corrupt during the later Middle Ages as a result of the influence of Rome. The process of Reformation was therefore seen not as a breach but as a restoration of the original purity of the church of the apostles. Ussher demonstrated this by considering matters such as confession, the Eucharist and married clergy as they appeared in the Lives of early Irish saints and in other texts relating to the church. He found substantial similarity between the Protestant church of his own day and the church of the early sources. The argument was not a specifically Irish one but was regularly used by European Protestant theologians in the seventeenth century. Ussher's contribution was to anchor the argument firmly in historical evidence, and it thus forms a prelude to his more substantial work on the history of the early church in Britain and Ireland, *Britannicarum ecclesiarum antiquitates*, published in 1639. BC/RG

Display: title-page.

**Further reading:** Lotz-Heumann 1996; McCafferty 1997/8.

*31.*
## JAMES USSHER NOTEBOOK

TCD 574. Seventeenth century. Paper. 32cm x 22cm. 720 pages.

James Ussher was an avid collector of historical source material of Irish interest. A significant collection of his miscellaneous historical notes is preserved in the library of Trinity College Dublin. Where original documents were in the Irish language, he sometimes employed scholars to translate texts into Latin for him. In this example, a portion of the Annals of Ulster, commencing in AD 431, was transcribed in Irish on the left-hand page, and a Latin translation was provided on the right-hand page. This is just one of numerous extracts from various annals in this volume, many of them in Latin. While Ussher had arranged for a lengthy portion of the Annals of Ulster to be transcribed in Irish, the accompanying Latin translation was abandoned before completion when it had reached the year AD 489. Something of Ussher's eagerness to know what the remaining portion contained can be seen in his scribbled notes to the first page of the untranslated Irish text. BC

Display: pp 446–7. Opening page of a transcript from the Annals of Ulster, in Irish, with parallel Latin translation, made for James Ussher, archbishop of Armagh.

**Further reading:** Cunningham and Gillespie 2004–5; O'Sullivan 1956.

28　29

30　31

31

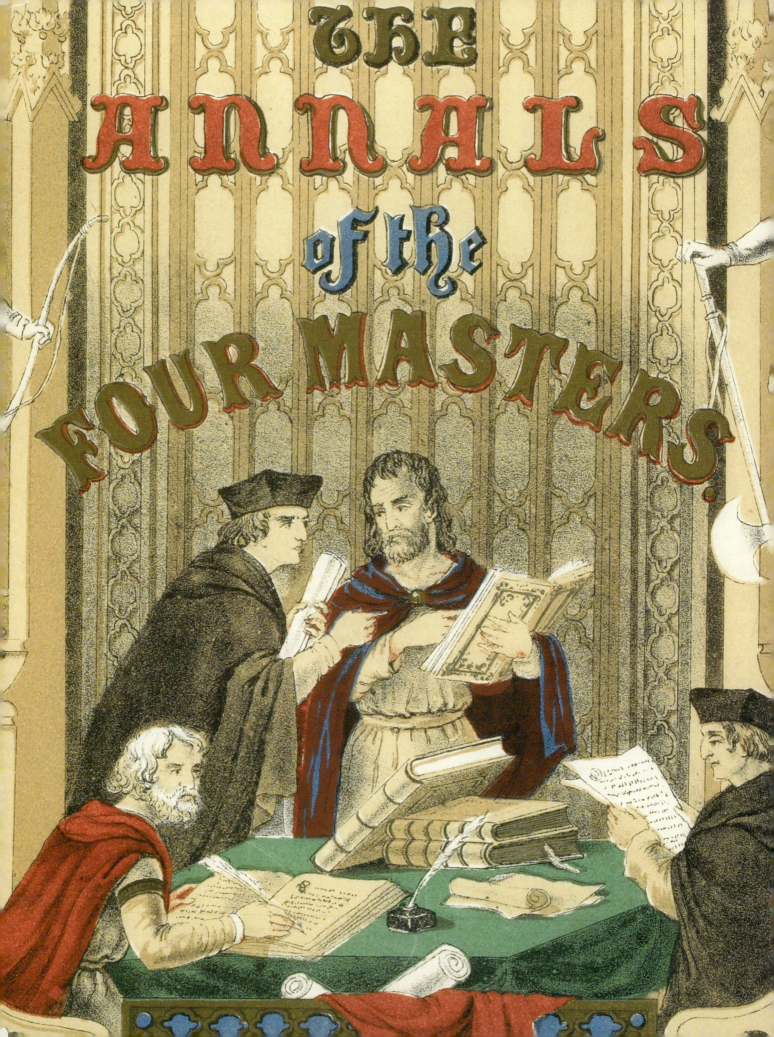

## five

Section 5

# The legacy of the Four Masters

From the time they were completed in the early seventeenth century, scholars were interested in having access to the historical material contained in the Annals of the Four Masters. The Annals were used by the genealogist Dubhaltach Mac Fhirbhisigh in the 1640s and were cited extensively by Roderic O'Flaherty in the 1680s when he wrote the first major history of Ireland to be published abroad (**32**). O'Flaherty, too, was one of those who sought to improve the original manuscript of the Annals by making additions to the text. Various transcripts of the Annals were made during the late eighteenth century, largely under the influence of the antiquary Charles O'Conor of Belanagare (**33**). By the early nineteenth century there was a strongly felt need to have the full text of the Annals of the Four Masters available to scholars in print. This was finally achieved by John O'Donovan's classic dual-language text, issued in seven volumes in 1851 (**37**). The impetus to bring editions of classic national texts into the public sphere was not an exclusively Irish one, and similar projects in editing major sources of national history were undertaken in other European countries at about the same time. Once O'Donovan's edition of the 'Annals of the Kingdom of Ireland' was published, the achievement of Mícheál Ó Cléirigh and his associates was given due recognition. The Annals became a foundational text for research in Irish history and archaeology, O'Donovan's extensive notes and comprehensive index creating a reference work of lasting value for medieval Irish history. At a popular level, too, the reputation of Ó Cléirigh continued to grow. By the 1880s, for instance, Louvain was one of the 'sights' in a travelogue by Eugene Davis entitled 'Souvenirs of Irish footprints in Europe', published in the *Evening Telegraph*, in which Mícheál Ó Cléirigh featured strongly amongst a miscellany of saints, scholars and national heroes. In the course of the early twentieth century the Ó Cléirigh story was further enhanced as Irish history became an important element of the national ideology of the fledgling Free State. In 1943/4 the tercentenary of the death of Mícheál Ó Cléirigh provided the opportunity for the first major public celebrations (**41**, **42**, **43**, **44**) of the achievements of the seventeenth-century Irish scholars known to all as the Four Masters.

Frontispiece of Owen Connellan's edition of the *Annals of the Four Masters,* 1846 (cat. no. 19) (*opposite*).

## 32.
## RODERIC O'FLAHERTY

Roderic O'Flaherty, *Ogygia seu, rerum Hibernicorum chronologia*. London, 1685. Printed work.

Roderic O'Flaherty, from Moycullen, Co. Galway, was an important bridge between the manuscript tradition of Gaelic historians such as the Four Masters and eighteenth-century antiquarians. In his youth he was closely associated with the genealogist Dubhaltach Mac Fhirbhisigh, while in later life he was in contact with the Dublin scientist and political philosopher William Molyneux and the Welsh manuscript-collector and philologist Edward Lhuyd; indeed, Molyneux arranged for the publication of his work. O'Flaherty himself had ready access to one of the autograph sets of the Annals (**18, 19**) and made some additions to it from annalistic sources available to him that had been compiled by the learned family of Mac Fhirbhisigh of Lecan, Co. Sligo. O'Flaherty's own major work, *Ogygia*, was the first scholarly history of Ireland to be published in Latin for an English audience. It includes regular citations from the Annals of the Four Masters, which he termed '*Annales Dungallenses*' (Annals of Donegal). O'Flaherty took the opportunity to elaborate on the Milesian ancestry of the Stuart monarchy, but the essence of his argument was that the kingdom of Ireland was more ancient than the kingdoms of Scotland or England. His method involved drawing on modern research on universal chronology and applying this to the Irish sources, including the *Leabhar Gabhála* origin-legend and the place-lore recorded in the *Dinnsheanchas*. BC

Display: pp 206–7. In Roderic O'Flaherty's *Ogygia* the marginal notes on sources include references to the Martyrologies of Tallaght, Gorman and Donegal, as well as the Annals of the Four Masters, which he calls the Annals of Donegal.
Further reading: Ó Muraíle 1996b.

## 33.
## CHARLES O'CONOR

Charles O'Conor, *Dissertations on the antient history of Ireland, wherein an account is given of the origine, government, letters, sciences, religion, manners and customs, of the antient inhabitants*. Dublin, 1753 and 1766. Printed work.

Charles O'Conor (1710–91) of Belanagare, Co. Roscommon, was an avid collector of Irish manuscripts and a former owner of an autograph manuscript of the Annals of the Four Masters (**18, 19**). He made extensive annotations to his set, particularly on matters relating to his own ancestors, the O'Conors of Connacht. His influential history of Ireland was first published in 1748 in separate parts, issued anonymously. It was later published in book form in 1753, with further editions in 1766 and later. The approach adopted in O'Conor's historical essays on pre-Norman Ireland was influenced by Geoffrey Keating's *Foras feasa ar Éirinn* (**25**), in that the reputation of the Irish people was stoutly defended and their civility emphasised. O'Conor was also preoccupied by issues of chronology, and he sought to

present his account of the Irish past in the context of international chronology. Thus, for example, he drew comparisons between the work of Sir Isaac Newton and the chronology of Irish history preserved in Gaelic sources. BC

Display: pp 14–15. 'The earliest account . . . Isaac Newton'.
Further reading: Ward *et al.* 1988.

## 34.
## REVD CHARLES O'CONOR

Revd Charles O'Conor (ed.), *Quatuor Magistrorum annales Hibernici usque ad annum MCLXXII ex ipso O'Clerii autographo in Bibliotheca Stowense servato*. Rerum Hibernicarum Scriptores Veteres III. Buckingham, 1826. Printed work.

One autograph manuscript of the Annals of the Four Masters (**18**) was acquired for the library of the duke of Buckingham at Stowe through the network of contacts of the librarian there, who was a grandson of the antiquary Charles O'Conor of Belanagare (**33**). The younger O'Conor translated the pre-Norman section of the Annals into Latin and published his Irish and Latin edition in 1826. His rendering of the Irish text was severely criticised by scholars, prompting calls for a more accurate edition. His use of an italic font to represent the Irish letters was also deemed inadequate, and prompted George Petrie to design a Gaelic type especially for use in the printing of Irish texts. BC

Display: pp 68–9. The opening entries for the Christian era. O'Conor abridged the Annals, omitting AD 2–8, for instance. He provided a translation from Irish into Latin, and his notes were also in Latin.

## 35.
## OWEN CONNELLAN

Owen Connellan (ed.), *The annals of Ireland translated from the original Irish of the Four Masters*. Dublin, 1846. Printed work. [Fig. 7.2]

This edition, published by Bryan Geraghty, was originally conceived as a periodical publication. The colour frontispiece illustration was designed and engraved by W. H. Holbrooke. The text was in English only, and the notes that accompanied it were in the nature of general essays on Irish history rather than explanations of the Annals themselves. Each new section of the periodical publication opened with a decorated initial capital, designed for this purpose and claiming to follow the style of lettering of the Book of Kells. The cumulative volume, issued in 1846, contained a striking, if historically inaccurate, colour frontispiece. This imaginative nineteenth-century image shows the Four Masters in an implausibly elaborate Gothic setting, far removed from the humble cottages that were the temporary location of the Donegal Franciscans who accommodated the historians and scribes during their work on the Annals. BC

Display: frontispiece.

## 36.
### IRISH PENNY JOURNAL

*Irish Penny Journal,* 16 January 1841. Printed work. [Fig. 7.4]

An illustrated weekly magazine, the *Irish Penny Journal* was founded by George Petrie in 1840 and lasted just a year. Petrie was also directly involved in an earlier initiative, the *Dublin Penny Journal* (1832–7). Established 'with national as well as useful objects in view', Petrie's popular magazines contained biographies, folklore, legends and topographical descriptions. They were intended to bring topics of historical, antiquarian and literary interest to a wide audience. Among the contributors were Petrie himself and John O'Donovan, who drew on his detailed knowledge of the Annals of the Four Masters and other manuscript sources for his essays. The magazine included engravings by Robert Clayton from sketches by Petrie. Popular publications such as these were an important channel for disseminating knowledge of Irish history among a wider Irish readership. They were significant in impressing on popular consciousness the special value attaching to historical sources such as the Annals of the Four Masters. A rival weekly publication, the *Irish Penny Magazine*, was issued in a similar format during 1833 and reissued in 1841. BC

**Display:** *Irish Penny Journal*, vol. 1, no. 29 (16 January 1841). This issue featured Kilbarron Castle, Co. Donegal, an Ó Cléirigh castle, believed to have been the birthplace of Mícheál Ó Cléirigh.

**Further reading:** Hayes 1911.

32   33

Cathir, the great g[...]
monarch of Ireland, t[...]
king of Ireland three y[...]
Conn of the hundr[...]
Fedlim, monarch of I[...]
Thofe who allow h[...]
the commencement of [...]
Moylenen.
180. L. Ælius A[...]
profligate and abando[...]

TE CHRISTI.
, et octavus annus regin[...]
tus Criomthani in regimi[...]
in Edar, (hodie *Hoath*,)[...]
[u]m Antiquarios. Expedit[...]
memorantur. Pretiosum[...]
[r]elata, cum 300 gemmis l[...]

DISSERTATIONS
ON THE
ANTIENT HISTORY
OF
IRELAND:
WHEREIN
An ACCOUNT is given of the
Origine, Government, Letters, Sciences;
Religion, Manners and Cuftoms, of the *antient* Inhabitants.

34   35

36

32

Cathir, the great great grandfon of Conquovar, monarch of Ireland the laft of the Leinfter line, king of Ireland three years *.

## 37.
## JOHN O'DONOVAN

John O'Donovan (ed.), *Annála Ríoghachta Éireann. Annals of the Kingdom of Ireland, by the Four Masters, from the earliest period to the year 1616, edited from MSS. in the library of the Royal Irish Academy and of Trinity College Dublin, with a translation and copious notes* (1st edn, 7 vols). Dublin, 1848–51. Printed work. [Fig. 7.3]

Plans to publish the full Irish text of the Annals of the Four Masters together with an English translation were actively discussed in scholarly circles in Dublin from the early 1830s. John O'Donovan was selected to translate and edit the Annals, and he was paid for his work by George Smith of the publishers Hodges and Smith. Because of his expertise in Irish place-names, developed during his work as a researcher for the Irish Ordnance Survey, O'Donovan was able to provide very extensive annotations to the text of the Annals, and these notes have proved to be of lasting value. When the first three volumes were issued in 1848—at the height of the Great Famine—sales of the work were less brisk than the publishers had hoped. They persisted with the project, however, publishing the full seven-volume set in 1851 in a lavish edition that won widespread critical acclaim. O'Donovan's work in producing a scholarly dual-language edition of the Annals has not been surpassed. His edition is still in use today, and for over 150 years has made the work of the Four Masters accessible to a wide readership. When it was first published, O'Donovan's edition of the Annals was a truly pioneering undertaking. It helped to bring the Irish language and early Irish history into the public sphere for the first time in generations. BC

Display: pp 1436–7. This portion of the Annals of the Four Masters contains part of the text of the Annals for 1536–7 in Irish, with translation on the facing page.

Further reading: Cunningham 2006a.

## 38.
## MARTYROLOGY OF DONEGAL

J. H. Todd and W. Reeves (eds), *The Martyrology of Donegal: a calendar of the saints of Ireland: Félire na naomh nErennach*, translated by John O'Donovan. Dublin, 1864. Printed work.

A martyrology is a list of names of saints, arranged in a calendar according to their feast-day—that is, the day of the year on which they died. The information supplied about each saint often included details of the place of death, and in some instances selected stories associated with the saint were also noted. The Martyrology of Donegal was prepared by Mícheál Ó Cléirigh in association with Cú Choigcríche Ó Cléirigh. Working with older martyrologies, the Ó Cléirigh scholars completed their first version of this work in manuscript in 1628, and later prepared an enlarged version that was dated 1630.
This martyrology was originally entitled *Féilire na naomh nErennach: Martyrologium Sanctorum Hiberniae*. It was the Donegal Franciscan John Colgan at Louvain who gave it the title 'Martyrology of Donegal', by which name it is now better known. The text of the 1630

recension was published by the Irish Archaeological Society in 1864, based on a translation prepared by John O'Donovan. BC

Display: title-page.

Further reading: Ó Riain 2006.

## 39.
## MICHAEL Ó CLÉIRIGH AND HIS ASSOCIATES

Brendan Jennings, *Michael Ó Cléirigh, chief of the Four Masters, and his associates*. Dublin, 1936. Printed work.

Brendan Jennings's meticulously researched work on the travels and writings of Mícheál Ó Cléirigh has proved very influential. A beautifully written book, it succeeded in capturing a national sense of fondness for the historical achievements that Ó Cléirigh represented. The presentation of Ó Cléirigh as a scholar hero was all the more convincing because of Jennings's mastery of his subject and obvious enthusiasm for the topic. Jennings was keen to stress the status of Ó Cléirigh as one of Ireland's most important historians, concluding that:

> this humble Brother, who hid himself so completely while accomplishing so much for Ireland, has fulfilled one of the noblest ambitions man can have. He has written his name large across the history of his country, and has left it engraved indelibly on the hearts of all his countrymen [p. 174].

Jennings's researches on the life and work of Ó Cléirigh had originally been serialised in *Assisi: Irish Franciscan Monthly* (**41**). The publication of a revised version of the essays in 1936 coincided with the tercentenary of the completion of the Annals of the Four Masters. The reception the book received from reviewers scarcely did justice to Jennings's achievement, some commentators concentrating almost exclusively on the 'hot topic' of where precisely in Donegal the Annals had been written. BC

Display: title-page.

## 40.
## AODH MAC AINGIL
## Hugh MacCaghwell

Tomás Ó Cléirigh, *Aodh Mac Aingil agus an scoil Nua-Ghaedhilge i Lobháin*. Dublin, 1936. Printed work. [Fig. 8.1]

This classic work on Aodh Mac Aingil (Hugh MacCaghwell) by Tomás Ó Cléirigh was influential in the twentieth century in making the Louvain story better known, particularly among Irish-language enthusiasts. Appearing in the same year as Brendan Jennings's study of Ó Cléirigh, the publication coincided with the tercentenary of the completion of the Annals of the Four Masters. Aodh Mac Aingil played an influential role in the foundation of a college (**14, 15**) for Irish Franciscans at Louvain in 1607, and he served as professor of theology and guardian of the college in its early years. In addition to his administrative and teaching duties, Mac Aingil published books in Irish and

Latin. In 1618 he published *Scáthán shacramuinte na haithridhe* or 'A mirror of the sacrament of penance', a devotional text in the Irish language. The book is of interest for Mac Aingil's political views on the Irish nation as well as being a work of devotional literature. As a theologian Mac Aingil made particular study of the works of John Duns Scotus, a medieval theologian who was then believed to have been Irish. Mac Aingil gained a high reputation in Europe for his Scotist scholarship, which included various theological tracts published in the 1620s under his Latinised name of Hugo Cavellus. BC

Display: title-page and frontispiece.

39    40

38

**41.**

*ASSISI*

*Assisi: Irish Franciscan Monthly.* September 1936. Printed work.

The tercentenary of the completion of the Annals of the Four Masters was marked by the Irish Franciscans in 1936. In September of that year a special issue of *Assisi*, the monthly magazine of the community, was devoted to a celebration of the achievement of the Four Masters. The phrase that had become an Ó Cléirigh motto, *Do chum glóire Dé agus onóra na hÉireann* ('For the glory of God and the honour of Ireland') was prominent on the cover. The contents include essays on the Four Masters, Louvain, the Annals, the Donegal Franciscan convent and the 'Epic story of Br Michael'. The focus was increasingly on the person of Ó Cléirigh—the sole Franciscan of the group—rather than on the Annals he had masterminded. Heroes were the order of the day, and every effort was made to bring the elusive Ó Cléirigh closer to the public mind. **BC**

Display: cover of *Assisi: Irish Franciscan Monthly*, September 1936.

**42.**

Ó CLÉIRIGH TERCENTENARY BROCHURE (1944)

*Comóradh i n-onóir Mhichíl uí Chléirigh, bráthair bocht, ceann na gCeithre Máistrí; Gaiety Theatre, Baile Átha Cliath, Dia Domhnaigh 25ú lá de Mhí an Mheithimh, 1944.* Dublin, 1944. Printed work. [Fig. 8.3]

The tercentenary of the death of Mícheál Ó Cléirigh was marked in Ireland in late 1943 and 1944 by a series of commemorative events, including radio broadcasts, publications, theatre performances, musical concerts and banquets. A special commemorative brochure was issued on the occasion of a gala concert at the Gaiety Theatre, Dublin, in June 1944. The concert included performances by the Raidio Éireann Orchestra of compositions by Aloys Fleischmann, Éamonn Ó Gallchobhair, Réamonn Ó Frighil and Hamilton Harty. An impressive list of dignitaries of church and state were present on the occasion, including the papal nuncio, Cardinal Maglione, and the taoiseach, Éamon de Valera. A speech on Ó Cléirigh was given by Eóin Mac Néill.

Beautifully designed and printed by the Three Candles Press, the brochure, issued in wartime Ireland, reminded patrons that:

In honouring Brother Michael, Ireland will be honouring Divine Providence for having given him to the Irish Nation, for having set him up and secured him in his labours. She will be honouring, too, that idea of peace-loving nationhood, that right of a people to be untruculently themselves which it was part of Michael's life work to establish. Above all, at this moment, she will be honouring in a world at war, the strength of the weak in confounding the weakness of the strong.

**BC**

Display: front cover.

**43.**

*MEASGRA MHICHÍL UÍ CHLÉIRIGH*

Sylvester O'Brien (ed.), *Measgra i gcuimhne Mhichíl Uí Chléirigh/Miscellany of historical and linguistic studies in honour of Brother Michael Ó Cléirigh, OFM, chief of the Four Masters, 1643–1943.* Dublin, 1944. Printed work. [Fig. 8.4]

This work was edited by Sylvester O'Brien on behalf of the Irish Franciscans to mark the tercentenary of the death of Mícheál Ó Cléirigh. That it was anticipated that it would be a work of national importance was evident in the advance publicity, which emphasised that it would be 'a volume of historical and linguistic studies, partly in Irish and partly in English, contributed by scholars of repute and edited by the Franciscan Fathers. It will have a foreword by Dr Douglas Hyde, President of Ireland, and a preface by An Taoiseach Eamon de Valera.'

Once published, the miscellany received mixed reviews. One commentator complained that the frontispiece depiction of Ó Cléirigh had 'no basis in life or fact', and several reviewers commented on the uneven quality of the essays. The involvement of Franciscan scholars was welcomed, however, the *Irish Ecclesiastical Record* reviewer noting that 'it is from their patriotic feeling for things Irish as well as from their scholarship that much is to be expected *do chum glóire Dé agus onóra na hÉireann*'. In a 1944 issue of *Studies*, the Jesuit quarterly, a parallel was again drawn between the unsettled state of Ireland in Ó Cléirigh's lifetime and Ireland during the Second World War:

They were troubled times in which Ó Cléirigh worked, but the compilation of this present miscellany too can have been no easy task. Paper for printing is rapidly approaching the degree of scarcity of vellum in Ó Cléirigh's day; our lines of communication with Celtic scholars on the Continent are even more difficult than his were; and while he could at least look at and copy Irish manuscripts, the scholar of to-day finds it impossible in these siren-punctuated times to do even that.

BC

Display: frontispiece and title-page. The frontispiece is a representation of Mícheál Ó Cléirigh based on a mural painting by the late Brother Juniper Arens OFM in the cloisters of the Franciscan Friary, Killarney. The title-page incorporates the elaborate seal designed in the late nineteenth century for the Franciscan Library, Dublin. The seal depicts the arms of the Franciscan order, together with three of the major Irish Franciscan publications of the seventeenth century: 'Father Luke Wadding's *Annales Minorum*, treasury of Franciscan history for all time; Father John Colgan's *Acta Sanctorum Hiberniae*, storehouse of Irish hagiography; *Annála Ríoghachta Éireann*, record of the story of the Irish race, compiled by Brother Michael Ó Cléirigh and his associates and known as the "Annals of the Four Masters"'.

**44.**

COMMEMORATIVE POSTAGE STAMPS, 1944

Original artwork by R.J. King for commemorative postage stamps, 1944. 7.3cm x 8.6cm. [Fig. 8.2]

On 30 June 1944, as part of the commemorative events organised to mark the tercentenary of the death of Mícheál Ó Cléirigh, specially commissioned postage stamps were issued in his honour. These were designed by an Irish artist, R.J. King, and depicted the scholarly friar at work on the Annals. The stamp also included the memorable phrase *Do chum glóire Dé agus onóra na hÉireann* ('For the glory of God and the honour of Ireland'), a phrase used by Ó Cléirigh himself in the patronal dedication of the Annals (**20**, **21**).

The message of the stamp was the centrality of history to Irish identity. The Minister for Posts and Telegraphs emphasised that the stamps were being printed in Ireland using Irish paper. It was noted that 'The stamp is a tribute not only to the great chronicler, Michael Ó Cléirigh, but it recalls to the minds of the present generation the very ancient traditions of our Nation and our civilization'. The stamps were issued in denominations of a halfpenny and one shilling, and formed part of the definitive series that remained in use until 1969. BC

Display: postage stamps, in denominations of a halfpenny and a shilling, issued in 1944 to mark the tercentenary of the death of Mícheál Ó Cléirigh, with original artwork by R. J. King.

Further reading: Buchalter 1972, 50–1; *Comóradh i n-onóir Mhichíl Uí Chléirigh, bráthair bocht, ceann na gCeithre Máistrí* (Dublin, 1944), [15].

41   42

43   44

41

**Assisi:**

*Franciscan Illustrated Monthly*

Vol. **VIII.** No. 9.          SEPTEMBER, 1936          TWOPENCE

## contributors

Edel Bhreathnach, UCD Mícheál Ó Cléirigh Institute (EB)
Bernadette Cunningham, Royal Irish Academy (BC)
Raymond Gillespie, National University of Ireland, Maynooth (RG)
Benjamin Hazard, National University of Ireland, Maynooth (BH)
John McCafferty, UCD Mícheál Ó Cléirigh Institute (JMcC)
Mícheál Mac Craith OFM, National University of Ireland, Galway
Colmán Ó Clabaigh OSB, Glenstal Abbey and UCD Mícheál Ó Cléirigh Institute (CÓC)
Nollaig Ó Muráile, National University of Ireland, Galway
Pádraig Ó Riain, University College Cork

## acknowledgements

The editors wish to acknowledge the many individuals and institutions who supported the production of this catalogue. The publication was funded by the Heritage Council and the Department of the Taoiseach and the Department of Arts, Sports and Tourism as part of the Louvain 400 celebrations. The authorities of the institutions involved in the exhibition 'Writing Irish History: the Four Master and their world' assisted in many practical ways and we are particularly grateful to Caoimhín Ó Laoide OFM, Joseph MacMahon OFM, Ignatius Fennessy OFM, John McCafferty, UCD Mícheál Ó Cléirigh Institute, Bernard Meehan, Trinity College Dublin, Siobhán Fitzpatrick, Royal Irish Academy, and Séamus Helferty, UCD School of History and Archives. We wish to acknowledge the dedication of the contributors, the designer Ger Garland and the publisher Nick Maxwell, Wordwell Books, for their work and also their understanding in working to a short deadline. Photographs were produced by Davison Associates and Declan Corrigan Photography. Many other people offered their advice and assistance and we are grateful to Emer Condit, Wordwell Books, Elizabeth Dawson, UCD Mícheál Ó Cléirigh Institute, Raymond Gillespie, NUI Maynooth, Raghnall Ó Floinn, National Museum of Ireland, Petra Schnabel, Royal Irish Academy, Orna Somerville, UCD School of History and Archives, and Karl Vogelsang, Royal Irish Academy, in this regard.

## photograph credits

## A

Allison, A.F. 1955 Franciscan books in English, 1559–1640. *Biographical studies* 3 (1), 16–65.

Anon. 1944 *Comóradh i n-onóir Mhichíl uí Chléirigh, bráthair bocht, ceann na gCeithre Máistrí; Gaiety Theatre, Baile Átha Cliath, Dia Domhnaigh 25ú lá de Mhí an Mheithimh, 1944.* Dublin.

## B

Bannerman, J. 1986 *The Beatons*. Edinburgh.

Baronius, C. 1601–8 *Annales ecclesiastici* (12 vols). Mainz. [Also Cologne, 1609; Antwerp, 1612.]

Bernard, J.H. and Atkinson, R. (eds) 1898 *The Irish Liber Hymnorum* (2 vols). Henry Bradshaw Society 13–14. London.

Best, R.I. and Lawlor, H.J. (eds) 1931 *The Martyrology of Tallaght*. Henry Bradshaw Society 68. London.

Best, R.I., O'Brien, M. and Bergin, O. (eds) 1954–67 *The Book of Leinster* (5 vols). Dublin.

Bhreathnach, E. 2002 Two contributors to the Book of Leinster: Bishop Finn of Kildare and Gilla na Náem Úa Duinn. In M. Richter and J.-M. Picard (eds), *Ogma. Essays in Celtic studies in honour of Proinséas Ní Chatháin*, 105–11. Dublin.

Bieler, L. 1948a The Irish Book of Hymns: a palaeographical study. *Scriptorium* 2, 177–94.

Bieler, L. 1948b John Colgan as editor. *Franciscan Studies* 8, 1–24.

Bradshaw, B. 1979 Manus 'the magnificent': O'Donnell as Renaissance prince. In A. Cosgrove and D. McCartney (eds), *Studies in Irish history presented to R. Dudley Edwards*, 15–36. Dublin.

Breatnach, L. (ed.) 1987 *Uraicecht na Ríar. The poetic grades in early Irish law*. Dublin.

Breatnach, P.A. 1999 An Irish Bollandus: Fr Hugh Ward and the Louvain hagiographical enterprise. *Éigse* 31, 1–30.

Breatnach, P.A. 2002 A seventeenth-century abridgement of *Beatha Aodha Ruaidh Uí Dhomhnaill. Éigse* 33, 77–172.

Buchalter, M.D. 1972 *Hibernian specialised catalogue of the postage stamps of Ireland, 1922–1972*. Dublin.

Byrne, F.J. 1974 Senchas: the nature of Gaelic historical tradition. In J. G. Barry (ed.), *Historical Studies 9: Papers read before the Irish Conference of Historians*, 137–59. Belfast.

## C

Charles-Edwards, T. 2005 *The Chronicle of Ireland* (2 vols). Liverpool.

Colgan, J. 1645 *Acta sanctorum veteris et majoris Scotiae seu Hiberniae sanctorum insulae*. Louvain. [Repr. with introduction by Brendan Jennings, Dublin, 1948.]

Colgan, J. 1647 *Triadis thaumaturgae, seu divorum Patricii, Columbae, et Brigidae . . . acta*. Louvain. [Repr. with introduction by Pádraig Ó Riain, Dublin, 1997.]

Colker, M.L. 1991 *Trinity College Library, Dublin: descriptive catalogue of the medieval and Renaissance Latin manuscripts* (2 vols). Aldershot.

Comyn, D. and Dinneen, P.S. (eds) 1902–14 *Foras feasa ar Éirinn: The History of Ireland, by Geoffrey Keating* (4 vols). Irish Texts Society. London.

Conlan, P. 1977 *St Anthony's College of the Irish Franciscans, Louvain, 1927–1977; 1607–1977*. Dublin.

Connellan, O. (ed.) 1846 *The Annals of Ireland translated from the original Irish of the Four Masters*. Dublin.

Corish, P.J. 1957 Father Luke Wadding and the Irish nation. *Irish Ecclesiastical Record* (5th ser.) 88, 377–95.

Cunningham, B. 2000 *The world of Geoffrey Keating: history, myth and religion in seventeenth-century Ireland*. Dublin.

Cunningham, B. 2004 Politics and power in sixteenth-century Connacht. *Irish Arts Review* 21 (4), 116–21.

Cunningham, B. 2005 The making of the Annals of the Four Masters. Unpublished PhD thesis, University College Dublin.

Cunningham, B. 2006a 'An honour to the nation': publishing John O'Donovan's edition of the Annals of the Four Masters, 1848–56. In M. Fanning and R. Gillespie (eds), *Print culture and intellectual life in Ireland, 1660–1941*, 116–42. Dublin.

Cunningham, B. 2006b Illustrations of the passion of Christ in the Seanchas Búrcach manuscript. In R. Moss, C. Ó Clabaigh and S. Ryan (eds), *Art and devotion in late medieval Ireland*, 16–32. Dublin.

Cunningham, B. and Gillespie, R. 2004–5 James Ussher and his Irish manuscripts. *Studia Hibernica* 33, 81–99.

## D

Davis, E. 1889 *Souvenirs of Irish footprints over Europe* (reprinted from the *Evening Telegraph*). Dublin.

de Blácam, A. 1929 *Gaelic literature surveyed: from earliest times to the present*. Dublin. [Repr. Dublin, 1973.]

Dillon, M., Mooney, C. and de Brún, P. 1969 *Catalogue of Irish manuscripts in the Franciscan Library, Killiney*. Dublin.

Doherty, C. 1991 The cult of St Patrick and the politics of Armagh in the seventh century. In J.-M. Picard (ed.), *Ireland and northern France AD 600–850*, 53–94. Dublin.

## F

Fennessy, I. 2004 Luke Wadding. In H.C.C. Matthew and B. Harrison (eds), *Oxford Dictionary of National Biography* (60 vols), vol. 56, 643–9. Oxford.

Fletcher, A.J. 2001 Preaching in late medieval Ireland: the Latin and English traditions. In A.J. Fletcher and R. Gillespie (eds), *Irish preaching, 700–1700*, 56–80. Dublin.

Franciscan Fathers (eds) 1957 *Father Luke Wadding: commemorative volume*. Dublin.

## G

Giblin, C. 1967 The Annals of the Four Masters. In [Anon.] (ed.), *Great books of Ireland*, 90–103. Dublin.

Gilbert, J.T. 1874 The manuscripts of the former college of Irish Franciscans, Louvain. In Historical Manuscripts Commission, *Fourth report*, pt 1, appendix, 599–613. London.

Gwynn, E.J. (ed.) 1903–35 *The metrical dindshenchas* (5 vols). Todd Lecture Series. Dublin. [Repr. Dublin, 1991.]

## H

Hayes, J. 1911 Old popular pennyworths. *Irish Booklover* 2 (10), 149–51.

Hennessy, W.M. and MacCarthy, B. (eds) 1887–1901 *Annála Uladh: Annals of Ulster from the earliest times to the year 1541* (4 vols). Dublin. [Repr. Dublin, 1998.]

Historical Manuscripts Commission 1906 *Report on Franciscan manuscripts preserved at the convent, Merchant's Quay, Dublin*. Dublin.

Hughes, K. 1972 *Early Christian Ireland: introduction to the sources*. London.

Hyde, D. 1899 *A literary history of Ireland, from earliest times to the present day*. London. [Rev. edn 1967.]

**J**

Jennings, B. 1934 Documents from the archives of St Isidore's College, Rome. *Analecta Hibernica* 6, 203–47.

Jennings, B. 1936 *Michael Ó Cléirigh, chief of the Four Masters, and his associates.* Dublin.

Jennings, B. 1949 Florence Conry, archbishop of Tuam. *Journal of the Galway Archaeological and Historical Society* 23, 83–93.

Jennings, B. (ed.) 1953 *Wadding papers, 1614–1638.* Dublin.

Jennings, B. (ed.) 1968 *Louvain papers 1606–1827.* Irish Manuscripts Commission. Dublin.

**K**

Kelly, F. 1986 An Old-Irish text on court procedure. *Peritia* 5, 74–106.

Kenney, J.F. 1929 *The sources for the early history of Ireland, I: ecclesiastical. An introduction and guide.* New York.

Kinane, V. 1994 *A history of the Dublin University Press, 1734–1976.* Dublin.

Knott, E. 1948 An Irish seventeenth century translation of the Rule of S. Clare. *Ériu* 15, 1–187.

**L**

Lacey, B. (ed.) 1998 *Manus O'Donnell. The Life of Colum Cille.* Dublin.

Leerssen, J. 2002 *Hidden Ireland, public sphere.* Galway.

Lehmann, R. (ed.) 1964 *Fled Dúin na nGéd.* Medieval and Modern Irish Series 21. Dublin.

Lotz-Heumann, U. 1996 The Protestant interpretation of history in Ireland: the case of James Ussher's *Discourse.* In B. Gordon (ed.), *Protestant history and identity in sixteenth-century Europe, volume 2: The later Reformation*, 107–20. Aldershot.

**M**

Mac Airt, S. 1958 *Filidecht* and *coimgne.* *Ériu* 18, 139–52.

Mac Airt, S. and Mac Niocaill, G. (eds) 1983 *Annals of Ulster to AD 1131: text and translation.* Dublin.

Macalister, R.A.S. (ed.) 1950 *The Book of Mac Carthaigh Riabhach.* Dublin.

Macalister, R.A.S. and Mac Neill, J. (eds) 1916 *Leabhar Gabhála, the Book of Conquests of Ireland, the recension of Micheál Ó Cléirigh,* part 1. Dublin.

McCafferty, J. 1997/8 St Patrick for the Church of Ireland: James Ussher's *Discourse.* *Bullaun* 3 (2), 87–101.

McCarthy, D.P. 1998 The chronology of the Irish annals. *Proceedings of the Royal Irish Academy* 98C, 203–55.

McCone, K. 1995 OIr. *senchae, senchaid* and preliminaries on agent noun formation in Celtic. *Ériu* 46, 1–10.

McDonnell, J. 1997 *Five hundred years of the art of the book in Ireland.* Dublin.

McGuinne, D. 1992 *Irish type design: a history of printing types in the Irish character.* Dublin.

McKenna, L. (ed.) 1916–18 *Iomarbhágh na bhFileadh* (2 vols). Irish Texts Society 20–21. London.

McNeill, C. 1930 Reports on the Rawlinson collection of manuscripts in the Bodleian Library, Oxford. *Analecta Hibernica* 1, 12–178.

Mac Neill, J. 1913 Poems by Flann Mainistrech on the dynasties of Ailech, Mide and Brega. *Archivium Hibernicum* 2, 37–99.

Mac Niocaill, G. 1975 *The medieval Irish annals.* Dublin.

Matthew, H.C.C. and Harrison, B. (eds) 2004 *Oxford Dictionary of National Biography* (60 vols). Oxford.

Messingham, T. 1624 *Florilegium insulae sanctorum: seu vitae et acta sanctorum Hiberniae.* Paris.

Millett, B. and Lynch, A. (eds) 1995 *Dún Mhuire, Killiney, 1945–95: léann agus seanchas.* Dublin.

Mooney, C. 1944 The golden age of the Irish Franciscans, 1615–50. In S. O'Brien (ed.), *Measgra i gcuimhne Mhichíl Uí Chléirigh,* 21–33. Dublin.

Mooney, C. 1958 The writings of Father Luke Wadding, OFM. *Franciscan Studies* 18 (3–4), 225–39.

Murray, D. 2000 *Romanticism, nationalism and Irish antiquarian societies, 1840–80.* Maynooth.

**N**

Ní Bhrolcháin, M. 2005 Leinster, Book of. In S. Duffy (ed.), *Medieval Ireland, an encyclopedia,* 272–4. New York.

Nicholls, K. 1990 Introduction to the Annals of the Four Masters. In J. O'Donovan (ed.), *Annála Ríoghachta Éireann: The Annals of the Kingdom of Ireland* [reprint], vol. 1. Dublin.

**O**

O'Brien, C. 1992 *The history of the glorious virgin Saint Clare.* Galway.

O'Brien, S. (ed.) 1944 *Measgra i gcuimhne Mhichíl Uí Chléirigh/ Miscellany of historical and linguistic studies in honour of Brother Michael Ó Cléirigh, OFM, chief of the Four Masters, 1643–1943.* Dublin.

Ó Buachalla, B. 2006 *The crown of Ireland.* Galway.

Ó Buachalla, B. 1982–3 *Annála Ríoghachta Éireann* is *Foras Feasa ar Éirinn*: an comhthéacs comhaimseartha. *Studia Hibernica* 22–3, 59–105.

Ó Clabaigh, C.N. 2002 *The Franciscans in Ireland, 1400–1534: from reform to Reformation.* Dublin.

Ó Clabaigh, C. 2006 The cult of St Francis in late medieval Ireland. In R. Moss, C. Ó Clabaigh and S. Ryan (eds), *Art and devotion in late medieval Ireland,* 142–62. Dublin.

Ó Cléirigh, T. [c.1936] *Aodh Mac Aingil agus an scoil Nua-Ghaedhilge i Lobháin.* Dublin.

O'Connor, T. 1999 Towards the invention of the Irish Catholic *natio*: Thomas Messingham's *Florilegium* (1624). *Irish Theological Quarterly* 64, 157–77.

O'Connor, T. 2002 'Perfidious Machiavellian friar': Florence Conry's campaign for a Catholic restoration in Ireland, 1592–1616. *Seanchas Ardmhacha* 19 (1), 91–105.

O'Conor, C. 1753 *Dissertations on the antient history of Ireland, wherein an account is given of the origine, government, letters, sciences, religion, manners and customs, of the antient inhabitants.* Dublin. [Rev. edn 1766.]

O'Conor, Revd C. (ed.) 1826 *Quatuor magistrorum annales Hibernici usque ad annum MCLXXII ex ipso O'Clerii autographo in Bibliotheca Stowense servato.* Rerum Hibernicarum Scriptores Veteres III. Buckingham.

Ó Corráin, D. 1978 Nationality and kingship in pre-Norman Ireland. In T.W. Moody (ed.), *Nationality and the pursuit of national independence: Historical Studies 11,* 1–35. Belfast.

Ó Cuív, B. 1976 The Irish language in the early modern period. In T.W. Moody, F.X. Martin and F.J. Byrne (eds), *A new history of Ireland, iii: early modern Ireland,* 509–45. Oxford.

Ó Cuív, B. 1984 Ireland's manuscript heritage. *Éire-Ireland* 19, 87–110.

Ó Cuív, B. 2001–3 *Catalogue of Irish language manuscripts in the Bodleian Library at Oxford and Oxford College Libraries* (2 vols). Dublin.

O'Curry, E. 1861 *Lectures on the manuscript materials of ancient Irish history.* Dublin.

O'Donnell, T. (ed.) 1959 *Father John Colgan, OFM, 1592–1658.* Dublin.

O'Donovan, J. (ed.) 1848–51 *Annála Ríoghachta Éireann. Annals of the Kingdom of Ireland, by the Four Masters, from the earliest period to the year 1616, edited from MSS. in the library of the Royal Irish Academy and of Trinity College Dublin, with a translation and copious notes* (1st edn) (7 vols). Dublin.

O'Flaherty, R. 1685 *Ogygia seu, rerum Hibernicorum chronologia*. London.

O'Grady, S.H. and Flower, R. 1992 *Catalogue of Irish manuscripts in the British Library* (3 vols). Dublin.

O'Keeffe, J.G. (ed.) 1931 *Buile Shuibhne*. Medieval and Modern Irish Series 1. Dublin.

O'Kelleher, A. and Schoepperle, G. 1918 *Betha Colaim Chille: Life of Columcille*. Illinois. [Repr. Dublin, 1994.]

O'Leary, P. 2004 *Gaelic prose in the Irish Free State*. Dublin.

Ó Muraíle, N. 1987 The autograph manuscripts of the Annals of the Four Masters. *Celtica* 19, 75–95.

Ó Muraíle, N. 1996a *The celebrated antiquary Dubhaltach Mac Fhirbhisigh (c. 1600–71): his lineage, life and learning*. Maynooth.

Ó Muraíle, N. 1996b Aspects of the intellectual life of seventeenth-century Galway. In G. Moran (ed.), *Galway: history and society*, 149–211. Dublin.

Ó Muraíle, N. (ed.) 1998 *Cathal Óg Mac Maghnusa and the Annals of Ulster*. Enniskillen.

O'Neill, T. 1984 *The Irish hand*. Portlaoise.

Ó Raghallaigh, T. (ed. and trans.) 1927–9 Seanchus na mBúrcach [History of the Burkes]. *Journal of the Galway Archaeological and Historical Society* 13 (1927–8), 50–60, 101–37; 14 (1928–9), 30–51, 142–67.

O'Rahilly, C. (ed.) 1952 *Five seventeenth-century political poems*. Dublin.

O'Rahilly, T.F. *et al.* 1926–70 *Catalogue of Irish manuscripts in the Royal Irish Academy*, Fasc. 1–27. Dublin.

Ó Riain, P. (ed.) 1978 *Cath Almaine*. Medieval and Modern Irish Series 25. Dublin.

Ó Riain, P. (ed.) 2002 *Beatha Aodha Ruaidh: the Life of Red Hugh O'Donnell, historical and literary contexts*. London.

Ó Riain, P. 2006 *Feastdays of the saints: a history of Irish martyrologies*. Subsidia Hagiographica 86. Brussels.

O'Sullivan, A. (ed.) 1983 *The Book of Leinster*, vol. 6. Dublin.

O'Sullivan, W. 1956 Ussher as a collector of manuscripts. *Hermathena* 88, 34–58.

O'Sullivan, W. 1966 On the scripts and make-up of the Book of Leinster. *Celtica* 7, 1–31.

O'Sullivan, W. (ed.) 1994–5 Correspondence of David Rothe and James Ussher, 1619–23. *Collectanea Hibernica* 36–7, 7–49.

O'Sullivan, W. 1997 A finding list of Sir James Ware's manuscripts. *Proceedings of the Royal Irish Academy* 97C, 69–99.

O'Sullivan, W. 1999 The Slane manuscript of the Annals of the Four Masters. *Ríocht na Mídhe* 10, 78–91.

P

Parry, G. 2004 Sir James Ware, 1594–1666. In H. C. C. Matthew and B. Harrison (eds), *Oxford Dictionary of National Biography* (60 vols), vol. 57, 386–7. Oxford.

Petrie, G. 1831 Remarks on the history and authenticity of the Annals of the Four Masters. *Transactions of the Royal Irish Academy* 16, 381–93.

Plummer, C. (ed.) 1922 *Bethada náem nÉrenn* (2 vols). Oxford.

Plummer, C. 1925 *Miscellanea hagiographica Hibernia*. Subsidia Hagiographica 15. Brussels.

Power, P. (ed.) 1914 *Life of St Declan of Ardmore and Life of St Mochuda of Lismore*. Irish Texts Society 16. London.

R

Rochford, R. 1625 *The life of the glorious bishop St Patricke . . . together with the lives of the holy virgin S. Bridgit and of the*

*glorious abbot Saint Columbe*. English Recusant Literature 210. St Omer. [Repr. London, 1974.]

S

Sharpe, R. 1991 *Medieval Irish saints' lives*. Oxford.

Simms, K. 1998 Charles Lynegar, the Ó Luinín family and the study of *seanchas*. In T. Barnard, D. Ó Cróinín and K. Simms (eds), *A miracle of learning: studies in manuscripts and Irish learning. Essays in honour of William O'Sullivan*, 266–83. Aldershot.

Spettman, H. 1923 Das schriften 'de oculo morali' und sein verfasser. *Archivum Franciscanum Historicum* 16, 309–22.

Stanihurst, R. 1587 *De vita S. Patricii Hiberniae apostoli*. Antwerp.

Steggle, M. 2004a Bentley, Catharine [Magdalen Augustine] (1591–1659). In H.C.C. Matthew and B. Harrison (eds), *Oxford Dictionary of National Biography* (60 vols), vol. 5, 276. Oxford.

Steggle, M. 2004b Evelinge, Elizabeth [Catharine Magdalen] (1596/7–1668). In H.C.C. Matthew and B. Harrison (eds), *Oxford Dictionary of National Biography* (60 vols), vol. 18, 768. Oxford.

Stokes, M. 1871 *On two works of ancient Irish art known as the Breac Moedog (or Shrine of St Moedog) and the Soiscel Molaise (or Gospel of St Molaise)*. London.

T

Todd, J.H. and Reeves, W. (eds) 1864 *The Martyrology of Donegal: a calendar of the saints of Ireland: Féilire na naomh nErennach* (translated by John O'Donovan). Dublin.

U

Ussher, J. 1631 *A discourse of the religion anciently professed by the Irish and British*. London.

Ussher, J. 1639 *Britannicarum ecclesiarum antiquitates*. Dublin.

W

Walsh, P. 1918 *Genealogiae regum et sanctorum Hiberniae, by the Four Masters, edited from the manuscript of Michél Ó Cléirigh*. Maynooth.

Walsh, P. 1929 Two Irish manuscripts. *Studies* 18, 292–306.

Walsh, P. (ed.) 1948–57 *Beatha Aodha Ruaidh Uí Dhomhnaill: the Life of Aodh Ruadh Ó Domhnaill* (2 vols). Irish Texts Society. London.

Walsh, P. 2003 *Irish leaders and learning through the ages* (ed. Nollaig Ó Muraíle). Dublin.

Ward, R.E., Wrynn, J.F. and Coogan Ward, C. (eds) 1988 *Letters of Charles O'Conor of Belanagare: a Catholic voice in eighteenth-century Ireland*. Washington DC.

Ware, J. 1639 *De scriptoribus Hiberniae*. Dublin.

Ware, J. 1656 *S. Patricio, qui Hibernos ad fidem Christi convertit Adscripta opuscula quorum aliqua nunc primùm, ex antiquis MSS. codicibus in lucem emissa sunt, reliqua, recognita: omnia, notis ad rem historicam & antiquariam spectantibus, illustrata*. London.

# abbreviations

| | |
|---|---|
| AD | *Anno Domini* |
| AM | *Anno mundi* |
| *Cat. Ir. MSS FLK* | Myles Dillon, Canice Mooney and Pádraig de Brún, *Catalogue of Irish manuscripts in the Franciscan Library, Killiney* (Dublin, 1969) |
| *Cat. Ir. MSS RIA* | T. F. O'Rahilly, Kathleen Mulchrone *et al., Catalogue of Irish manuscripts in the Royal Irish Academy*, Fasc. 1–27 (Dublin 1926–70) |
| FLK | Franciscan Library, Killiney, Dublin |
| NLI | National Library of Ireland, Dublin |
| OFM | Order of Friars Minor |
| RIA | Royal Irish Academy, Dublin |
| TCD | Trinity College Dublin |
| UCD | University College Dublin |
| UCD-OFM | University College Dublin, Franciscan Collection |

*References to manuscripts exhibited are given to their relevant catalogue number, highlighted in bold. Where manuscripts are cited or illustrated elsewhere in the book reference is given to page number. Page numbers in italics indicate illustrations.*

BIBLIOTHÈQUE ROYALE, BRUSSELS
2324–40 Irish saints' Lives. 37.
4190–200 Irish saints' Lives. 37.
4369 Martyrology of Donegal 1628. 37, 38, 44, 46, 104.
5095–6 Martyrology of Donegal 1630. 37, 44, 104.
5100–4 Martyrology of Gorman. 37–8, 44.

BODLEIAN LIBRARY, OXFORD
Laud 615. 108
Rawlinson B 503 Annals of Innisfallen. 55
Rawlinson B 514. 108
Rawlinson B 482, B 488, B 502 Annals of Tigernach. 55.
Rawlinson B 489 Annals of Ulster. 106.
Rawlinson C 320. 45.

BRITISH LIBRARY, LONDON
Add. 4792 Annals of Loch Cé, AD 1568–9. 27, 44.

NATIONAL LIBRARY OF IRELAND, DUBLIN
G 1. 107
G 2 – G 3. 22.
G 488. 124.

NATIONAL LIBRARY OF SCOTLAND, EDINBURGH
Advocates 72.1.29. 108.

ROYAL IRISH ACADEMY, DUBLIN
A iv 1 Saints' Lives. 36.
B iv 2 Mícheál Ó Cléirigh miscellany. **6**.
C iii 3 Annals of the Four Masters, AM 2242–AD 1171. 27–30, *33*, 44, *60*, 61–2, 69, 71, 117, 119, 130, **18**.
D i 2 Rule of St Clare. **12**.
23 F 2–3 Copy of Annals of the Four Masters. 62.
23 F 4–6 Copy of Annals of the Four Masters. 64.
23 M 70 Book of Invasions. 22, 28, *32*, 117.
23 P 2 Book of Lecan. 46, 55, 104.
23 P 6 Annals of the Four Masters, AD 1170–1499. 27–30, *63–4, 67, 68,* 69, *94–5,* 117, 119, **21**.
23 P 7 Annals of the Four Masters, AD 1500–1616. 27–30, *63–4,* 69, 117, 119, **22**.
23 P 12 Book of Ballymote. 55, 104.
23 P 16 *Leabhar Breac*. 37.
23 P 24 Life of Red Hugh O'Donnell. *96–7,* 123, **24**.

STADTBIBLIOTHEK, SCHAFFHAUSEN
Generalia 1 Adomnán's Life of Colum Cille. 36.

TRINITY COLLEGE DUBLIN
58 Book of Kells. 69, 130.
97 Miscellany including Rule of St Francis. **9**.
109 Irish Observant Franciscan antiphonary. *110*, **11**.
347 Franciscan vade-mecum. *90–1,* **10**.
574 James Ussher notebook. 55, **31**.
667 Franciscan miscellany. 45.
1279 Copy of Annals of the Four Masters. 62.
1282 Annals of Ulster. *23, 25,* 55, **5**.
1293 Annals of Loch Cé. 27, 44.

1300 Copy of Annals of the Four Masters. 62.
1301 Annals of the Four Masters, AD 1334–1605. 27–30, 62–3, 64, **65**, **19**.
1339 Book of Leinster. *18,* 38, 103, 107, **1**.
1440 History of the Burkes. 45, *102,* 103, **8**.
1441 Book of Hymns. 103, **4**.

UNIVERSITY COLLEGE DUBLIN. FRANCISCAN COLLECTION
A 1 Psalter of St Caimin of Iniscealtra. 46, *50*.
A 2 Book of Hymns. 38, 46, *88–9,* 103, 106, 126, **3**.
A 3 Martyrology of Tallaght. *86–7,* **2**.
A 8 Life of St Colum Cille. 37, 103, **7**.
A 13 Annals of the Four Masters, AM 2242–AD 1169. *26,* 27–30, *31,* 44, 63, *66,* 71, 117, **20**.
A 14 Geoffrey Keating's *Foras feasa ar Éirinn*. 30, 52, 54, 55, 56, *57,* 123, 126, 130, **25**.
A 16 Genealogies of Saints and Kings. *24,* 29, *40,* 44, 47, *51,* 104, 117, **23**.
A 19 Copy of Life of St Colum Cille. 108.
C 11 Commendation for Florence Conry. *92–3,* **17**.
C 11 Foundation letter of St Anthony's College, Louvain. *5,* **14**.
C 11 Permission to receive fish from Sant Vliet. **16**.
G 9 Papal Bull of Foundation, **15**.
R.J. King artwork for 1944 postage stamps. 79, *81,* **44**.

IN PRIVATE OWNERSHIP
Book of Mac Carthaigh Riabhach (Book of Lismore). 36, 46.

# exhibits / illustrations

Cat. no. 1     Book of Leinster. *Leabhar na Núachongbhála* (TCD 1339), Fig. 1.1.

Cat. no. 2     Martyrology of Tallaght (UCD-OFM A 3), pp 86–7.

Cat. no. 3     Book of hymns. *Liber Hymnorum* (UCD-OFM A 2), pp 88–9.

Cat. no. 4     Book of hymns. *Liber Hymnorum* (TCD 1441).

Cat. no. 5     Annals of Ulster. *Annála Uladh* (TCD 1282), Figs. 1.2; 1.4.

Cat. no. 6     Ó Cléirigh miscellany (RIA B iv 2).

Cat. no. 7     Life of St Colum Cille. *Beatha Cholm Cille* (UCD-OFM A 8).

Cat. no. 8     History of the Burkes. *Seanchas Búrcach* (TCD 1440), p. 102.

Cat. no. 9     Rule of St Francis (TCD 97), Fig. 4.2.

Cat. no. 10     Franciscan vade-mecum (TCD 347), pp 90–1.

Cat. no. 11     Irish Observant Franciscan antiphonary (TCD 109), p. 110.

Cat. no. 12     Rule of St Clare. *Riaghail ár Máthar Naomhtha S. Clara* (RIA D i 2).

Cat. no. 13     *History of St Clare* (Douai, 1635).

Cat. no. 14     Foundation letter of St Anthony's College, Louvain (UCD-OFM C 11), Fig. 0.2.

Cat. no. 15     Bull of Foundation (UCD-OFM G 9).

Cat. no. 16     Permission to receive fish from Sant Vliet (UCD-OFM C 11).

Cat. no. 17     Commendation for Florence Conry (UCD-OFM C 11, document O 1), pp 92–3.

Cat. no. 18     Annals of the Four Masters. *Annála Ríoghachta Éireann* (RIA C iii 3), Figs. 2.4; 6.1.

Cat. no. 19     Annals of the Four Masters. *Annála Ríoghachta Éireann* (TCD 1301), Figs. 4.1; 6.2.

Cat. no. 20     Annals of the Four Masters. *Annála Ríoghachta Éireann* (UCD-OFM A 13), Figs. 2.1; 2.2; 6.3.

Cat. no. 21     Annals of the Four Masters. *Annála Ríoghachta Éireann* (RIA 23 P 6), Figs. 6.4; 7.1; pp 94–5; p. 116.

Cat. no. 22     Annals of the Four Masters. *Annála Ríoghachta Éireann* (RIA 23 P 7).

Cat. no. 23     Genealogies of Saints and Kings (UCD-OFM A 16), Figs. 1.3; 3.2; 4.4.

Cat. no. 24     Life of Red Hugh O'Donnell (RIA 23 P 24), pp 96–7.

Cat. no. 25     Geoffrey Keating's *Foras feasa ar Éirinn* (UCD-OFM A 14), Fig. 5.2.

Cat. no. 26     Thomas Messingham, *Florilegium insulae sanctorum* (Paris, 1624), Fig. 3.1.

Cat. no. 27     Pierre de Limoges, *De oculo morali* (Viterbo, 1656), p. 122.

Cat. no. 28     John Colgan, *Triadis thaumaturgae ... acta* (Louvain, 1647).

Cat. no. 29     James Ware, *De scriptoribus Hiberniae* (Dublin, 1639).

Cat. no. 30     James Ussher, *A discourse of the religion anciently professed* (London, 1631).

Cat. no. 31     James Ussher notebook (TCD 574).

Cat. no. 32     Roderic O'Flaherty, *Ogygia* (London, 1685).

Cat. no. 33     Charles O'Conor, *Dissertations on the antient history of Ireland* (Dublin, 1766).

Cat. no. 34     Charles O'Conor (ed.), *Quatuor Magistrorum annales Hibernici* (Buckingham, 1826).

Cat. no. 35     Owen Connellan (ed.), *The annals of Ireland* (Dublin, 1846), Fig. 7.2; p. 128.

Cat. no. 36     *Irish Penny Journal*, 16 January 1841, Fig. 7.4.

Cat. no. 37     John O'Donovan (ed.), *Annála Ríoghachta Éireann, Annals of the kingdom of Ireland by the Four Masters* (7 vols, Dublin, 1848–51), Fig. 7.3; pp 98–9.

Cat. no. 38     J. H. Todd and W. Reeves (eds), *Martyrology of Donegal* (Dublin, 1864).

Cat. no. 39     Brendan Jennings, *Michael Ó Cléirigh and his associates* (Dublin, 1936).

Cat. no. 40     Tomás Ó Cléirigh, *Aodh Mac Aingil agus an scoil Nua-Ghaedhilge i Lobháin* (Dublin, 1936), Fig. 8.1.

Cat. no. 41     *Assisi: Irish Franciscan Monthly*, September 1936.

Cat. no. 42     *Comóradh i n-onóir Mhichíl uí Chléirigh* (Dublin, 1944), Fig. 8.3.

Cat. no. 43     Sylvester O'Brien (ed.), *Measgra i gcuimhne Mhichíl Uí Chléirigh* (Dublin, 1944), Fig. 8.4.

Cat. no. 44     R.J. King artwork for commemorative postage stamps, 1944, Fig. 8.2.

Florence Conry OFM, fresco from aula of St Isidore's, Rome, Fig. 0.1.

*Leabhar gabhála Éireann* (RIA 23 M 70), Fig. 2.3.

John Colgan OFM, fresco from aula of St Isidore's, Rome, Fig. 3.3.

Sir James Ware, Fig. 5.1.

James Ussher, archbishop of Armagh, Fig. 5.3.

Luke Wadding OFM, Fig. 5.4.